SIGNS AND MEANING

Other interview books from Automatic Press ♦ VIP

Formal Philosophy
edited by Vincent F. Hendricks & John Symons
November 2005

Masses of Formal Philosophy
edited by Vincent F. Hendricks & John Symons
October 2006

Political Questions: 5 Questions for Political Philosophers
edited by Morten Ebbe Juul Nielsen
December 2006

Philosophy of Technology: 5 Questions
edited by Jan-Kyrre Berg Olsen & Evan Selinger
February 2007

Game Theory: 5 Questions
edited by Vincent F. Hendricks & Pelle Guldborg Hansen
April 2007

Legal Philosophy: 5 Questions
edited by Morten Ebbe Juul Nielsen
October 2007

Philosophy of Mathematics: 5 Questions
edited by Vincent F. Hendricks & Hannes Leitgeb
January 2008

Philosophy of Computing and Information: 5 Questions
edited by Luciano Floridi
Sepetmber 2008

Epistemology: 5 Questions
edited by Vincent F. Hendricks & Duncan Pritchard
September 2008

Complexity: 5 Questions
edited by Carlos Gershenson
September 2008

Probability and Statistics: 5 Questions
edited by Alan Hájek & Vincent F. Hendricks
September 2009

See all published and forthcoming books in the 5 Questions series at
www.vince-inc.com/automatic.html

SIGNS AND MEANING
5 QUESTIONS

edited by

Peer Bundgaard
Frederik Stjernfelt

Automatic Press ♦ VIP

Automatic Press ♦ $\frac{V}{I}$P

Information on this title: www.vince-inc.com/automatic.html

© Automatic Press / VIP 2009

This publication is in copyright. Subject to statuary exception
and to the provisions of relevant collective licensing agreements,
no reproduction of any part may take place without
the written permission of the publisher.

First published 2009

Printed in the United States of America
and the United Kingdom

ISBN-10   87-92130-11-9   paperback
ISBN-13   978-87-92130-11-2   paperback

The publisher has no responsibilities for
the persistence or accuracy of URLs for external or
third party Internet Web sites referred to in this publication
and does not guarantee that any content on such
Web sites is, or will remain, accurate or appropriate.

Typeset in $\LaTeX 2_\varepsilon$
Photo and graphic design by Vincent F. Hendricks

Contents

Preface   iii

Acknowledgements   vii

1   Per Aage Brandt   1

2   Marcel Danesi   9

3   Terrence Deacon   19

4   John Deely   25

5   Jørgen Dines Johansen   29

6   Gilles Fauconnier   45

7   Groupe μ 51

8   Jesper Hoffmeyer   61

9   Patrick Colm Hogan   71

10 Robert E. Innis   87

11 Mark Johnson   101

12 John Michael Krois   109

13 Kalevi Kull   113

14 Jean Petitot   121

15 Roland Posner   125

16 François Rastier   139

17 Eleanor Rosch   153

18 Lucia Santaella	165
19 John Searle	179
20 T.L. Short	189
21 Barry Smith	199
22 Göran Sonesson	207
23 John F. Sowa	219
24 Frederik Stjernfelt	229
25 Leonard Talmy	237
26 Eero Tarasti	247
27 Mark Turner	257
28 Wolfgang Wildgen	273
29 References	279
About the Editors	311
Index	313

Preface

Signs and Meaning: 5 Questions is an interview book which collects the answers to five broad and simple questions given by outstanding semioticians, linguists and philosophers of language. As in the other issues of the *5 Questions Series* the questions are set up so as to allow each contributor both to sketch his or her own intellectual biography–in more or less detail, in a more or less pronounced memoir-genre way–and to outline his or her conception of the state of the art of the field as well as of the theoretical challenges of the future. Contributors have been free to answer the questions point by point or to write a full essay on the basis of the questionnaire.

The title of the present book does not designate any established discipline nor any well delineated and methodologically homogeneous field of research. There is no unified theory of signs (*pace* both Peirce and Saussure), nor is there any of meaning. This is probably far from contingent: just as being, as Aristotle had it, is what can be said in multiple ways, meaning is what can, and should, be conceptually accessed in multiple ways, according to its various fundamental aspects. Therefore a theory of meaning can, in one conception, be considered as a theory of signs and of the interpretive processing of signs; a major task would, accordingly, consist in developing a sound typology and/or ontology of signs and their interpretive use. A theory of meaning can all as well address the way in which language use is hooked up with those mental acts in and through which we intend the objects of our experience, and thereby aim to define the intentional or conceptual structure thanks to which humans shape their experiences, carve their *Umwelt* in conceptually graspable forms, and the means thanks to which such structure is specified in language. A theory of meaning can, of course, also consider it as its major task to determine those mental processes by virtue of which humans combine, configure, or conflate the constituents of their experiences and thereby construct meaningful mental contents. And a theory of meaning may, all as evidently, consider and try to lay down what it takes, formally, a priori, for something to pertain to the domain of meaningfulness. Finally, a theory of meaning may perfectly well–as the contributors to this book clearly illustrate it–combine aspects from several or all of the above-mentioned approaches while adding yet new dimensions to the study of meaning. One such possibility consists in pushing the lower limits of the concept 'meaning' (and 'sign interpretation') even lower so as to determine microbiological processes in semiotic terms or so as to define the neural circuits underpinning higher order mental processes. Another possibility would, correlatively, consist in pushing investigations in the other direction, upwards, as it were, and consider the supra-personal constitution of higher order, social meaningful objects.

This state of affairs is probably what explains the great many different scientific disciplines, currents of thought and rational domains directly or indirectly dealt with by the contributors to this book while developing their approach to signs and meaning; just to mention a few: cognitive semantics, cognitive linguistics, philosophy of language, metaphysics, epistemology, biology, antropology, ethology, computer sicence, cybernetics, sociology, mathematics,...

There is no reason to hide that we, the editors, consider "semiotics"–freed from all its contingent poststructuralist connotations–a term which could suitably accommodate the various investigations into the fundamental dimensions of meaning phenomena: in our view, all contributors do indeed "do" semiotics, even though many don't use that term. However, the point of this book is not to champion our take on this issue. The aim of this book is to allow the reader to get acquainted with major strands in contemporary theories of signs and meaning, without being submitted to the rigor of scholarly presentation. Therefore we have chosen not to organize the material under general headings, defining the membership of this or that contributor to this and that line of thought (an endeavor which–aside being awfully arduous–would have made it more difficult to acknowledge the wealth of fertile crossovers between the different traditions and approaches). Reading this book may therefore be a somewhat erratic experience, leading one from cellular semiosis to the meaning of money via the rhetoric of images, or from Saussure to Peirce via Frege, Wittgenstein, and Austin ... and back again. We are nevertheless convinced that the excursion into the landscape of meaning phenomena and their landmark theories, represented by the contributors, will prove challenging; be it only because the crash courses in these theories along with the intellectual flash biographies provide us with an insight into essential aspects of meaningfulness and meaning construction.

Peer Bundgaard
Aarhus
November 2008

Acknowledgements

We are particularly grateful to the contributors for devoting time to writing such erudite, enlightening and often thought-provoking interviews and grateful to the philosophical community in general for showing interest in this project. In addition we would like to express our gratitude to Christopher M. Whalin and Elizabeth Pando for proof-reading the manuscript and to our publisher Automatic Press ♦ $\frac{V}{I}$P, in particular senior publishing editor V.J. Menshy, for continuing to take on these 'rather unusual academic' projects.

Peer Bundgaard & Frederik Stjernfelt
Aarhus
November 2008

1
Per Aage Brandt

Professor

Department of Modern Languages and Literatures

Department of Cognitive Science

Case Western Reserve University, USA

---

1. Why were you initially drawn to the theory of signs and meaning?

I studied at the University of Copenhagen (1963-71) and chose Romance philology, rather than linguistics, psychology or philosophy, while attending many fine lectures and courses in these fields. I had chosen the humanities, over physics or mathematics, for a couple of reasons: 1) I wanted to scientifically study meaning and language, 2) I believed that a scientific approach to meaning required 'formalization', modeling, theoretical work, and I found nothing such yet really established: a nice challenge. An early introduction to philosophy of science, by the great Helmuth Hansen, who durably inspired generations of students; solid grammar (served by top Romance philologists like Knud Togeby, Ebbe Spang-Hanssen, P. Hyllested, V. Sten, Højby, Sven Skydsgaard ...), literary analysis on phenomenological grounds (Svend Johansen, Einar Tassing), new French structural theories of meaning as existing in social, cultural, discursive, textual frameworks — all this, plus psychologist Edgar Tranekjær Rasmussen's lectures on consciousness, the general phonetics course by Eli Fischer-Jørgensen, and the legendary Louis Hjelmslev's methodological course — captured me and fueled my early intellectual passion. This university was for some beautiful years an incredible condensation of highly qualified and productive activities: teaching, research, discussion, and publication.

There was no 'theory of signs and meaning' to be drawn to, as I then saw it, but instead a huge lot of good problems to develop. An interdisciplinary group of students meeting regularly in the diner *The Cannibal* in Nørregade, we founded the journal *Poetik* which became a framework for heated debates and risky theorizations. I think my first article there was "Strukturalisme på empirisk grundlag" [Structuralism empirically based]. It appeared to me that the structure of meaning is a deeper problem than the structure of sign systems; so, semiology, Saussure's suggestion, could only be a tip of the semiotic iceberg. While we were of course discussing narrativity, discourse and enunciation [diegese, diskurs, udsigelse] and their role in the analysis of political ideology and socio-symbolic processes, from Mauss to Lévi-Strauss, and soon in the perspective of the new structuralists, Greimas, Barthes, Foucault, Lacan, Derrida, I was also, in parallel, deeply engaged in considerations in view of understanding the relation between linear manifestations of syntax and grammatical meaning (Chomsky versus Tesnière, accompanied by Derrida's grammatological critique of a 'metaphysics' of the linearity of meaning: the sequentiality of concatenated lexical items does not per se create meaning, as if the linear 'soufflé', the breath, were really the Spirit...). The latter realm of research led to my book *L'analyse phrastique* (1973) and the stemmatic project, which is still alive and kicking (2008), albeit now in a context of cognitive linguistics and conceptual robotics.

As to the signs and their classification, we of course discussed C. S. Peirce versus Saussure, and Umberto Eco's and others' flashy or arcane interpretations; my feeling was that Peirce was as tricky as Jacques Lacan, and that these eccentric thinkers and bizarre writers should be read after midnight, when their mesmerized followers are asleep. A special problem was the relation between Marxism and semiotics: is money a sign system? What is value? — It soon appeared that iconicity, not social symbolicity, was the deepest problem and the most important phenomenon to consider. I found out that Nelson Goodman was misleading. What was right? Years went by, before the implicitly phenomenological theory of mental spaces and conceptual integration finally started shedding some light on this, and my new Aarhus-based group, in this respect particularly driven by my daughter Line Brandt, started developing a new model of semiotic blending; the issue is cognitively rather complicated and touches philosophically on the ontological status of *representations*.

Can I give my present view of signs here, in a short version?

Let me try. We have to take a deep breath and go down to the level of human consciousness as such. Consciousness is a huge architecture but is basically built with two 'panes', one being perceptual, and the other imaginary, that is, representational. Human communication constitutively poses that subjects knowingly share this condition; so, the addressed other will invest his imaginary pane in decoding input from the addressing subject who expresses contents of his own imaginary pane. Subjects have and can consciously hold many indirect representational panes, housing imaginary scenarios behind other imaginary scenarios, interrelated through signs. To believe that contents are shared — and that we therefore 'communicate' — is to believe that some structure present in some of these representational panes is quasi-identical, in that it involves quasi-identical scenarios, built of shared categories, properties, and relational schemas. Such beliefs are foundational in iconicity. The privilege of iconic communication is that it does not imply knowledge of codes or causal knowledge but only some representational imagination and some sensitivity to the possible and plausible intentions of the communicating other. Icons are thus signs, signifiers linked to signifieds not by codes or by causes, but by allo-mental intuitions. Ideally, iconic communication is performed face to face and therefore allows on-line negotiation of 'meant meaning' (utterance–interpretive suggestion — accepted/rejected). In most contexts, however, the same process of interpretation is active, over large distances in time and space; which is why culture is possible. Icons are expressions of evaluations, concerns, fears, desires, plans, or just thetic and hypothetic thoughts. By contrast, symbols are in fact basically instructions, as Eco suggests; to symbolize is to give instructions or orders. But all expressed signs are icons. To express a symbolic meaning, we of course need to communicate *an icon of the symbol* or string of symbols (cf. writing). If indices, in the Peircean sense, deserve to be called signs, we cannot express these 'signs' without again signifying them, simulating them, through icons (cf. coughing, symptom, and simulated coughing, icon of symptom). So in fact, only icons communicate; they can contain symbols or indices, or both, or they can contain other icons, or nothing else. Linguistic signs, words and sentences, are icons of conceptual instructions and also icons of indices of the state of mind and representational states of the speaker. Why is all this important? Because most of what we experience in the human world is the result of expressive activity and therefore, precisely, iconic — in one or more of these senses. The noble art of cognitive semiotics is the study of the way in which conscious beings cognize, apprehend, interpret the experienceable world and the manifestations of its conscious beings, including their signs.

2. What do you consider your contribution to the field?

Maybe primarily to communicate my passionate interest in this field. And an invincible anti-skepticism. I have tried to show in many ways that meanings can indeed be modeled — graphically, mathematically, or at least in discourse. The point is that what has so often been left untouched because it seems hopelessly open-ended and immediately infinite (meanings referring to life, feelings, values, etc.), can often be grasped in terms of finite formal cognitive phenomena and thus has a real chance of being analyzed and understood. If science as such is collaboration in the elementary human quest for knowledge, then a scientific approach to meaning and to cultural activities should be perfectly possible; we can achieve new knowledge in this domain by more systematically grasping, exchanging and comparing, coordinating, and further examining what we know from 'experience'. While meaning often appears unstable and infinitely plastic–and therefore too 'historical' for analysis–on local cultural levels, it still relies on underlying cognitive and cross-cultural, cross-historical stabilities that make is possible for humans to think out of the immediate local boxes, to deviate from the local cultural standard fixations, and thus allow independent, inventive creativity, such as fiction, art, and science itself.

What may I have contributed to the discovery of such underlying stabilities? So far, I have worked on finding basic principles of enunciation, of semio-syntactic (stemmatic) structure, of modal dynamics, of narrative diegetics, of semantic domains, of metaphor and metonymy, of mental architecture; tonal organization in music; semiotic and cognitive aesthetics. And some philosophical issues concerning the ontology of meaning, and therefore including dualism versus monism: lately, I have been working on a project to show that (monist) analytic philosophy, which opposes research on meaning and therefore is of a certain methodological interest, is historically grounded particularly and specifically in Spinoza's ontological thinking, whereas Descartes as a defender of the study of *representation* (again) and a founder of phenomenology, is a rational thinker of cognition, mind, and meaning, too often unjustly set aside in current research on meaning and mind; which explains much of the theoretical confusion in semiotic and cognitive philosophy: so for instance, analytic, truth-conditional semantics cannot account for meaning as signified sign-immanent meaning as mental, imaginary, representational content. Paradoxically, Descartes turns out to be the real monist, in the sense that his philosophy, and its modern developments, including Husserl's, Merleau-Ponty's, and certain contemporary thinkers (Michel Serres, Jean Petitot, and John Searle, rather than David Chalmers) entail the possibility of *causally* uniting the study of meaning and the study of matter (or: to develop a pheno-physics of human reality). This possibility has been ruled out for a century, I claim, by analytic Spinozism (see Damasio, but also 'flesh philosophers' like Lakoff and Johnson).

Just to give an idea of the way in which I found the logico-linguistic modalities to function: bits of logos, whatever you want to call them (semantic propositions), refer to mental maps. Those involving MUST refer to the idea of states of a system such that a plurality of states is reduced, and the system is forced to ('must') be in one of the remaining states. The 'force' in MUST is cognized topologically, as a *shrinking map* of possible states. MAY appears in ideas of enlarging the number of states available to a system, that is, corresponds to a *growing map*. The epistemic values of NECESSARY and POSSIBLE can be analyzed in the same way as MUST and MAY. The epistemic value of IMPOSSIBLE means, formulated in these terms, that no states are available for the system (all have disappeared), all roads are closed, the referent system cannot 'go' anywhere. NEGATION is basically the critical transition from POSSIBLE to IMPOSSIBLE, by closing the open; from NECESSARY to POSSIBLE, from shrinking to growing; or from IMPOSSIBLE to POSSIBLE, by opening the closed. Though not from POSSIBLE to NECESSARY–it does not make sense to both close and shrink. Negation thus expresses and can be modeled topologically as modal criticality. The value CAN is a little different; it contains a negation of a negation, namely a reopening of a closed; therefore it often feels as involving the addition of a supplement of force. In this view, modal thinking is grounded in topological imagination and can therefore be described by mathematical topology, such as René Thom's catastrophe theory, as also shown by Wolfgang Wildgen and Jean Petitot. There are, in my analysis, basically four different types of forces that produce these state changes: physical causality, social (deontic) normativity, mental (epistemic) force, and speech act force. My guess is that speech act force is primordial and gave rise to the other types when the set of *basic semantic domains* became stable. Modality is a driving force in narrative structure, in argumentation, in causal description, i. e. in thinking altogether. Language would be almost useless in the human world without modal expressions and the modalization of contents. So the closed class of modal signs in a language is — across interlingual variations — a semiotic universal.

3. What is the proper role of a theory of signs and meaning in relation to other academic disciplines?

Well, theories of signs and meaning do hardly define any academic discipline in itself. These theories appear in philosophy, social science and anthropology, psychology, etc.–and indeed in linguistics. Cultural studies in general rely on implicit semiotic theories if not on explicit elaborations. The objects of perception, reflection, memory, communication, and interaction, are mainly semiotic: signs or sign-borne meanings. Diagrams, for example, seem to be more direct manifestations of thought than language; when language expresses thought, it most often refers to implicit or explicit diagrams that manifest thought. Diagrams using arrowing, containment, channeling, partitioning, binding, and spatial mapping — expressions (graphics and gestures) that manifest operations like these — are much more characteristic of human constructive imagination than operations on symbol strings. By contrast, diagrams do not express emotional states very well.

In the future, I am convinced that successors of naïve 'artificial intelligence', including what we are currently developing as cognitive or conceptual robotics, will rely on meaning models such as the representations of modal dynamics, temporal schemas, spatial navigation schemas, speech act schemas, narrative schemas of self and other, etc. Cognitive robotics currently develops Cartesian simulations of consciousness along these lines.

Future linguistics will be a semiotics. Meaning, originating in the processes of thinking, and represented in language as 'semantics', is already signified mentally by other signs — diagrams and icons of all kinds. This is why writing was unjustly expulsed from the study of language, as Derrida's early luminous remarks on Saussure showed. 'Pure' thinking is therefore already semiotic; 'writing' is truly a part of language, not an external supplement. Rejecting this insight would be giving up the study of thinking, and of semantics.

4. What do you consider the most important topics and/or contributions in the theory of meaning and signs?

Let me just mention two lines of research. As Umberto Eco asks: why do we think that image theory, theory of causal reasoning, and theory of symbolization should be considered aspects of one and the same theory of meaning? Why would three theories have to be or become one theory? Well, because we have only got one brain, per person, and it is only thanks to this organ that humans have minds that can think and use imagery to do so, to reason causally, and to freeze concepts in symbols allowing shared thinking. Roman Jakobson's approach to semiotics, poetics, and linguistics as grounded in neuroscience is one of the most important ways to answer that question. Ernst Pöppel's studies of time in brain and mind are beautiful specimens of this approach.

Marcel Mauss' discovery of the symbolic dimension of exchange, the aspect of 'giving' that affects 'being', not only 'having', is crucial to everything that followed, from Claude Lévi-Strauss to Georges Bataille and to current studies of social cognition. Ernst Cassirer's monumental work belongs to the same line, as I see it. It is impossible to study actions–hence narratives–without paying attention to this dimension. The identification of this specific relation between behavior and meaning is perhaps the most important contribution of structuralism to current research.

5. What are the most important open problems in this field and what are the prospects for progress?

My refrains or mementos: We don't yet know how to model the human psyche as such (Freud tried). We don't yet know how to model the human society as such (Marx tried). And we don't yet know how to model human language as such (Chomsky tried). Those who tried to unify Freud's, Marx's, and Chomsky's views, technical constructions, or theories are even more astray, I think. One thing we do know, however, is that the three problems are to be treated in the framework of human semiotic *evolution*. Not unlike astronomical speculations, theories of meaning are theories of how things came about, not of systems for classifying them. For example, what we habitually consider the systematic components of language may be of totally different age, like the parts of the human brain. The lexical part of our linguistic memory may be younger (or older, which is less likely) than the nodes of meaningful syntax; the morphological connections between the lexical and the syntactic part of grammar may have happened at an even later time—and could also have failed to happen altogether. Language would then not have occurred, at least not the sort of expressive behavior we now call language. This view is, I believe, radically different from Louis Hjelmslev's, or Knud Togeby's. Lévi-Strauss' notion of *bricolage* comes closer to the biologically and thus evolutionarily produced configurations our ancestors liked to see as systems or 'immanent structures' (Togeby).

One question I would like to examine closely is the relation between the genres of long-term *memory* (Tulving) and the components of language: memory is either procedural (like phonetics), episodic (like sentence meanings), or 'semantic' (like semantic). What does this parallelism indicate? Apparently that language lives in the compartmentalized house of memory—apart from the fact that there is no such house.

Another question is: how did human imagination become such an autonomous intellectual and forcefully constructive (or destructive) instance? I would include brain imaging in the methodology and investigate along at least the two following lines: Compare to cognition in states of psychosis—apparently involving processes of uncontrolled blending between the mental spaces of perception and of imagination.—Compare to cognition during human eroticosexual excitement, which offers the singularity of discarding world knowledge from the semantic memory to such an extent that the subject experiences a desemanticized and highly concentrated present experience dominated by phantasies (French: 'fantasmes'); Freud may still have a point here. The theme is likely to imply major moral obstacles under the current circumstances; but it could very well be an appropriate path toward an understanding of so-called abstract thinking.

Finally, we still need to know what *money* is; a semiotics of general economy would be useful in a globalizing and ecologically uncertain world.

2
Marcel Danesi

Professor of Semiotics and Communication Theory
University of Toronto, Canada

---

1. Why were you initially drawn to the theory of signs and meaning?

I received my doctorate in historical linguistics in 1974 from the University of Toronto, with a specialization in Italian, and started teaching full time at the university in the same year. From the outset, I was dissatisfied with the mainstream generative approach to language, which at the time ignored non-literal meaning phenomena (and still largely does so to this day). I thought then (and I still do now) that such models of language were evasive in how they treated the presence of such phenomena in language as metaphorical discourse, labeling them as mere deviations from more basic rules of literalist meaning. I need not go into the problems of the generative approach to meaning here. I have discussed these myself at some length in *Poetic Logic: The Role of Metaphor in Thought, Language, and Culture* (2004). I simply mention them because of the fact that my dissatisfaction with generativism changed my career. By the late 1970s I had become fascinated by meaning phenomena of all types (verbal and nonverbal) and the role they played in everyday life.

I also discovered the writings of the Neapolitan philosopher Giambattista Vico (1668-1744) at about the same time. I became especially intrigued by his *New Science* (1725). Vico taught me that metaphor was a product of our "poetic mind," as he called it, constituting a verbal residue of primordial thinking that continues to build into words how we discover the world through sense-based associations. So, I started researching and writing about metaphor at a time when the topic was just starting to come into the domain in linguistics, that is, right after Lakoff and Johnson's watershed publication of 1980 (*Metaphors We Live By*).

Because of my work on metaphor, I was invited in the early 1980s by the Institute for Semiotic and Structural Studies, which held advanced courses, seminars, and conferences during the summer months at Victoria College of my university, to teach a graduate seminar on metaphor. The seminar was an enriching experience for me. I discovered the power of a relatively simple framework—sign theory—for investigating all kinds of meaning phenomena. I had very little formal knowledge of semiotics before actually teaching that course. But I soon became absorbed in the discipline. Right after the course, I took over the editorship of the Monograph Series of the Toronto Semiotic Circle and then met the late Thomas A. Sebeok, who converted me completely over to semiotics. In the mid-1980s, Victoria College, which had instituted an undergraduate program in semiotics a few years earlier, invited me to teach and eventually to coordinate the courses in the program. I have been teaching in, and coordinating, the program ever since.

What has always made semiotics attractive to me is its flexibility. As Jack Solomon put it in his excellent introductory book to the field, *The Signs of Our Times* (1988), "semiotics never tells you what to think, only how to think and how to probe beneath the surface" (p. 13). It has also taught me that Homo sapiens is, more accurately, Homo signans, "the signer." The Stone Age carvings on cave walls of jumping and dying animals give unequivocal testimony to how truly advanced and sophisticated we have always been as "representers" or "modelers" of the world. Indeed, I have come to understand, through semiotics, that the distinguishing characteristic of the human species has always been its remarkable ability to represent the world through pictures, vocal sounds, hand gestures, and the like. This ability is the reason why, over time, our species has come to be regulated not by force of natural selection, but by "force of history;" that is, by force of the accumulated meanings that previous generations have captured and passed on in the form of signs. As opposed to nature, culture is everywhere meaningful, the result of our need to seek meaning and order to existence. It is this "quest for meaning" that fascinates me and, I believe, the students that take my courses at the university.

Semiotics has also taught me that meaning is something that we produce ourselves. Nevertheless, in so doing, maybe signs are small-scale models of hidden patterns in the world. Studying the *raison d'être* of the latter has always been—and continues to be—

the aim of philosophy, mathematics, and various other disciplines; studying the *raison d'être* of the former is the specific goal of semiotics. The central task of semiotics is, in fact, to unravel the meanings built into signs and sign assemblages, from words, symbols, narratives, symphonies, paintings and comic books, to scientific theories and mathematical theorems. At first blush, this task would seem to be a daunting one, encompassing virtually all the creative and knowledge-making activities that make up human social life. But it is not, as I myself have found out, because semiotics focuses more narrowly on the use, structure, and function of the signs used in such activities. Even so, it ultimately produces insights that relate to the larger question of the meaning of existence.

2. What do you consider to be your contribution to the field?

This is a very difficult question to answer. I have been doing semiotics because I truly enjoy it, not because I have to. I would like to think that my writings on Vico and metaphor have had an impact on the field, even if it might be a miniscule one. However, given the feedback and responses I have received in recent years, it would seem that the work I have published on puzzles has been my most important contribution to the field. The reason is probably that puzzles have rarely (if ever) been studied from the semiotic perspective. Although I do not mention semiotics explicitly in my book *The Puzzle Instinct* (2002), any semiotician will instantly see that I have used sign theory to flesh out the meanings of puzzles in human life.

Puzzles are considered, typically, to be part of recreational or ludic culture. But, if so, how similar or different are they from other ludic texts, such as jokes, satirical poems, etc.? Or do puzzles reveal something much more fundamental about human cognition and the quest for meaning? These questions have rarely been studied in any depth, even though puzzles have been around since recorded history. One of the oldest mathematics textbooks (the Egyptian *Rhind Papyrus*), which dates back to 1650 BCE, turns out to be essentially a collection of mathematical brainteasers. The Biblical kings Solomon and Hiram were renowned for organizing riddle contests. Benjamin Franklin, the American inventor, and Lewis Carroll, the English writer known for his two great children's novels *Alice's Adventures in Wonderland* and *Through* the Looking-Glass, contrived ingenious puzzles that continue to befuddle and intrigue people to this day.

My purpose in focusing on puzzles has been to draw attention to their importance for sign theory, for what are puzzles if not intriguing kinds of signs that are constructed with every possible medium available—verbal and nonverbal? Everything from riddles and anagrams, to crosswords and sudoku, would constitute the subject matter of *enigmatological semiotics*, as it can be called. I will continue to work in this subfield.

3. What is the proper role of a theory of signs and meaning in relation to other academic disciplines?

I see sign theory as guiding our understanding of all the mysteries that life presents to us. This is what the other disciplines must eventually come to realize (if they already haven't)—namely that sign-construction guides all human knowledge. Does this mean, therefore, that our sign-constructs imprison us cognitively or creatively, as post-structuralists are inclined to claim? Are they true descriptors of reality, or the result of mind games that we play in our interactions with reality? On the one hand, our signs are indeed imaginary constructs that influence how we perceive reality, as the post-structuralists would claim; on the other hand, however, they turn out to be veritable "tools of discovery." Real discoveries happen all the time in mathematics and science, serendipitously unraveling patterns within nature. The invention of the mathematical ratio π ($=$ approximately 3.14) was motivated by the need to calculate the area of a circle. It is a construct. But, as it turns out, this very same construct turns out to be a "descriptor" of such physical phenomena as the motion of a pendulum or the vibration of a string, among many other naturally-occurring phenomena. This synergy between signs and reality is a remarkable one indeed. Thus, sign theory, in my view, should comprise the epistemological center of any academic discipline, including mathematics and science. Charles Peirce, as always, was right when he pointed out that, as a species, we are programmed to "think only in signs." In so doing, moreover, we discover reality—or at least culture-specific versions of that reality. It is when we add up all the cultural versions that we might eventually develop a universal system for penetrating the mysteries of life.

4. What do you consider to be the most important topics and/or contributions in the theory of signs and meaning?

Today, there are two trends that have come to the forefront—*biosemiotics*, or the study of semiosis across species, and what can be called *cybernetic semiotics*, or the study of sign-use in new media, such as the Internet. Among the leading figures in biosemiotics I mention the great Estonian semioticians, from Yuri Lotman to Kalevi Kull, as well as the late American semiotician Thomas A. Sebeok. In the area of cybernetic semiotics, I mention, for example, the work of Søren Brier and semioticians who are currently involved in studying the relation between reality and simulation—the significant work being conducted on diagrams (by Frederik Stjernfelt, for instance) is leading the way in showing how simulation and reality are linked. In an age where "virtual living" is becoming more and more of a reality, examining the role of diagrams (icons, avatars, etc.) is clearly of utmost importance.

The psychological power of the "simulative environments" that technology has brought into existence has, of course, been a target of interest of artists and cinematographers (as can be seen in the 1999 movie *The Matrix*), as well as of some so-called "posthuman" philosophers. But it is semioticians, I believe, who are leading the way in showing the impact of the new media on human meaning-making. I should mention here that it was probably Marshall McLuhan (1911-1980), who taught at my university, who foresaw the power of media to transform human life. McLuhan did so in a way that is consistent with semiotic ideas, even though he never claimed to be a semiotician. Before the advent of alphabets, people communicated and passed on their knowledge through the spoken word. But even in early oral cultures, tools had been invented for recording and preserving ideas in durable physical forms. These were invariably pictographic. So intuitive and functional is pictography that it comes as little surprise to find that it has not disappeared from our own world, as the study of diagrams has shown. McLuhan was among the first to realize that changes in media lead to changes in social structure and knowledge systems. The invention of alphabetic writing around 1000 BCE brought about the first true radical change in human social structure. The philosopher Thomas Kuhn (1922-1996) called such a change a "paradigm shift." The move away from pictographic to alphabetic writing was, to use Kuhn's appropriate term, the first paradigm shift of human history, since it constituted the initial step towards the establishment of a worldwide civilization.

Simply put, alphabetic writing made print the first viable global medium for storing and exchanging ideas and knowledge. The second step was taken in the fifteenth century with the development of movable type technology. McLuhan designated the type of social order that ensued from that momentous technological event the "Gutenberg Galaxy," after Johann Gutenberg (c. 1400-1468) the German printer who invented movable type in Europe. The Gutenberg Galaxy did indeed, as McLuhan suggested, establish printed books as the primary tools for recording and preserving information and knowledge. But it did more than that. It also established the book form as the first true "mass distraction" device of history. And, indeed, to this day we read books not only for educational or professional purposes, but also to while away our leisure hours. The third step was taken at the start of the twentieth century, after advancements in electronic technology established sound recordings, cinema, radio, and (a little later) television as new media for communicating information and, above all else, for providing distraction to larger and larger masses of people. Since electronic signals can cross borders virtually unimpeded, McLuhan characterized the world that was being united by electronic media as the "global village." Near the end of the twentieth century, the fourth step was taken right after computers became widely available and the Internet emerged as the most dominant of all currently-employed media.

Biosemiotics and cybersemiotics have come forward, arguably, to expand the McLuhnian legacy. Tools are signs. As such, they are extensions of the biology and psychology of the human organism making them. An ax, for instance, extends the power of the human hand to break wood; the wheel of the human foot to cover distances; and so on and so forth. McLuhan claimed that the tools developed to record and transmit messages determine how people process and remember them. Human beings are endowed by nature to decipher information with all the senses. Our *sense ratios*, as he called them, are equally calibrated at birth to receive information. However, in social settings, it is unlikely that all the senses will operate at the same ratio. One sense ratio or the other increases according to the dominant modality employed in a culture to record and transmit information. In an oral culture, the *auditory sense ratio* is the one that largely shapes information processing and message interpretation; in a print culture, on the other hand, the *visual sense ratio* is the crucial one. This raising or lowering of sense ratios is not, however, preclusive. Indeed, in contemporary digital culture, we are constantly activating various sense ratios in tandem.

So, what can semiotics contribute to the study of new media? In my view, it can detect patterns within it instantly, and lay them bare for others to reflect upon them. For example, a study of linguistic signs in cyberspace has revealed a growing tendency towards "sign compression," as it can be called—a phenomenon that manifests itself in such phenomena as abbreviations, acronyms, and the use of numbers in place of words, all of which are designed to make the delivery of linguistic messages rapid. With few, if any, corrective forces at work in cyberspace two relevant questions emerge: Is this "economizing of form" a contemporary phenomenon or has it always existed as a general semiosic tendency? Is it influencing not only the mode of delivery of language as used in cybernetic communications, but also language in all its structural, cognitive, and expressive dimensions?

The answer to both questions would appear to be in the affirmative, as I have discussed in a recent study titled "Alphabets and The Principle of Least Effort" (published in *Studies in Communication Sciences* 6, 2006, pp. 47-62). Scholars and scientists have always used abbreviations and acronyms of various kinds to facilitate technical communications among themselves, enhancing their rapidity and precision. Abbreviations such as *etc., et al., op. cit. N.B.,* are still part and parcel of "scholarspeak," as it may be called. But what sets the compression tendencies in Netlingo, as the British linguist David Crystal (*Language and the Internet,* 2006) calls linguistic communication in cyberspace, apart from all economizing tendencies of the past, is the speed and extent to which reduced forms are spreading and becoming part of general communicative behavior. In effect, the semiotic study of Internet style reveals the operation of a Principle of Least Effort—a principle that was made somewhat famous in the 1950s by the French linguist André Martinet, who claimed essentially that languages change as a result of the operation of economic tendencies *(Économie des changements phonétiques,* 1955). Calling it the Principle of Economic Change, Martinet posited that complex language forms and structures tended towards reduction, abbreviation, compression, leveling, or elimination over time. Distinctions of meaning were preserved nonetheless, but with less phonic material. Grammatical change, Martinet argued, is usually a consequence of previous phonetic change. A classic example of this is the loss of the Latin declension system in the Romance languages. As a result of phonetic changes, such as the elimination of the final /-m/ in accusative forms and the dropping of final consonants generally, the suffixes used in declensions no longer signaled grammatical distinctions as early as the fourth century. Over time, this led to the reconstitution and even elimination of the entire declension system. More economical devices were developed by the Romance languages to maintain case distinctions, such as prepositions and determiners.

The fact that a Principle of Least Effort may be operative in human communication was, actually, first identified in the 1930s by the Harvard linguist George Kingsley Zipf (1902-1950). Essentially, Zipf claimed that many phenomena in language could be explained as a tendency in the human species to make the most of its lexical and grammatical resources with the least expenditure of effort. This tendency was independent of individual and culture. Zipf started by demonstrating empirically that there exists a statistical correlation between the length of a specific word (in number of phonemes) and its rank order in the language (its position in order of its frequency of occurrence in texts of all kinds). The higher the rank order of a word (the more frequent it is in actual usage), the more it tends to be "shorter" (made up with fewer phonemes). For example, articles *(a, the)*, conjunctions *(and, or)*, and other function words *(to, it)*, which have a high rank order in English (and in any other language for that matter), are typically monosyllabic, consisting of 1-3 phonemes. What is even more intriguing is that this compression force does not stop at the level of function words. It can be seen to manifest itself in the tendency for words and phrases that come into popular use to become abbreviated *(hi, bye, ad, photo, 24/7,* etc.) or changed into acronyms *(aka, VCR, DNA, laser, GNP, IQ, VIP,* etc.). It can also be seen in the spread of diagrams in digital communication contexts, since these have the ability to compress huge amounts of information economically and effectively. In effect, the general version of "Zipf's Law," as it is commonly called, proclaims that the more frequent or necessary a form for communicative purposes, the more likely it is to be rendered compressed, diagrammatic, or economical in physical structure.

Nowhere is the operation of this Principle as apparent today as it is in the forms that are created in Netlingo. To increase the speed at which messages can be inputted and received, a series of common abbreviations, acronyms, and other compressed structures have crystallized in it. Here are a few common English cyberforms, as they can be called: b4 = before, f2f = face-to-face, 2dA = today, ruok = Are you OK? g2g = gotta go. Writing takes time and effort. In the Internet Age, both come at a premium. Not answering the barrage of e-mails or text messages that people receive on a daily basis is perceived negatively. Slowness in response is, at times, even penalized by social ostracism or various other forms of reprobation. Logically, form compression helps counteract the situation by making it possible to "get back" to one's sender of messages quickly and rapidly.

In no way does compression imply diminishment. Indeed, once alphabet characters came into existence as compressions of pictographs they took on a semiotic life of their own. This kind of assessment of change in sign systems probably characterizes how many (if not all) innovations are made in representation and communication generally. General conditions seem to exist in sign systems that determine the equilibrium of the systems in terms of their forms and meanings. It is the specific conditions that shift with time and place, not the general semiotic tendencies. Internet-Age phenomena, such as Netlingo, will become more and more the target of investigation inside and outside semiotics. The latter will provide a "philological barometer," so to speak, for inferring evolutionary patterns in sign systems.

5. What are the most important open problems in this field and what are the prospects for progress?

In my view, we need a more compressed sign theory (no witticism intended, given the foregoing discussion). As Sebeok and I attempted to show in a 2000 work *(The Forms of Meaning: Modeling Systems Theory and Semiotic Analysis)*, we at least need a reduced terminology that will allow semiotics to tap into a broader academic domain. The traditional goal of semiotic theory has been to figure out how signs are constituted and how they encode referents. The theoretical frameworks developed by Saussure and Peirce stand, to this day, as the standard ones for pursuing this objective. But over the last five decades, a perusal of the major journals of semiotics reveals that the field has become cluttered with terminological inconsistencies, partisan factions, and a host of neologisms and arcane trends that (in my view) may have tarnished its image as a scientific enterprise. The basic premise held by Sebeok and myself is that many (if not most) of the apparently disparate terms and concepts used haphazardly within the field can be easily integrated into the theoretical framework called *Modeling Systems Theory* (MST). The actual physical form of a sign can, as we suggested, be called simply that—a *form*. The linkage of a form to its referent (or referential domain) can be called, simply, a *model*. The crux of MST is the claim that models are subject to both biological and psychological process (simulation, indication, etc.) and that these will vary in nature and complexity depending on function.

To conclude, let me say that. I feel privileged to be a member of the community of semioticians, accepted by them as an active contributor to the field. Semiotics has stimulated several questions in me that have guided my mode of inquiry and will probably guide it in the future: Why does there seem to be continuity between mind matter (semiosis) and physical matter? Is it possible to discover the larger pattern from which the fabric of our models of reality have been cut to produce a "broader picture" of the universe? I will look for answers to such question, not in broad terms, but by studying our "micromodels" of reality, such as puzzles. When we solve a puzzle, we may unconsciously be modeling how our brain thinks.

3
Terrence Deacon

Professor

Biological Anthropology and Linguistics

University of California, Berkeley

The Five Questions

1. Why were you initially drawn to the theory of signs and meaning?

My early college interests were in physics and biology, but this was in the mid 1970s and a new approach was beginning to encroach into both: systems thinking, exemplified by cybernetics and the early days of computer technology. The impact on biology was two-fold: first there was a growing recognition that both ecosystems and organisms were complex systems, and second there was the rapidly growing understanding of molecular genetics which seemed to demonstrate that at its very most basic levels life involved something like information. As a student I organized study groups in which we read many of the seminal works in these areas including Waddington's series of Volumes on Theoretical Biology, W. Ross Ashby's books on information theory and cybernetics, books by von Bertalanffy and others promoting General Systems Theory, Aurthur Koestler's critiques of reductionism, and many seminal papers by such folks as Claude Shannon, Philip Anderson, Michael Polanyi, and Paul Weiss. I dug into symbolic logic going back to Boole's *Laws of Thought* and up to the exciting *Laws of Form* by G. Spencer Brown. Gregory Bateson became an influence as well, though I was not his student, I had a few contacts with him through one of his former students, Anthony Wilden, whose book *System and Structure* was also influential. But in all of this the concept of meaning was missing, and there didn't seem to be a clear link between the physics and the referential aspects of the theories. Koestler's criticisms continued to bother me.

Then at the insistent urging of a book store employee, I picked up a collection of papers by Charles Sander Peirce, though I had long resisted digging into philosophy. It was a revelation. I saw that these modern efforts were beginning–only beginning–to find ways to formalize some of the problems Peirce was analyzing. But Peirce had gone further in his conceptualization of the problem, though lacking the tools that developed in the 20th century. I felt he was a generation ahead of me; not a century earlier. Basing his semiotics on a highly general theory of "habit," arguing that the semiotics of extrinsic communication was continuous with the communication that constitutes mind, systematically trying to avoid the tendency to appeal to psychologism and homuncular arguments to "explain" interpretation processes, and conceiving of semiotic processes as growing naturally out of the fabric of the physical universe–these visionary ideas astounded me. I dropped out and spent a year just reading through the collected papers, then in 1976 I wrote a BA thesis attempting to show the links between Peirce's semiotics and cybernetic theory.

I was subsequently accepted to graduate school at Harvard University where I hoped to be able to study the unpublished papers of Peirce, then stored in the Houghton Library. I thought that philosophers like Scheffler, Quine, and Putnam, who were there, and each had at some point in their works mentioned Peirce and Pragmatism, would find this interesting. But I never got these conversations going, and had little opportunity to read the papers. Instead, I took classes from them and from folks like Chomsky and Fodor at MIT and from the neuroanatomist Walle Nauta and psychologists like Sheldon White and others. I became intrigued by the thought that I could pursue the ideas inspired by Peirce empirically, by understanding brain function. My PhD work on the neural architecture of brain structures in humans and primates relevant to the evolution of language, had this as its background. The systems and Peircean framing of my thinking about evolutionary, neural, and linguistic issues, has always led me to be critical of simple reductionistic approaches and computational metaphors for mental and neural processes.

2. What do you consider your contribution to the field?

I think that my development of a Peircean approach to language evolution and brain function still stands as unique. In my struggles in the 1980s to integrate Peirce's semiotics with an understanding of these problems, but informed also by cybernetic and systems thinking and particularly Bateson's use of Russellian logical type theory I realized that the current categorical conception of icons, indices, and symbols could be reformulated as a logical type hierarchy (in that order) such that interpretation of a sign as a symbol required prior interpretations of its component relations in indexical terms, which in turn required prior interpretations of the indices' component relations in iconic terms. The relationship was constructive, emergent, and internal not external.

This was implicit in the Peircean First, Second, Third logic which he used to organize his various semiotic taxonomies, but of course the logical type analysis was not yet conceived. I realized that this was an important clue to the evolution of language mystery, and that it also would help me reconceptualize regional brain function in semiotic terms as well. Though I have not to date formalized this approach for brain function generally, because of the immensity of the task (though this work is soon to be published), I recognized in the early 1990s that this could form the basis for a semiotic cognitive neurosciences, that would eventually overthrow the hegemony of computationalist theories.

Perhaps the other important contribution has been my turning the Chomskyan paradigm on its head, by paying attention to the self-organizing and meme-like nature of linguistic processes outside brains, and how languages themselves have evolved to be learnable by immature brains. This has been part of a larger reframing of evolution in more systemic terms, in which I have explored the distributed multileveled nature of the emergence of adaptive functional organization in biology as well as language and culture. This has also grown from a Peircean understanding of semiotic processes as "alive" in some sense—or to put it another way, a realization that life is semiosis.

3. What is the proper role of a theory of signs and meaning in relation to other academic disciplines?

Semiotics is currently treated mostly as a branch of the humanities, and less often as relevant to the social sciences. It has not really penetrated deeply into general psychology, cognitive sciences, or biology. This is in my opinion largely due to the fact that it has never been formulated as a scientific theory, where the process we describe as semiosis (the generation, transmission, and interpretation of signs) is cashed out in its physical details, in a way that fully avoids both eliminative reduction and yet does not merely provide semiotic terminological glosses analogizing concepts and processes in the science to mentalistic and communicative processes described in human terms. Consequently, scientists generally see it as a a philosophical renaming game of little significance and even an obfuscation, which in any case makes no additional contribution to empirical research. I believe this is about to change. As information and adaptation concepts have become more and more critical to our understanding of biological processes, a use of these concepts that is vacant of any theory of content, reference, meaning, interpretation, etc., will become a serious limitation. The sciences of life and cognition, and even computation, will eventually need to be founded on semiotic principles yet to be articulated. Moreover, this will allow insights from these natural science fields to become more easily integrated with those of the "special sciences" and humanities, where theory is currently stagnating, in need of new foundation.

4. What do you consider the most important topics and/or contributions in the theory of meaning and signs?

1. The relentless demand that representation relationships and interpretive processes be treated as critical components of any approach to biology, psychology, linguistics, or social science.

2. The recognition that the technical notions of information and computation are inadequate for these fields of study.

3. The insistence that one cannot adequately analyze symbolic and linguistic phenomena without also analyzing the wider context of iconic and indexical phenomena.

4. The realization that homuncular and phenomenological accounts that allow mentalistic concepts as unanalyzed primitives in our theories of communication and cognition are necessarily incomplete and ultimately circular, and require unpacking in process terms (e.g. a theory of interpretants, not merely interpreters).

5. What are the most important open problems in this field and what are the prospects for progress?

We currently lack a scientific theory of semiosis, that demonstrates how semiotic relationships emerge from and causally influence more basic physical-chemical processes. We need to expand physics to make this connection, not reduce semiosis to physics. This requires a systematic and thorough understanding of the problem of emergence. Current theories about information and computation are seriously inadequate, but current taxonomic and structural approaches to semiotics are inadequate as well. Semiotic theory must ultimately be shown to be an inevitable component of a full physical theory of the world. Semiotic phenomena cannot be treated as unanalyzed givens, as in panpsychic theories (e.g., variants of Whiteheadian cosmology) nor as reducible or epiphenomenal relationships, nor as dualistic aspects of the physical world. We ultimately need an emergent account of semiosis as a physical processes that explains how content, reference, meaning, value, and subjective experience have a clear efficacious role to play in the working of the cosmos. We need a physics in which we, and all our semiotic and subjective features, make sense.

4
John Deely

Professor
Center for Thomistic Studies
University of St. Thomas

---

1. Why were you initially drawn to the theory of signs and meaning?

As a graduate student, I had been steeped in philosophical studies of evolution, phenomenology, and Latin Age thought via the work of Thomas Aquinas. As a university professor, I felt a kind of lack in the area of "linguistic" or "Analytic" philosophy. So when Mortimer J. Adler offered me a position as Senior Research Fellow in his Chicago-based Institute for Philosophical Research, charged to write a book on philosophy of language, it struck me as a golden opportunity to fill in the gap, as it were, in my graduate education. After months spent reading the likes of Russell, Wittgenstein, Ayer, Ryle, Strawson, Quine, Alston, the literature of the later "linguistic turn" (Rorty *et al.*) and such authors as Chomsky and Max Black, I was beginning to feel like an athlete confined to a diet of cereal with no milk. On my shelf from graduate days was a Latin volume authored by one John Poinsot titled *Ars Logica*, which I remembered from an essay by Jacques Maritain I had chanced to read years before (someone had left his book, *Quatre Essais sur l'Esprit*, containing his essay on signs, in a choir stall to which I was assigned in a priory) contained an early 17th century *Tractatus de Signis*. I took the volume off the shelf and turned to the pages comprising the *Treatise on Signs*, and began to read for comic relief.

However, the more I read the more I came to feel that here at last in the literature on language, though far from a contemporary tract, I had stumbled on a work of fundamental importance, indeed, as I read on, of revolutionary significance, laying out foundations of signification that did not even enter into the purview of the contemporary Analytic and linguistic philosophers, nor the linguists of the contemporary scene.

About this same time I received in the mail an advertising flyer for the Mouton "Approaches to Semiotics" series, edited by one Thomas A. Sebeok of Indiana University, Bloomington, and dedicated to the publication of monographs and translations of classics in the theory of signs (as I recall the advertisement). I wrote to the editor, Tom Sebeok, at his university address, telling him of my discovery of this early "semiotic of John Poinsot", and he responded with guarded interest "in principle" in seeing a translation of the work.

We met in person three years later at a linguistics conference in a Chicago hotel, where I also met the Mouton official who accepted my argument that the complexity in terminology of the work (its key Latin expressions containing four words required fifteen words in English to be intelligibly rendered) required parallel Latin-English columns of matching text. Twelve more years were to elapse before I was able satisfactorily to complete the work and see it in print. But I did have the satisfaction the following year of seeing Poinsot's *Tractatus* presented in the Feature Review in the *New York Times Book Review* for 30 March 1986, pp. 14–18. By this time, I had participated in a number of projects and meetings with Tom Sebeok, including the founding to the Semiotic Society of America in 1975–76, and semiotics had become the focal point of my intellectual interests.

2. What do you consider your contribution to the field?

Well, this is perhaps not a question concerning which I am the best judge. Besides making available for the first time outside the Latin language of what seems to have been the definitively first work to establish the thematic unity of semiotics as a subject of inquiry and the being of signs as consisting in an irreducibly triadic relation, as Charles Peirce also argued, I have also shown in my later book, the *Four Ages of Understanding*, the relevance of semiotics to the whole history of philosophy and its role as, arguably, the positive essence of a postmodern era of philosophy and intellectual culture; and I have challenged the frontiers of semiotic inquiry by proposing, based on arguments in the texts of both Charles Peirce and John Poinsot, that the action of signs is in fact coextensive with the being of the physical universe, at work (as "physiosemiosis") even prior to and preparatory for the advent of life in the universe as an influence of the future constantly re-arranging the relevance of the past to the present as chance and causality work together to constantly change the state of the universe.

3. What is the proper role of a theory of signs and meaning in relation to other academic disciplines?

Semiotics is the first and only perspective that is inherently interdisciplinary, precisely because not only is the whole of knowledge and experience a network woven of sign relations but also the very boundaries of the disciplines at any given time depend upon sign relations. It is not that the whole universe consists of signs, but simply that whatever comes to be known of the universe becomes known in and through the action of signs. For these reasons, semiotics is the most important intellectual development since the beginnings of modern science in the 17th century, and precisely as the antidote or remedy for the demand for specialization that scientific development entails. Far from being "imperialistic", semiotics makes possible a *wholistic* understanding of intellectual and university life. It is, as Sebeok best said, an enhancing discipline, not a substitute for any other discipline concerned with a specific subject matter, such as physics, biology, literature, or political science. But I think it will be some considerable time before semiotics comes to be generally understood and assigned its proper place within the university, just as it took some centuries for science in the modern sense to find its "institutional place".

4. What do you consider the most important topics and/or contributions in the theory of meaning and signs?

Undoubtedly the realization that signs are a distinctive mode or form of being and that, as with every being, there is an action proper to and distinctive of signs that is consequent upon this distinctive being. Thus the study of signs, as it widened and deepened in contemporary intellectual culture, overcame the semiological notion that human culture alone provided a realm within which signs are properly to be found at work. Sebeok in the early 1960s introduced the distinction between "anthroposemiosis" as the human use of signs and "zoösemiosis" as the action of signs throughout the animal world. Then Krampen expanded the realization of sign-action still further to include also the realm of plants in "phytosemiosis", completing the groundwork for the establishment today of *biosemiotics* in the work of such pioneers as Hoffmeyer, Emmeche, Kull, Barbieri, Favareu, and others; while Nöth opened the 21st century with a colloquium in Kassel dedicated to the question of the "Semiotic Threshold", where I was able to propose anew the consideration I had originally raised first at the 1989 Harvard Peirce Congress, then in the sixth chapter of my 1990 text, *Basics of Semiotics*, namely, the notion mentioned above that there is an underlying "physiosemiosis" that not only accompanies but indeed preceded biosemiosis.

Thus semiotics is nothing less than a revolution within intellectual culture, the final results of which are far from fully realized and have global implications for our understanding of the whole of experience and life. In this respect, the notion of the human being as a *semiotic animal* — with which I both opened and closed my 1990 text — replacing the modern notion of human beings as "thinking thing", detached from and superior to the rest of nature, represents a huge stride toward integrating human responsibility with the environmental requirements for the health of life on earth.

5. What are the most important open problems in this field and what are the prospects for progress?

The whole of nature involves the action of signs, but human beings are the only part of the universe (wherever human life may arise in this universe, for it is hardly likely that semiotic animals are confined only to earth) which is able to know that there are signs and not only make use of signs in order to thrive and survive. Thus *responsibility* not only arises in the universe with the advent of semiotic animals, but turns out to extend to the relation of human beings not only among themselves or in their own behavior but also to the whole of nature insofar as they are involved with it. Thus the semiotic animal is also, and at the same time, perforce — in the felicitous expression introduced by Susan Petrilli and Augusto Ponzio — a *semioethic* animal. And I think that, even as the notion of *physiosemiosis* represents for the sciences of nature the best chance for completing the understanding of evolution as more than a *vis a tergo*, so the exploration and development of this notion of *semioethics* represents on the human side the most important immediate prospect for semiotics today.

5

Jørgen Dines Johansen

Professor of General and Comparative Literature

Center for Literature and Semiotics

University of Sourhtern Denmark

---

1. Why were you initially drawn to the theory of signs and meaning?

For two reasons: Before changing to studying literature I studied psychology and philosophy, and hence hermeneutic questions concerning interpretation and questions concerning validity in text interpretation have always been central to me.

Second, in the late sixties in Denmark structuralism was all over the place. A very strong Danish-French connection, going both ways, existed: Barthes and Greimas, among others, were very much influenced by Hjelmslev (and Brøndal), and the young generation of linguists and especially literary scholars, to which I, at that time, belonged, were influenced both by Hjelmslev and by French structuralism. At that time, I belonged to a group of students at Copenhagen University that published a Danish journal *Poetik (Poetics)* that was, in the first few years, fighting for structuralist semiotics, first and foremost as it was defined by Greimas. In Denmark, within the humanities and within literary studies, the late sixties were the heydays of structuralism (and within literary studies Russian formalism and Prague structuralism exercised a strong influence).

What attracted my generation was the promise that structuralist semiotics made a scientific study of texts and specifically literary texts possible. In contradistinction to impressionistic readings of literature, semiotics offered simultaneously a theory and a method of text interpretation, and concrete tools allowing us to approach and analyze texts systematically. I still think that semiotics offers an access to text interpretation that is basically sound.

However, to me, semiotics today is certainly different from that continental semiotics of the sixties and seventies.

Ten years later the situation was very different. First of all, a plethora of competing theories were at play: Structuralism (dethroned, but, of course, still practiced), poststructuralism (French and American), Peircean semiotics, the semiotics of Nelson Goodman, the Moscow-Tartu-school. And, in addition to these different varieties of semiotics, or at least theories somehow linked with semiotics, within the study of literature both Marxism and psychoanalysis were playing an important role.

Both poststructuralism and Marxism challenged continental semiotics. And while I respected Marxist literary studies, although for me Habermas became the most important figure, I didn't find the poststructuralist and postmodern thinking very appealing. In the seventies I also lost faith in the semiotics of the Paris School. It seemed to me that there were the following reasons to abandon the structuralist paradigm: 1. Although it was recognized, of course, that signs were used for communication, strict structuralism sought to transform a text into a system, into "un micro-univers sémantique." 2. This meant, among other things, the suppression of enunciation in the objectivation of the text (Greimas: L'objectivation du texte). 3. The trouble of showing the exact transformations between the levels of generation (le parcours génératif, e.g. between the fundamental, the narrative, and the discursive semantics). 4. The narrowing down of the sign concept: "Si on admet, [...], que l'exclusion du référent est un préalable nécessaire à l'exercise de toute sémiotique, on doit reconnaître que l'indice, [...] entre dans la catégorie des non-signes" (Greimas in *Dictionnaire* I, 1979: 186) 5. The will to building a total and closed theory, although in a sense laudable, made many scholars turn their backs to the project because: a. They didn't want to pledge their allegiance to what, to them, appeared to be an almost Byzantine theory building. b. They didn't want to get involved in discussions that would primarily concern terminological questions and procedures. c. The structuralist paradigm seemed self-contained and self-sufficient. It had no ambition to link with other approaches and other theories. d. The self-imposed limits of the structuralist approach made it doubtful whether it could, indeed even wanted, to deal with important dimensions of the texts.

Hence, unwilling to give up semiotics, but rejecting the approaches of both the Paris School and poststructuralism and postmodern thinking, I turned to the semiotic project of C.S. Peirce. In 1982 I stayed for a year to study his MSS at the Peirce Edition Project in Indianapolis, and during this time I learned to know many American semioticians, Tom Sebeok, John Deely, Nathan Hauser, Floyd Merrell, and many more. And since that time I have kept in touch with North American semiotics.

An important reason for the skepticism concerning the structuralist project was also a change of interest from the study of sign systems to the study of sign processes, and consequently, from the study of texts as systems to studying them as processes and as utterances embedded in a historical context.

My own path within semiotics has been from structuralism to a semiotic-pragmatic, or semio-pragmatic, approach to texts. And in addition to Peirce's semiotics and pragmaticism, I have also been influenced by the pragmatic turn took place from the 70ties onward within linguistics, philosophy, and within the study of literature. Pragmatics is a vague term, and it has many origins: In antiquity rhetoric is definitely an ancestor. The semiotics and pragmaticism of C.S. Peirce and the American pragmatic philosophers are important, and so is the semiotics of Charles Morris with its tripartition of semiotics into syntax (sign-sign), semantics (sign-object), and pragmatics (sign-interpretation). However, also the theories of communication of the German philosophers Karl-Otto Apel and Jürgen Habermas have been instrumental in shaping my position.

2. What do you consider your contribution to the field?

For two reasons, at least, it is always hard to point to what one has achieved: First you may be deluded concerning the significance of what you have done. Second, it is very difficult to speak about your own work because it may seem like praising it. However, in order to answer the question anyway, I would like to point to three related areas:

First, I have for many years, from 1973 in fact, worked on creating a model, a diagram, that will bring together the elements and relationships that are involved in Peirce's conception of semiosis as I understand it. My own point of departure was the triangle of signification as it has been known from Adam and Eve, and used among others by Ogden and Richards. With Peirce's terminology it becomes figure 1 below.

However, in order to model Peirce's more complex understanding of the sign, the following had to be added, obtaining figure 2.

32   5. Jørgen Dines Johansen

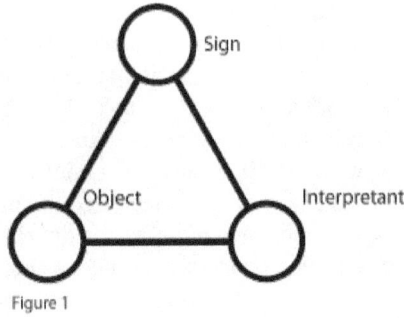

Figure 1

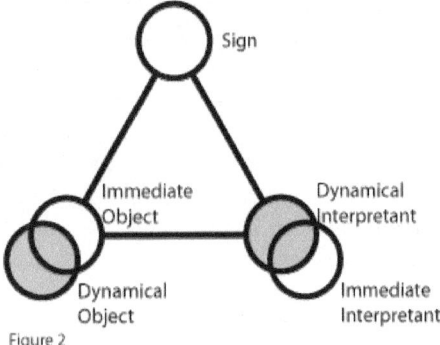

Figure 2

There is a curious asymmetry in this model the immediate object is linked, not with the immediate interpretant, but with the dynamical one (see below). Now, if we turn this model in a half-circle around its axis, we will get figure 3.

If we further split sender and receiver, like those of the interpretant and object, into immediate and dynamical, we will get figure 4.

The division of the sender into utterer and addresser, and the division of the receiver into addressee, is obviously necessary in order to make possible an answer to how it is possible to tell a lie, because it is exactly the split between utterer and addresser makes dissimulation and fraud possible. The split between addressee and interpreter will be between the utterer's presuppositions about the interpreter, the persona of him that he produces in the sign, i.e., a role that the interpreter is supposed to fit into. Obviously the interpreter in flesh and blood may not understand this role, or he may refuse to play it. The joke about the nun and the sailor you can tell to sailors, but not to nuns.

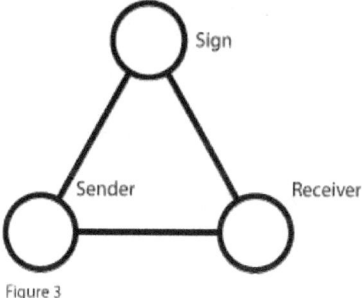

Figure 3

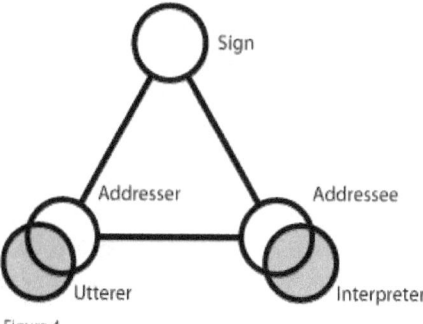

Figure 4

Finally, we have to split the sign (sign-vehicle) because we have to distinguish between the sign as it is actually pronounced or written, the token, and the type. Listening to Japanese or Danes speaking English is enough to justify a distinction between what is actually produced, and what is supposed to be in accordance with the different rules of pronunciation.

Hence, we get a distinction between five immediate and five dynamical elements of the semiosis of human communication:

- token vs. type
- dynamical object vs. immediate object
- dynamical interpretant vs. immediate interpretant
- utterer vs. addresser
- interpreter vs. addressee

These oppositions may also be understood as the difference between the external and the internal side of semiosis:

The token is what is actually produced, it is what reaches the ear or eye of the receiver, i.e., the token is a force that influences the other party. It is supposed, however, to be linked with and to be an actualization of a type, to the set of rules that governs the semiotic in question, and for communication to succeed the parties must both possess at least some knowledge of these rules (although they may not be able to explicate it).

The dynamical object is what influences the perceiver, the immediate object, however, is the outcome of the sign action, i.e., the immediate object is an interpretation of what the dynamical object may be. Hence the immediate object is the outcome of the action of the dynamical object together with the mechanisms of interpretation at hand. It goes without saying that the immediate object may misrepresent the dynamical one.

The dynamical interpretant is the outcome of a process consisting in, maybe unconsciously) weighting the possibilities and the pros and cons triggered by the influence of the dynamical object on the immediate interpretants that it elicits and activates. The immediate interpretants, in the plural, are the already deposited interpretive habits that are used to make sense of what presents itself to the mind. Interpretive habits are species specific, and partly culture specific, and some may even be idiosyncratic. Important immediate interpretants are deposited interpretive habits such as conventions, rules, scripts, scenarios, prototypes, and models.

Interpretive habits may be, and are, modified through interaction with the outer world including other people. The difference between the dynamical and the immediate interpretant is that the immediate interpretant is a set of possibilities that is activated, whereas the dynamical interpretant is the actual outcome of a process that takes place, and, as Peirce reminds us, the dynamical interpretant may be influenced by factors external to the sign, hence there is something occasional and fallible in actual interpretation.

The utterer is the agent, the doer, in flesh and blood (or the reconstruction of the interpreter). As such he is, like the other dynamical elements of semiosis, opaque; you never know whether you have fully understood his motivations and intentions in uttering what he does. In fact, he becomes a possible sign of something else. The addresser is what is revealed of the utterer in the sign action, most often what the utterer wants to reveal in order to reach his objective, but sometimes also something that is unintentionally revealed.

Like utterers, interpreters are external to the sign, and they cannot be fully controlled by it. They interpret the sign according to their interpretive habits, and these habits will never fully coincide with those of the utterer. The interpreter, as he or she is represented in the sign, i.e., the addressee is a representation of an imagined interpreter, i.e., a construction produced by the utterer that may or may not fit the actual interpreter.

The combination of these ten elements make up the *semiotic pyramid*:

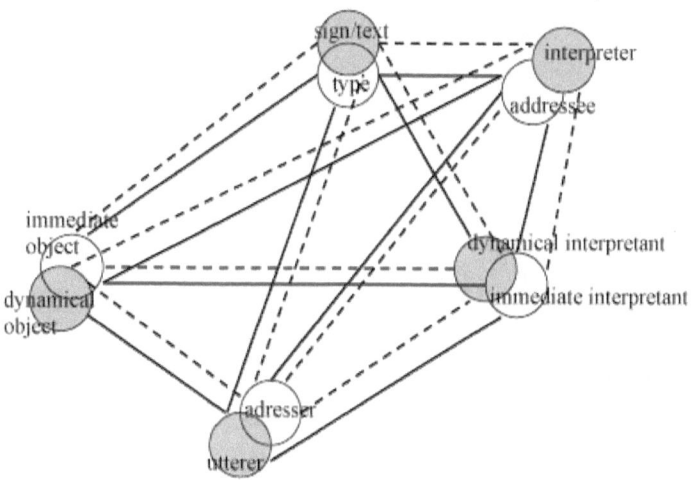

On this model of Peircean semiosis I have, in order save another representation, mapped the four so-called universal pragmatic validity claims that, according to Jürgen Habermas, are presupposed in dialogue, or other forms of communication. According to Habermas, there are four such claims, namely *understandability, truth, normative rightness, and sincerity*. Of course Habermas knows that texts may be incomprehensible, that assertions may be false, that propositions for conduct and interaction may be unethical, and that utterances may be insincere. His point is, however, that for non-strategic communication to take place at all, these four claims have to presupposed, until the contrary is proven. The mapping of *understandability, truth, and sincerity* should be self-evident, whereas it might be claimed that *normative rightness* should rather have been placed with the interpretants. However, from a dialogical point of view, the interpreter is the judge deciding whether what is claimed or recommended is in accordance with his or her norms. The fact that the interpreter's norms are themselves developed within a certain society and a certain culture is quite true, but it is another matter.

Second, on the basis of my work with the semiotic pyramid, I have further attempted to define the subject matter of the semiotic-pragmatic approach to the study of texts. In my view the Semiotic-pragmatic approach to texts favors and investigates the following 15 points:

1. The communicative & interactional aspects of signhood
2. The texts' groundedness in the lifeworld
3. The purposiveness of sign production
4. The interrelatedness of facts and values
5. The commitments of the parties of dialogue
6. The vested interests of the interlocutors
7. Signs are uttered either in order to persuading the other party to share one's view point (this is valid both for genetically produced sign sequences such as, for instance, mating rituals in animals, and for human dialogue),
8. or for persuading a third party to trust and prefer one's arguments over those of the other party (also male animals fly their colors in order to be preferred over others by the female)
9. The point is to give the listener/viewer probable reasons for adhering to one position rather than to another (to procure assent and collaboration),
10. in order to do so, in human dialogue, the discursive, narrative, structural, and figurative resources of speech are explored
11. In human beings, signs are produced with the purpose to globally influencing another party, i.e., to provoke responses involving cognitive, imaginative, emotional, and bodily reactions, both conscious and unconscious
12. The importance of effectively making one's point is due to the fact that dialogue normally is about decisions concerning actions and interactions, and about decisions that can be debated

13. Thus, the raison être of dialogue implies that it is possible to choose among different possible decisions,

14. and hence, man is understood as having a freedom of choice, but also to be responsible for it

15. Hence, on this view, the study of semiosis is primarily seen as purposeful, often intentional sign production, sign interpretation, and sign interaction

The purpose of the semiotic-pragmatic approach to texts is to study sign processes and sign interpretations as utterances, in the broad sense. This does not mean neglecting the systematic aspects of texts, literary scholars are certainly aware of those, but it does mean semiosis, on this view, should be studied as purposive processes.

The third and final contribution I would like to mention is my work with iconicity, especially in literature. I find that although literature, like other kinds of linguistic texts, is made up of symbolic signs, it nevertheless works extensively with iconic structures. I distinguish between two kinds of iconicity, mimetic iconicity, i.e. the text is in some ways isomorphic with non-linguistic states of affairs or events that it represents. Caesar's "veni, vidi, vici" mimes , as Jakobson has pointed out, by its linguistic order, the order of the chain of events as they were supposed to have occurred, hence, I call this form of iconicity *mimetic*. "Veni, vidi, vici" also illustrates, however, the other kind of iconicity that literary and rhetorically structured texts very often exhibit. Again, according to Jakobson, we see in "veni, vidi, vici" a systematic exploration of the internal similarity of the signs themselves. In "Linguistics and Poetics" Jakobson says that the "symmetry of three disyllabic verbs with an identical initial consonant and identical final vowel add splendor to Caesar's laconic victory message: Veni, vidi, vici (Jakobson in Sebeok 1960, 358). Let us call this kind of internal iconicity, the fact that linguistic signs are symmetrical and mirror one another for *systemic iconicity*. Very often literature combines both kinds of iconicity, and the emotional and aesthetic effect of such a combination is often stunning.

The second dimension that I have attempted to elaborate, takes its point of departure in Peirce's distinction between three kinds of iconic signs, images, diagrams and metaphors. Images have qualities in common with their objects, diagrams share structural features and relationships with their objects, and, a metaphor, according to Peirce, is a relation between sign and object, or a sign and another sign, in which the representative character of the former is expressed through, and by virtue of, the latter. A thermometer is primarily an indexical sign (because it is influenced by body temperature), but this indexical relationship is expressed in a metaphor because heat, which can be felt, but not seen, is transformed and represented as height. The height to which the pillar of mercury raises corresponds to the intensity of the fever, and so the pillar of mercury represents body temperature as a parallelism in something else.

Hence, processing linguistic texts in general and literary texts in particular by relating symbolic signs to iconic ones is a necessity because symbolic sign would signify nothing if they were not linked with iconic and indexical signs. We have, however, three different, but cooperating processes of iconization, namely a. *imaginization*: The production of mental images (partly) triggered by the text. b. *diagrammization*: conceiving the text as a relational structure, a network, and c. *allegorization*, through which the signification and the represented world of the text is linked with other conceptual structures.

Imaginization covers all perceptual modes, e.g. listening to sounds and seeing images with the mind's eye. Furthermore, imaginization linked with personal knowledge. It highlights the apparent paradox of reading: the fact that readers are thrilled by visions and stories coming from the outside, but realized by bringing in the readers own fantasies and memories. Imaginization is probably unavoidable and valuable when controlled. Hence, it seems useful to look at a text as a set of different instructions for iconization, as Shakespeare asks us to do:

> Piece out our imperfections with your thoughts;
> Into a thousand parts divide one man,
> And make imaginary puissance;
> Think when we talk of horses, that you see them
> Printing their proud hoofs i' the receiving earth;
> For 'tis your thoughts that now must deck our kings,
> Carry them here and there, jumping o'er times,
> Turning the accomplishments of many years
> Into an hour-glass [...]
>
> (Henry V, prologue)

Literature favors imaginization because attention is turned inward; there is no matching with perception, but rather a creation of images, using memory and fantasy. Texts differ very much in the number of clues they offer for imaginization. However, even the most generous text will leave an indefinite number of ways open to imaginize it, it will always call for creative collaboration.

Imaginization seems little accessible for investigation because of its private and personal nature. It is, however, possible to hypothesize about it because texts normally delimit what can and what cannot count as a valid imaginization, because to be valid an iconic exemplification must, among other things a. conform to a. a given order of events, b. pay attention to the fact that the text may highlight certain details whereas others are not described. Imaginization must also c. conform to text's mood and emotional tenor. And finally, d. imaginization is limited by the fact that objects, scenes, and actions have sets of typical realizations within a culture, and knowing them are part of a necessary cultural competence. Accordingly, it may possible to describe pertinent and important features even of individual imaginization, because even if imaginization is subjective, subjectivity shouldn't be confused with either the private or the unique. It is related to age, gender, class, knowledge, and cultural level. An indication that readers may imaginize literature in similar ways is the discussions about book illustrations and movies based on novels. These discussions indicate that we possess vague ideas about how to imaginize the texts since we may object to or be thrilled by concrete realizations.

There are, however, limits to imaginization. For instance, are people really able to experience, say *War and Peace* as a movie? And is translating words into sensuous images all that is needed to understand a text? Rejecting that imaginization suffices to interpret texts brings us to the second way of iconizing the text: *diagrammatization*:

Diagrammatization is abstractive, systematic and concerned with the text as a whole. It keeps track of relations and their transformations, and, instead of imaginizing, readers may look at the text as a kind of algebraic structure. Although meaning depends on the interaction between iconic, indexical, and symbolic signs, different signs and sign system, e.g. language may have a relative autonomy, i.e., we may understand without any conscious translation into other sign systems. We do need, however, to keep track of relations between and transformations of signs in order to understand a text:

> What is it men in women do require?—
> The lineaments of gratified desire.
> What is it women do in men require?—

5. Jørgen Dines Johansen

> The lineaments of gratified desire
> (Blake 1971, 167)

We need not remember our partners' look of gratified desire in order to understand this poem; we do need, however, to notice its repetitions and parallelisms: proportion and reciprocity are the main features of this gnomic poem. The poem is not preoccupied with images, but with sound because its sound pattern supports its meaning and significance. Furthermore, its basic structure is analogical: a: b:: b: a. The semiotic tradition from Russian formalism to the cognitive study of literature has cultivated the diagrammatic analysis in an effort to discover text properties, not in order to add something to the text.

Let Maranda and Maranda's model concerning the fairytale exemplify the extraordinary power of diagrammatization:

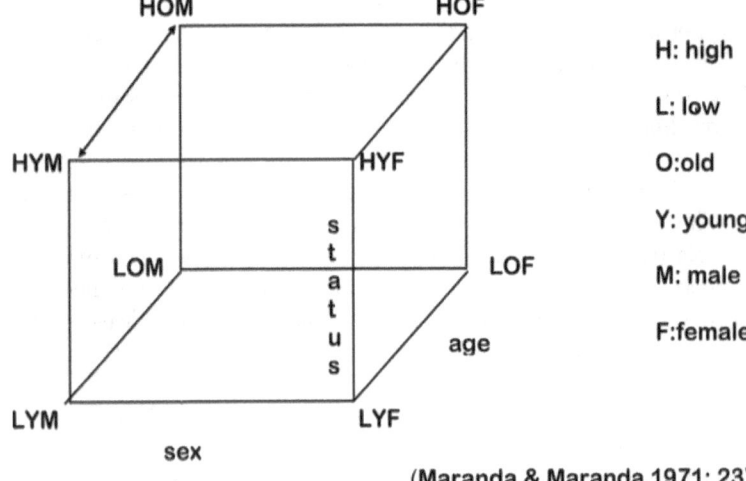

(Maranda & Maranda 1971: 23)

The eight tale roles, and the plot and conflict, are created by three binary oppositions of *age, sex,* and *status.* The strength of such a diagram is that it both shows, even literally, basic relations within this type of tale, and furthermore, contemplating and modifying this diagram may, indeed will, produce new knowledge, because it may be used to systematically explore the relations the different roles. Diagrammatization, then, is a most powerful device for producing new knowledge by laying bare the internal relationships of an object of research.

Whereas diagrammatization may experiment upon the object of research, it does not correlate it with other systems of signification. This, however, is precisely what metaphorical text interpretation, here called *allegorization* does. Metaphors, like similes, are semantically interpreted analogies that link different conceptual domains. When Peter, the Apostle is called the Rock it is a metaphor built on an analogy: Peter: Church:: rock: building. Hence, allegorization means looking a second meaning, one ,or more, sensus plenior (as the schoolmen said) in addition to the text's literal meaning (sensus litteralis). Allegorization is an attempt to make a text say something that is deemed aesthetically, morally, or epistemologically relevant, and, at the same time, often avoiding the difficulties that would arise from sticking to its literal meaning. For instance, according to Saint Augustine passages in the *Bible* that, when taken literally, does not contribute to the love of God and one's neighbor should be read allegorically: "Whatever there is in the word of God that cannot, when taken literally, be referred either to purity of life or soundness of doctrine, you may set down as figurative." (*De doctrina* . . . III,40).

Allegorization may be brought to the text from other systems of signification, it may, however, just as well be a dimension of the text itself:

> Pray, why do you look askance at me, my Thracian filly, and shun me so resolutely as though I knew nothing of my art? I would have you to know I could bridle you right well and take rein and ride you about the turning-post of the course. But instead you graze in the meadows and frisk and frolic to your heart's content; for you have no clever breaker to ride you (84 in Lyra graeca 1944: 181).

This poem by Anachreon does not reveal its allegorical nature. However, already the commentary in the *Lyra Graeca* does not doubt that it is about a nubile maiden who is going to be given in marriage or sexually initiated by the speaking male. It explores preexisting cultural stereotypes: 1. rider is to horse as man is to woman (very far from Blake's non-allegorical proportion woman: man:: man: woman) and 2. to make a newlywed woman obedient is like domesticating and breaking in a precious animal.

The thirst for allegorization is a part of our general quest for meaning. And even if we might not believe in the truth and revelatory force of second meanings such a transcategorical linking is found precious. There are two reasons for this: 1. The comparison of the different domains discover and explain each others characteristics (Anachreon does offer grim information about the relation between the sexes in ancient Greece). 2. Second meanings are felt to enrich the text because being simultaneously one self and something else adds to the complexity of the sign, and such complexity is often felt to be profound. Kafka's *The Trial* is not only about Joseph K.'s falling victim to the weird courts. It may also be about the mechanisms of dictatorship, about a person succumbing to his cruel superego, or about the relation between man and a cruel father-god.

Allegorization, in contradistinction to imaginization, furthers the quest for the generic. In allegorizing the text we most often do not link it with personal memories and fantasies, but with culturally shared patterns of interpretation. Hence, what is allegorized becomes an example of what is generally believed to be the case.

Even if, in different readers, one mode of iconizing the text may become predominant, the concrete reading process will switch between these levels. Sometimes the reading provokes a vivid image, or a series of images, whether visual, auditory, even olfactory or of taste and touch, or weak feelings of pleasure or pain. Sometimes the text is experienced as a diagram, an equation, or a parallelogram of forces; and sometimes it is taken to allegorize states of affairs or mind in the lifeworld contemporary with that of the text or with that of the reader. All three ways of reading are not only valuable, they are necessary since the very process of understanding literature calls for them all. If nothing in the text's representation of settings, props, and actions can be recognized to correspond to what can be retrieved as memory or fantasy images; if elements and parts cannot be related to each other; and if the issues of the text cannot be typified and mapped onto situations, dilemmas, and conflicts in the lifeworld then the text will remain black marks on the paper.

3. What is the proper role of a theory of signs and meaning in relation to other academic disciplines?

I think each and every of the sciences studying life, from the theory of literature to biology, has a semiotic dimension. This does not mean, however, that semioticians can make valid contributions to fields that they do not know, just by being semioticians. In order to apply semiotic insights to a field, it goes without saying, but, nevertheless, it is worth while saying, one should be thoroughly familiar with the academic discipline as it is studied by its non-semiotic researchers.

4. What do you consider the most important topics and/or contributions in the theory of meaning and signs?

I think that Peirce's ideas about semiotics still constitute the single most important contribution to the field. It would, however, be a harmful mistake to stick only to Peirce, after all it is almost a hundred years since he died, and the different academic disciplines have during this time developed their own questions and their own problems that were not thought of when he lived. Hence, semiotics must proceed by combining the general semiotic perspectives as they are outlined, fore and foremost by Peirce, but also by the Saussurean tradition, with present day knowledge of the disciplines in question.

5. What are the most important open problems in this field and what are the prospects for progress?

Since I do not think that Peirce succeeded in fully developing a general theory of signs there is much work to be done here. On the one hand, it is a question of Peirce philology as it, for instance, is done at The Peirce Edition Project in Indianapolis, i.e., to produce reliable editions of his works and make plausible hypotheses concerning how the different texts are related to each other, here the work of the late Max Fisch and Nathan Hauser should be mentioned. Another task is to give a general interpretation of Peirce's doctrine of signs, and here the works of Karl-Otto Apel, David Savan, Joseph Ransdell are certainly important. Lately the book by Thomas L. Short *Peirce's theory of signs* (2007) offers a both profound and eye-opening study of this subject.

Furthermore, both as a semiotician and as a literary theorist, I find a semiotic text theory that integrates the study of signs, of mind, and that of the institutional preconditions for different types of texts very much needed. Concretely, I think that the present combination of the theory of evolution and the cognitive study of mind is promising (e.g. the works of Terrence Deacon and Ellen Dissanayake). This double approach should, in my opinion, be linked with a semiotic-pragmatic study of human sign use, in an effort to understand both what makes text production possible, and why certain types of texts are developed in every known society.

6

Gilles Fauconnier

Research Professor
Department of Cognitive Science
University of California, San Diego

---

1. Why were you initially drawn to the theory of signs and meaning?

At 19 years old, in 1963, I was a student at the Ecole Polytechnique in Paris, a school founded during the French Revolution and militarized by Napoleon a few years later with the aim of training artillery officers and furthering the study of mathematics. Indeed, the school has counted many famous mathematicians among its alumni, but also pianists, monks, tennis champions, and even linguists. To broaden the horizons of students heavily steeped in mathematics, the general commanding the school had the idea of bringing in lecturers from the worlds of art, humanities, and politics. Among these invited speakers, I remember Salvador Dali and his trademark mustache, future president Giscard d'Estaing, historian Charles Morazé, and psychoanalyst Jacques Lacan. But the one who made the deepest impression on me was Roland Barthes, a remarkably subtle literary scholar who had bypassed the traditional French educational system and forged a highly original world view during years spent in a sanatorium. In the talk Barthes gave to an audience of young math students, he outlined the research he was developing on the semiology of fashion (which was to become *Système de la Mode*). His analysis was based on Martinet's linguistic theory of "double articulation," and more broadly on the structuralist paradigm, as developed by Saussure, Jakobson, Hjelmslev, Trubetzkoy, and many others. I discovered through Barthes a fascinating realm of thinking I had been utterly unaware of: semiology, linguistics, ethnology–an approach that sought to be scientific in understanding everyday social life and its signs and meanings. On the other hand, I was decidedly unimpressed by the linguistic theories that were then in vogue. The new star in the field was Noam Chomsky and I remember reading *Syntactic Structures*, and finding it totally uninspiring. The discipline was trapped in a bizarre paradox: both structuralism and generativism advocated and practiced a study of language that dealt exclusively with form at the expense of any attention to meaning. This patent absurdity was a curious consequence of a flawed view of science imported into the social sciences by behaviorist methodology. Paradoxically, I was not drawn into linguistics by admiration for any of its leading thinkers, but rather because it seemed like an area that was in fact poorly explored and therefore open to novel and exciting research.

In the nineteen-seventies, a few of us started this exploration, including Len Talmy, Ron Langacker, and George Lakoff. The research on force dynamics and fictive motion, cognitive grammar, metaphor, and mental spaces, would lay the foundations for cognitive linguistics and more generally contribute to the third wave of cognitive science, with its focus on the embodied mind, distributed cognition, and conceptual mappings.

2. What do you consider your contribution to the field?

The most significant breakthrough that cognitive linguists, including myself, were able to make was to focus attention on backstage cognition, the extraordinarily complex cognitive operations that take place as we think, talk, and engage in action. External signs, such as words, sentences, and conscious discourse, do not directly correspond to the infinitely more elaborate constructions of the mind that underlie human activity. Rather, they serve to prompt the mental constructions in a remarkably parsimonious way.

My own work inside this general approach has dealt in detail with mental space phenomena: how mental spaces are set up in discourse, connected by partial mappings, and blended to yield novel spaces. The approach is a fruitful way of looking at reference, tense and aspect, counterfactuals and hypotheticals, but also extends to non-linguistic aspects of thought found in art, science, technology, and religion. The theory of conceptual blending, developed initially by Mark Turner and myself, has proven to be exceptionally rich in its range of predictions and applications. It opened up another area of research, the properties of vital relations and their compression. There seem to be on the order of fifteen vital relations, such as identity, cause-effect, part-whole, representation, role/value. Within integration networks, vital relations are systematically compressed into other vital relations or into scaled versions of themselves. Compression is a powerful aspect of human thinking, and it brings into play mental and material representations, including what we think of as signs. For example, our conception of time compresses the analogy of successive days into the uniqueness of the cyclic day, which in turn maps onto culturally devised mechanical artifacts (e.g. rods rotating at uniform speed around a dial). The conception of the cyclic day blends with the perceivable properties of the artifact to yield the compressed notion of "timepiece." And this blend yields rich emergent structure for time, such as "hours," "minutes," "seconds," etc., and the notion of universal shared time.

3. What is the proper role of a theory of signs and meaning in relation to other academic disciplines?

This clearly varies with each discipline. The account we've proposed for the emergence of mathematical ideas–successive conceptual integrations over cultural time–illuminates the practice of mathematicians and helps to understand how highly abstract systems of thought can emerge from embodied human activity. Should mathematicians themselves be aware of this? Not necessarily–they can be excellent practitioners of their art without any conscious awareness of the cognitive processes that make it possible, just as humans in general need not have any knowledge of the linguistic theories behind the language they speak. But as soon as mathematicians wish to study the history or the teaching of mathematics, then serious attention should be focused on the cognitive operations and semiotic processes at work.

Other disciplines, of course, demand in principle a genuine understanding of meaning construction. This is manifestly true of psychology, anthropology, sociology, or cognitive neuroscience. It is also true of political science and history. But taking meaning and signs into account is easier said than done: people in general, and social scientists in particular, vastly underestimate the complexities of meaning construction. They bring into their disciplines notions of meaning that feel right but are in fact profoundly misconceived or outrageously simplified. Each discipline tends to use a notion of meaning that is implicitly or explicitly shared by practitioners of that discipline and therefore not easily called into question. Scholars in linguistics, semiotics, philosophy of language, have touched on deeper, more subtle, and counterintuitive aspects of meaning construction, but they have been incapable of agreeing on a unified view that could be exported straightforwardly to other fields, in the way for example that physics is exported to chemistry, and chemistry to biology.

Literature and theater explore meaning in sometimes far deeper ways, but without the scientific and theoretical goals of the social sciences. Clearly, the insights of literary studies are valuable for students of meaning. Conversely, recent work on literature, poetics, and theater has benefited from semiotics, cognitive science, and linguistics. This is not a mainstream trend, however, for reasons that have to do with the vastly different methodologies that operate in the fields concerned.

4. What do you consider the most important topics and/or contributions in the theory of meaning and signs?

This question presupposes a theory that would be "the theory of meaning and signs." I'm not aware of a widely accepted and established theory of this nature, comparable to broad theories of modern physics or biology. What we have so far are valiant efforts to uncover a multitude of aspects of meaning construction that remain elusive and difficult to deal with empirically and theoretically. At this point we should perhaps talk about approaches and frameworks rather than full-fledged theories. Nevertheless, there are reasons to be optimistic for the reasons mentioned in section 2. We are coming to grips with issues that were never formulated in traditional semantics or analytic philosophy. This is happening because we can go far beyond the overt manifestations of meaning through words and sentences, and ask deeper questions about conceptual systems, mental operations, and backstage cognition. I am understandably partial in this regard to the research done under the umbrella of cognitive semantics. The crucial contributions that have advanced the program include Fillmore's pioneering work in frame semantics and construction grammar, Langacker's extensive development of cognitive grammar, Talmy's highly original work on fictive motion, force dynamics, and event integration, Lakoff and his collaborators' far-reaching conceptual metaphor theory, and our own work on mental spaces and conceptual integration. Although the cognitive linguistics research program had its starting points in linguistics, it has extended in remarkably fruitful ways to other fields: the study of magic and religion, the cognitive underpinnings of mathematical thought, the understanding of material culture and distributed cognition, technological innovation and design, performance and creativity in theatre, to mention just a few.

Major empirical and methodological shifts are happening within this approach. The focus on cognitive operations rather than structural description makes empirical data and explanation in one area relevant to all others. Language, mathematics, technology, yield visible surface products that share fundamental cognitive, cultural, and biological invisible organizations. Empirical observation cuts across domains, and so does theoretical explanation. The notion of sign, dear to semiotics, will also change profoundly. It turns out, as Ed Hutchins has shown, that material artefacts serve to anchor conceptual integration networks. Extending Hutchins' approach, one can see material objects of all kinds, including sound waves and writing, or real space as studied by Scott Liddell, or traffic lights and visual displays as also anchoring such networks. In this light, "signifiant" and "signifié" are not separable: the dynamics of integration networks includes the manipulation, perceptual and conceptual processing of material objects in building integration networks and creating successive layers of conceptual thought. The traditional notion of sign is only a subcase of this general scheme.

5. What are the most important open problems in this field and what are the prospects for progress?

From the perspective outlined above, the challenges that lie ahead are colossal. The problems are not defined in advance. They emerge when theoretical accounts achieve generalizations and uncover theoretical conceptions that run counter to our folk-theoretic intuitions and classifications. While I am enthusiastic about the new paths we have discovered, it must be acknowledged that the study of meaning is not a "field" in the optimal scientific sense. What we have is a large array of frameworks with often starkly different assumptions and methods. In each one, problems emerge defined in theory-internal ways. From the perspective of one framework, problems highlighted in another can seem artificial or at best marginal and at worst unintelligible. In everyday life, we live under the illusion that we know clearly what meaning is and isn't. At a different level, in scientific life, our frameworks create similar illusions.

7
Groupe μ

Centre d'études poétiques
University of Liège

---

1. Why were you initially drawn to the theory of signs and meaning?

During the first few years of its existence at the end of the 1960s, Group μ (known in French as Groupe μ) was concerned mainly with questions of poetics. Following the aims of this discipline, the group was interested in taking a step back from the literary work as an aesthetic concept by revealing the very general structures that turn a given linguistic pattern into a literary occurrence. This kind of approach was thus clearly in line with the ideas of Roman Jakobson, Roland Barthes and Algirdas Julien Greimas. The concepts elaborated in the group's first major publication (*Rhétorique générale*, 1970) contributed to the revival of rhetoric at the time, by providing an explanatory model of rhetorical figures, a model which drew on contemporary concepts of linguistic structure.

This contribution was significant in two ways. The first was that the work was that of a group operating under one name (like Bourbaki in mathematics, for example). Yet the members of this group came from disciplines as diverse as linguistics, biochemistry, cultural sociology, philosophy, aesthetics, and the history of cinema. A common interest for symbolic productions, as well as an ambition to contribute to the development of a new paradigm in the humanities, fueled at the time by the structuralist impulse, brought us together. From this diversity, another specific feature of the work being undertaken was revealed: its transdisciplinary aims. The goal was, from the start, that of a "general rhetoric" applicable to all these disciplines: the aim was to expand the notion of the trope, together with that which the idea of the trope presumes (a cognitive goal and a theory of pragmatic interactions), to other categories of utterances such as the static image or the cinema. The original hypothesis was, therefore, semiotic in nature: if general laws of signification and communication exist –the premise in fact on which semiotics is founded–then it is possible that one will find in these utterances phenomena of polyphony which are comparable to those observed in oral language. Thus, the underlying hypothesis was that there are very general mechanisms involved: general, and therefore independent of the particular sphere in which they occur. Consequently, the aim of a general rhetoric is to describe the rhetorical function of all aspects of semiotics in terms of robust operations, which are the same whatever the field of application.

It was, therefore, for circumstantial reasons–the background of many members of the group and the advances in linguistic studies– that linguistic communication appears to have been privileged in the group's first collaborative works. But it should be noted that these works were already suggesting advances in general semiotics, thanks to contributions on narrative (cinematographic narrative as much as linguistic), on the system of the person or, as we shall see below, on the principles of semantic analysis.

From the outset, Group μ had thus been concerned with the facts of visual communication since this area corresponded to the experience and interests of various members of the group. However, the situation now was certainly different to how it was when *Rhétorique générale* was first published. In the Sixties, there was a corpus of linguistic concepts which were, admittedly, diverse but which were available for immediate use, so all that was necessary was to use this corpus in order to develop a contemporary linguistic rhetoric. Nothing similar existed for a rhetoric of the visual, however. What went under the name of visual semiotics– if one excludes the more open-minded suggestions of Christian Metz and Umberto Eco–was, largely, only the subjective criticism of art, which appeared in the intimidating disguise of an often obscure, and in any case approximate, technical language. Before launching itself into a "Rhetoric of the Image", Group μ had to painstakingly develop the necessary theoretical framework.

This was the origin of the group's contribution to visual semiotics: the *Traité du signe visuel* (1992) sought to elaborate a general grammar of the image, independently of the type of corpus being considered. This semiotic of the visual contributed, in its turn, to semiotics in general: indeed, a question encountered by the group at this stage was that of the relationship between (sensory) experience and signification, a question which certainly reveals something of this degree of generality since it comes up against the question of the origin of meaning itself.

2. What do you consider your contribution to the field?

The work within rhetorics of Group μ thus provided a powerful explanatory model of figures which took the form of a table where, on the Y-axis, we find the logical operations that are involved in the transformation of which the figure consists, and, on the X-axis, the linguistic objects on which such an operation has a bearing. The pedagogical exploitation of such a table was quite easy. It was no doubt this, as much as the efficiency of the template, which led to the belief that the group only thought of the figure in terms of atomic units (see for example Paul Ricoeur in *La métaphore vive*). In fact, the definition given of the figure–as a rupture of isotopy– certainly presumes a textualist position, and the description of the dynamic of production and reception of the figure was already introducing a pragmatic aspect to the project.

A pragmatic dimension, but also a cognitive one: in fact, the work on figures–and in particular those which affect the level of content or tropes–presumed a sound knowledge of the elementary structures of signification. This need led to the distinction (which was not really recognised at the time) between articulating units according to the $\sum$ form and according to the $\prod$ form. The $\sum$ structures are certainly familiar: they are those which characterise experience according to genres and species, and which are represented by Porphyry's Tree. Familiar, but mainly so because they had been privileged by a semantic linguistics that was still very close to Aristotelian logic: this was to the detriment of $\prod$ structures, which consider the relationship of parts to a whole and vice versa. These two semantic relations of a different nature, studied by cognitivists such as Palmer, turned up to be useful tools in a discipline already existing in its own right: mereology. But, above all, taking semantic relationships into consideration would later be extremely important in establishing visual semiotics.

The group separated itself even further from formal structuralism with the publication of *Rhétorique de la poésie* (1977), which showed that, although the presence of certain linguistic structures– and foremost amongst them poly-isotopy, made possible by rhetorical figures–was a necessary condition for the production of poetic effects, this condition was not enough, and that anthropological and social criteria would be needed to complete these structures.

The publication, subtitled *Lecture linéaire, lecture tabulaire*, therefore constituted a contribution to the study of textual dynamics. It is in this context that the group drew attention to the importance of the phenomenon of mediation, as used by Lévi-Strauss: this term designates the new conjunctions that can develop between the opposite terms of a structure. Certainly a very general process: mediations can exist in anthropological mechanisms just as they can be the product of discursive mechanisms. By questioning the oppositions which structure meaning and which therefore constitute the basis of encyclopaedias, all mediations in fact end up reorganising those encyclopaedias. The concept thus allows semiotics to be endowed with a dynamic and evolutionary aspect.

Concerning visual semiotics, a crucial achievement of the *Traité du signe visuel* (which Göran Sonesson said was to visual communication what Saussure's *Cours linguistique générale* was to linguistics) was to distinguish plastic signs from iconic signs (and for the study of these the $\prod$ structure was brought back into use, as we have seen).

From these points of view, one of the contributions of Group μ was to have provided the means for resolving the thorny question of motivation–which is, without doubt, one of the original and most recurrent themes of semiotic debates. The four-sided structure of the sign suggested by Jean-Marie Klinkenberg (*Précis de sémiotique générale*, 2000) effectively allowed arbitrary and motivated relations to be redistributed between the different components of the sign, without contradictions, and the concept of transformation allowed for a technical description of motivating facts.

But above all, the fundamental distinction posed by the group allowed for the autonomous conception of the plastic sign (which does not exclude the phenomena of icono-plastic interferences, which Hermann Parret considered as a major contribution). The plastic sign, which in its Peircean taxonomy can sometimes play the role of a symbol, sometimes that of an index, has three parameters: form, texture and chromaticism, with each of these parameters having its own modalities of articulation, syntactical relations and semanticisation.

As has already been said, an important question that was encountered during the examination of visual meaning was that of the relationships between signification and sensory experience. This question is, moreover, necessarily raised by that of iconism. The question of experience (in the German sense of "Erlebnis") had already been addressed at the beginning of the twentieth century by Charles Sanders Peirce (among others) but, given the knowledge of cognition (and in particular of visual cognition) at the time, he was unable to provide an answer. The originality of the group's contribution has consisted in creating a link between these disciplines and a semiotics often caught up in the dogma of immanentism. It showed in effect that meaning develops from elementary percepts, integrating and organizing stimuli from specialised perceptive mechanisms, in an abstracting approach concerned with categorising experience. The group had thus strived for the advent of cognitive semiotics.

3. What is the proper role of a theory of signs and meaning in relation to other academic disciplines?

Semiotics plays no small part in the social sciences. But this is not to the point of wanting to replace–as some would have it–disciplines like anthropology, sociology, psychology: more exactly, the aim of semiotics is to encourage a dialogue between all these disciplines, to act as a common interface. All these disciplines have, effectively, a shared premise: signification. Each one reveals how agents give meaning to practices which, from then on, become rites, channels, languages, and signs. Such is the task of semiotics: to create its own purpose from what is, for other disciplines, a premise: studying signification, describing the different ways it functions and the way it interacts with knowledge and action. This is a well-defined task and therefore a rational one. But it is also an ambitious task because not only is this agenda also that of other disciplines like philosophy but, in carrying it out, semiotics necessarily becomes a meta-theory: a theory of theories.

The discrepancies between different conceptions of semiotics derive, of course, from several factors and one of them is the manner in which semioticians understand this meta-theoretical role. It all depends on the distance they wish to establish with each of the disciplines to which their own is related. If semiotics is no more than the study of their common object, namely meaning, then it will be characterised by a high degree of abstraction (or of purity); it can even result in the idea that the portrayal of semiotics can be content with its own internal coherence in order to be appropriate for its object. The doctrine is thus founded upon an abstract and disembodied rationality, fearful for the purity of its models, which it wishes to protect from any referential contamination. If, on the other hand, it attempts a technical description of how meaning is constructed and circulates in each of the spheres in which it is found, then semiotics loses its ideal purity and runs the risk of being dismissed as claiming some scientistic or technical status.

Everyone would agree that this opposition securely structures (or seriously jeopardises, it all depends) the world of semiotics. But it appears that this opposition is not as final as it seems. In so far as the mechanisms allocating meaning are closely linked to the way an organism works, and in so far as they can be perceived at the level of the most elementary processes, a link is established between the extreme levels of the pyramid that has just been described. On the one hand, a semiotics thus conceived can rely on the precise descriptions of these processes provided by other disciplines. On the other, semiotics provides itself with the means to understand one of the most important problems with which philosophy has been concerned: the categorisation of experience, another name for meaning.

By bringing together, on the semiotic stage, the cognitive mechanisms as well as the social and cultural interactions which form the bedrock of meaning, Groupe μ was thus able to contribute not only to bringing down the wall that structuralism had put up between codes and social subjects, but also to bringing down that other, also seemingly impassable, wall which separates the social sciences from natural, even exact, sciences.

Indeed, in the field of what might be called 'pure' science, the importance of a coherent semiotic theory is no less great. In effect all sciences, at one stage or another, make use of sign systems.

Descriptive sciences, for instance, make use of representations, most often visual, to describe their object. However, the diagram of a cross-section in rock layers, just like the drawing of a plant or an animal, already implies an aspect of interpretation. Scientists are inclined to consider their diagrams as objective, and they therefore need to be made aware of the aspect of modelling that they contain. Has it not been said that the line is a tool of "cognitive simplification"? But they still have to know how to draw it differently from Dürer etching his *Rhinoceros*. In addition, if scientists wish to extract the maximum number of significant components from their sensations (that is to say those sensations susceptible to lead to a general interpretative construction), it would be useful for them to have a theory of indices.

Other disciplines, such as logic, mathematics, physics, astronomy, and chemistry traditionally have recourse to formalised languages. In their approach to the construction of univocal systems, those who practise these disciplines already behave like semioticians and would appear to have nothing to learn from our subject area. This, however, is not true, since semiotics in general has the upper hand in the majority of cases and, because of this, would help scientists to place their codes amongst the entire corpus of human codes.

As for the science of engineering, this is without doubt the area which would benefit most from the teaching of semiotics. Continually confronted with schemas, diagrams, and graphics, engineers forget or even completely ignore the conventional and constructed aspect of these representations and are often insufficiently warned of the potential dangers of perceptive illusions.

4. What do you consider the most important topics and/or contributions in the theory of meaning and signs?

In our answer to question 2 we pointed to what we feel to be our own contribution to semiotics. In fact, this discipline was, and continues to be, based on a number of key concepts, the contributions of various researchers each of whom has provided (and thus allowed the description and the understanding of) a whole category of utterances.

At various points in our research we have been fuelled by these beginnings. We have found large foundational concepts to be full of rich pickings. For example, to produce a model of the way figures function, we have made use of the Greimassian notion of isotopy, such as developed by François Rastier. But, if we want to avoid the risk of merely dabbling, we could not just take up a tool such as it was, without adapting it to our own purpose. Thus, we completed the concept of isotopy in three ways: first, by enlarging its field of application in the field of expression, second, by calling attention to its opposite–allotopy–and, third, by linking it to the pragmatic concept of cooperation.

A correct description of figures also summoned up the notion of articulation. And it is impossible to consider the question of the icon without revisiting the question of arbitrariness and of motivation. Here, then, we must remember that which usually goes without saying: that the fundamental principles of semiotics have intervened at every moment of our research, and it is not because they are part of a fairly generalised semiotic doxa that they should not be reconsidered. For example, when we were elaborating our typology of figures, it was necessary to mobilise the, now classic, Hjelmslevian opposition between expression and content. For the transforming dynamism of utterances (notably poetic or scientific utterances), other concepts have also intervened. That of mediation, for example, proposed by Lévi-Strauss for the interpretation of myths and then formally adapted for structural semantics by Greimas. From the point of view of visual semiotics, we have exploited the procedure of homologation outlined by Jean-Marie Floch, and through which it has been possible to associate an opposition of content with an opposition of expression.

The work thus undertaken has sometimes emerged out of interaction with other schools. The rhetorical dynamism to which we have drawn attention is also the goal of the concept of tension, explored and developed by Jacques Fontanille and his school, and which has also allowed for the formalising of what constitutes the motivation of utterances. In the same way, we have been able to retrieve, for our own purposes, Peirce's concept of infinite semiosis, which defines a common aim to the search for meaning.

As the example of mediation, originating in anthropology, quite frequently shows, it is not the ideas specifically labelled as semiotic that turn out to be the most fertile. Many other disciplines, in fact, have touched on the problem of meaning and they have been able to develop tools to understand sufficiently certain technical questions that have arisen therefrom. For example, contrary to what was believed at the time, semiotics had, in the Eighties, developed few tools suitable for dealing with the question of visual communication. Yet cognitive science had elaborated highly effective tools which could easily be appropriated by semiotics: for instance, the notion of form as developed by Gestalt psychology, Palmer's $\prod$ tree (being a counterpart to Porphyrus's $\sum$ tree, long since exploited by linguistics); and not forgetting the discovery of retinal detectors giving a physiological basis to the fundamental notion of opposition.

We have thus pointed out one of the main issues in semiotics, namely its relationship to interdisciplinarity. If, as is frequently said, the vocation of semiotics is to facilitate dialogue between the various social sciences, it cannot do so by crying, from its lofty position, an order such as "unite, all scientific disciplines!": it must do so through its own practices. This is why our group–which as we have seen is interdisciplinary and collaborative–has not been afraid to gather material from cognitive science and elsewhere, from the social history of science, with Kuhn, or mathematical science with the fractals of Mandelbrot.

5. What are the most important open problems in this field and what are the prospects for progress?

As has just been demonstrated, semiotics today has an arsenal of impressive tools at its disposal, the pertinence of which is continually demonstrated in ever-widening fields (for example, primitive writings, tattoos, and heraldry). But perhaps this abundance of resources is becoming cumbersome, or at least is starting to obscure the overall aim of the discipline. The publication of a vast treaty, in which all these concepts are clearly defined, would be welcome. And since, as a last point, semiotics is a branch of epistemology, we would gladly see this hypothetical work called *General Treatise on Knowledge*.

8
Jesper Hoffmeyer

Associate Professor

Department of Molecular Biology

University of Copenhagen

---

1. Why Were You Initially Drawn To The Theory Of Signs And Meaning?

As a young professor of biochemistry in the 1970s, I felt increasingly appalled by the rhetoric of my fellow experimental biologists. A decade earlier I had become attracted to the discipline of biochemistry because the conception of life as an outcome of dynamic interactions among myriads of truly miniscule particles, cells or molecules, wouldn't stop fascinating me. How could it be the case that 50.000 billions of cells–each of which were going to be replaced by new cells in a matter of few weeks–were capable of interacting in such a way as to keep alive a human being day after day through 8 decades? Having no inclination for religious explanations I found this to be the most challenging problem for science to solve–far more challenging, in fact, than the much better popularized problems of nuclear physics or space traveling. The challenge, by the way, remains unsolved to this day.

But the late 1960s also saw a strong intervention of new politically based kinds of criticisms in university life and, while these influences were obviously far more penetrating in the social sciences, also the natural sciences would gradually be drawn into the battle zone. For science is, of course, deeply involved in the technological development and was therefore, rightly or wrongly, accused of pulling the wires. Thus science was inherently involved in the development of petrochemical agriculture and in the chemical and pharmaceutical industries and could therefore be held responsible for all kinds of problems such as pollution or side effects of medical treatments. Science was also behind new reproductive techniques in the clinical practices, techniques that threatened classical conceptions of individual dignity and integrity, and it was involved in numerous conflicts at the labor market. Finally scientific conceptions of heritability of intelligence and other personality traits eventually sneaked into the structure of the educational system.

However, none of these accusations challenged science as science, they all rather challenged the way science was used, and scientists understandably rejected most of the criticisms on the grounds that it was unjustified to blame science for the errors committed by way of commercially motivated engineering practices. It nevertheless gradually occurred to me that science was perhaps in some way inherently disposed toward guiding our technical inventiveness in directions that tended to disregard important kinds of human concerns.

The controversy around the so-called 'sociobiology' launched by the entomologist Edmund O. Wilson in 1975 illustrates this point (Wilson 1975). Basically sociobiology was a new and more sophisticated version of the kind of biological determinism that had already been proposed by students of animal behavior such as Konrad Lorenz and widely popularized by for instance Desmond Morris (Lorenz 1974; Morris 1967). Contrary to ethology, however, sociobiology was based on a modern gene-centered understanding of evolutionary theory, and while several competent evolutionary biologists did argue for the inadequacy of the whole approach to support the far-reaching conclusions it claimed (notably Gould and Lewontin 1979), many if not most biologists embraced it as strong support for a genetic determinist conception of human nature. One might well oppose sociobiology for political and religious reasons–it certainly did not leave much space for the contribution of social factors or free will to the configuration of human behavior–but the theory was in many respects nothing but an extension of well-established reasoning patterns in evolutionary biology from the area of morphological or physiological adaptations to the area of animal and human behavior and further on to human mental properties. Opposing sociobiology at the biological level thus required one to search for possible unjustified biases built into the deep structure of the modern gene-based understanding of evolutionary theory.

This is not the place to go into a thorough analysis of this question (for details cf. Hoffmeyer 2008). Suffice it to say that one questionable presupposition that plays a central role in modern biology is the conception of 'information flow:' According to the so-called

'central dogma' the genetic information in a cell is transferred–
or 'passed on'–from DNA (genes) to RNAs to proteins–never the
other way around, i.e., the information flow in the cell is unidirectional. It is however not at all clear in what sense this entity,
'information,' actually flows. Usually genetic information is conceived as a sort of 'specification' causing a distinct phenotypic
trait, say a missing eye in a salamander or a damaged protein in
patients suffering muscular dystrophy. But since the actual biochemistry leading to the phenotypic trait is often quite well known
(as e.g. in the case of eyeless salamanders or muscular dystrophy)
it is hard to see what is added to our understanding by introducing the information metaphor. The idea of an 'information flow'
here simply substitutes for what is usually called causation.

There can be no doubt, however, that the information metaphor
does make biological sense. In fact, I don't think that one could
understand modern biology at all without the use of 'informational
language.' But whatever this added understanding consists in is
not part of cellular reality according to molecular biologists. At
the cellular level chemistry exhausts what goes on. The paradox
is solved, however, as soon as it is recognized that the heuristic
value of the information concept is connected to the role that
history (evolution) plays in the life of cells and organisms. What
happens is that 'history talks,' but history is not considered part
of biochemistry.

Evolution is an infinitely long series of unique events (e.g. extinctions of species, adaptations, speciations) whereby present organisms take advantage of the methods their ancestors used to get
success. By virtue of the genetic 'messages' (specifications) carried
forward from generation to generation through the reproductive
activity of individual organisms, the lineage (i.e., the population
seen as an evolving unit) maintains and continuously updates a
selective 'genomic memory' of its past that in most cases will be
a suitable tool for dealing with the future. The lineage in this
sense is a historical 'subject' capable of interpreting the changing
environmental conditions by adjusting the genotype distribution
in the next generation. The strangely paradoxical term 'natural
selection' (paradoxical because nature as such cannot of course
'select') may thus be justified to the extent it is understood that
the selective agents on this planet are the lineages. As a consequence of this selection process 'genetic information' is indeed
information in the sense that it is interpreted by the embryos of
the present generation as highly structured sets of messages from

countless previous generations concerning how to grow and produce functional organisms so that the lineage will survive.

Countering this line of argument, one might of course claim an ontology of absolute determinism with the implication that no true interpretative activity actually takes place, but one should be aware that such a claim is not in any way supported by modern science and certainly not by modern biology. Quite to the contrary, since we are here dealing with complex systems obeying so-called chaos dynamics, truly unpredictable contextual influences affect the embryonic interpretation of the hereditary texts in countless ways. And since the interpretation of the genetic information is a contextual process, it gives no meaning to imagine information as an entity that can 'flow.' Information is nothing like water in a river. In fact, genetic information doesn't move at all, of course, instead what goes on is that information is interpreted by the organismic systems as holistic subjects.

My dawning understanding up through the 1980s of the inadequacy of the biological concept of information thus not only served to legitimize a rejection of sociobiology but, more essentially, it brought me to study the *theory of signs and meaning*–or, in other words, to attempt reframing information biology as *biosemiotics* (Hoffmeyer and Emmeche 1991; Hoffmeyer 1996, 2008).

2. What do you consider your contribution to the field?

To answer this question very briefly I think my over-all contribution to *the theory of signs and meaning* (hereafter TSM), has been to develop biosemiotics as a biologically based general theory of life. The idea of biosemiotics as such was suggested several times up through the late 20th century (the first time, in fact, as far back as 1962 by the German medical psychologist Frederich Solomon Rothschild (Rotschild 1962; Kull 1999), and a semiotic approach had been applied to particular areas of biology, zoosemiotics (Sebeok 1963), phytosemiotics (Krampen 1981) or the semiotics of the immune system (Prodi 1988, Sercarz et al. 1988). In an important paper from 1984, a group of leading semioticians had agreed on a general statement of a 'semiotic perspective on science' as a step towards a new paradigm (Anderson et al. 1984), and in 1992 Sebeok and Umiker-Sebeok made biosemiotics the theme of their annual volume in the series *The Semiotic Web* (Sebeok and Umiker-Sebeok 1992). But to the best of my knowledge the paper Claus Emmeche and I published in 1991, *Code-Duality* and the Semiotics of Nature (Hoffmeyer and Emmeche 1991), was the first attempt ever made to make a Peircean semiotic understanding the very basis for the understanding of life as a biological phenomenon, and up through the next decades my work has been focused on developing this idea in all its myriad of theoretical aspects (Hoffmeyer 1996, 2008).

In a paper from 1995, I tried to formulate the biosemiotic approach to the study of life through 9 theses (Hoffmeyer 1995), and building on these theses Frederik Stjernfelt in 2002 summed up my conception of biosemiotics in 13 theses (Stjernfelt 2002). The first of these states that "Signs, not molecules, are the basic units in the study of life" (p.14). The second thesis is the thesis of Code-Duality: "As *analog codes* the organisms recognize and interact with each other in the ecological space, while as *digital codes* ('written' in DNA) they are passively carried forward in time between generations. In this sense, heredity could be seen as 'semiotic survival.' I went on to suggest that "this principle of code-duality ... can be taken as a definition of life" (argued in much more detail in Hoffmeyer 2008). Thesis 3 reads: "The simplest entity to possess real semiotic competence is the cell" (Stjernfelt, p. 16). In theses 5 and 6 it is claimed that "Subjectness is a more-or-less phenomenon" and that "subjectivity is embodied." Thesis 9 is the thesis of *semethic interaction:* "Wherever a new habit appears, it tends to become a sign for somebody else" (be it a species, a population, an individual organism, or even an organ, gland, or cell). This thesis, in fact, would be one of the backbones in a semiotic understanding of organic evolution. Thesis 11 concerns the idea of a 'semiotic niche' to complement the concept of an 'ecological niche.' And thesis 13 in Stjernfelt's summation holds that "biological evolution is a trend toward increased semiotic freedom" (p.23).

The biosemiotic conception summarized in these theses presents a strong argument for an emergentist view of life. By semiotic emergence, I mean the establishment of macro-entities or higher-level patterns through a situated exchange of signs between subcomponents. The important point here is that while the emergence of higher level patterns may seem to be slightly mysterious (or vitalist) as long as only physical interactions between entities are considered, the same outcome becomes quite understandable when based on *semiotic* interactions among entities at the lower level. Most importantly *semiotic emergence* in this sense may stand as a possible alternative candidate to natural selection as a mechanism for explaining the evolution of purposive behavior. The prominent example in sociobiological literature of so-called *altruistic behavior* may illustrate this point. The alarm calls of birds or monkeys are said to be altruistic in the sense that the callers themselves are supposed to increase their risk of being caught by a predator. The act of calling lowers the reproductive fitness of the caller and according to the Darwinian scheme any mutant that did not emit these dangerous alarm calls would quickly outcompete the altruists. So, how can altruism (in this sense) nevertheless persist in nature? The answer sociobiologists have given to this question is that evolution is not about the survival of individuals but about the survival of genes. And since every time an altruist gives up its life it will by this very act very probably save the lives of a several of its brothers and sisters (each having a 50% chance possessing the same altruist gene), the end result is that more copies of the altruist gene will survive than will copies of eventual mutant genes.

This hypothesis may perhaps have some value in the case of primitive animals such as bees or ants. But as soon as we turn to semiotically more sophisticated animals such as birds or mammals it strikes me that the hard problem disappears. 'Altruism' in these animals does not necessarily have to be connected to the presence or absence of particular genes but might instead simply be an unavoidable result of an emotional response that follows from the general communicative practices of the concerned animals. Thus, by assuming semiotic interactions among emotional individual organisms to be part of the natural world, many kinds of purposeful behavior patterns might emerge without natural selection to be concretely involved in the process. If such emergent behavioral pattern are sufficiently advantageous, natural selection might afterwards be expected to scaffold the patterns by favoring minor genetic adjustments that would facilitate the upholding and transmission of the concerned interaction patterns from generation to generation. But this does not detract from the fact that semiosis, rather than selection, in this case is the key to the evolution of end-directed behavior. And seeing natural semiosis, rather than natural selection, as the motive force behind the evolution of purposive behavior makes a decisive difference. For semiosis inescapably implies an element of Peircean Thirdness, i.e. mediation, whereas natural selection, as presently defined in evolutionary theory, remains safely inside the domain of Secondness. And while the domain of Secondness cannot, logically, evolve to produce creatures with consciousness and first person experiential worlds, the domain of Thirdness does not preclude, and might perhaps even entail, such an outcome. By assuming semiosic processes to be part of the natural world we might therefore, at least in principle, explain what natural selection is not capable of explaining: The existence in nature of life forms with experiential worlds and even human beings with inherently empathic social needs, moral inclinations and free will (Hoffmeyer in preparation).

3. What is the proper role of a theory of signs and meaning in relation to other academic disciplines?

From what has already been said it is obvious that I consider TSM to be a fairly fundamental theory. It in no way substitutes for the individual life sciences (from biochemistry to medicine) but it offers an indispensable resource base for the necessary work of reframing theoretical structures of the life sciences to accommodate the semiotic character of their subject matter. In this process, however, TSM must itself accommodate to the changed scope of its approach (more on this below).

In a broader perspective TSM should serve as a realistic input to the social and human sciences in general. As T. L. Short has recently formulated it, discussing Peirce's theory of signs, the philosophical significance of the theory is "to construct a naturalistic but non-reductive account of the human mind, and to explain and defend the claim that the sciences are objective in their mode of inquiry and in fact yield knowledge of an independently existing reality" (Short 2007, ix). By offering a realistic input to the humanities, TSM may once again serve to turn the focus of these sciences towards the implications it has for all kinds of human significative activity that such activity springs from bodies of 'flesh and blood'–or, more precisely, from an incredibly intricate interaction between different tissues and cells in the semiotically integrated psycho-neuro-immuno-endocrine landscape of the body. Such an endeavor may well run somewhat counter to the hegemonial trend in these sciences for the last three or four decades. For, again citing Short: "Continental writers, approaching Peirce from a background of Saussurean semiology, have systematically misrepresented his semeiotic. For the two doctrines are fundamentally incompatible ... The unholy union of Saussure's supposed conventionalism with the breadth of Peirce's mature semeiotic gave bastard birth to an extreme relativism and irrealism–a modern version of sophistry that Saussure and Peirce would both have rejected" (Short 2007, xiii).

4. What do you consider the most important topics or contributions in the theory of meaning and signs?

Presently, the semiotics of natural processes occupies a very marginal position in the general conception of semiotics–whether seen from outside or from inside the field. This is partly to be blamed on tradition, but it also reflects the simple fact that the sophistication of human semiotic activity is radically more pronounced than that of any other animal and, besides, that human semiotic activity for good reasons concerns us a lot more than does that of other species.

Not surprisingly, I suppose, I will nevertheless recommend an increased attention to the consequences it has for TSM that signs and meanings are rooted in bodies and, in the end, evolutionary dynamics. Nothing is subtracted from human semiotic freedom by the recognition that this freedom has earthly grounding. The fact that we cannot fly has been, and will in all future be, dealt with in human imagination and expressions in countless and truly unpredictable ways, but it remains a fact that our missing ability to fly does make up for a universal constraint that every human person must somehow accommodate to mentally. Biologists are in no particular position to specify what kind of more or less hidden universals in human nature that play games with our lives, for the essence of the fitness advantage it gave our remote ancestors to evolve linguistically competent minds exactly was to get rid of those hereditary restrictions on behavior that biologists are schooled to know about. Or, as Susanne Langer saw so many years ago: "There is a primary need in man, which other creatures probably do not have, and which actuates all his apparently unzoological aims, his wistful fancies, his consciousness of value, his utterly impractical enthusiasms, and his awareness of a 'Beyond' filled with holiness ... *this basic need, which certainly is obvious only in man, is the need of symbolization.* The symbol-making function is one of man's primary activities, like eating, looking, or moving about ... it is not the essential act of thought that is symbolization, but an act *essential to thought,* and prior to it. Symbolization is the essential act of mind; and mind takes in more than what is commonly called thought" (Langer 1942, 32-33).

But the fact that our semiotic life has evolutionary roots does, of course, influence the way we communicate and understand each other and this ought to be conceptualized by TSM. For instance, it immediately explains the apparent universal that we all feel deeply attracted to other semiotically free animals such as dolphins or apes whereas we rarely take pity on reptiles or fishes. The very fact that the psychological and corporeal reality of each individual is so tightly interconnected implies that the aesthetic and ethical needs of a human being can not any longer be coherently understood as 'incorporeal'–which is to say that, such needs cannot any longer be conceived as being based only on 'intellectual will power' but rather as always arising from a conjoined corporeal/intellectual effort. Accordingly, the role played by 'intellectual judgment" in this context is that of a *guide* rather than that of an *executive officer*. This does not, of course, imply a reduction of ethics to brute ethology–for the whole point of this argument is that the semiotization of the body has already pushed the potential for genuinely free action back *into* corporeal nature. Human semiotic life is enabled by its corporeal basis just as much as our corporeal life is in a deep sense semiotic. The corporeality of the human being is therefore, for better or worse (for not only the human good, but also the human evil, has human empathy as its precondition), the key to our ability to empathize with 'the Other.' This is not because the other *has* a body, but because he or she *is* a body just like I *am* a body myself.

By emphasizing the naturalistic aspect of TSM I am not attempting to make any judgments as to which aspect of TSM is the more important one. My concern rather is for TSM to consider the numerous implications of this anchoring of the theory in the realities of 'flesh and blood.' Not only is there no such thing as a free lunch, there isn't anything like a free phantasy either. Even phantasy is embedded in bodily frames– which however does not make our phantasies one bit less entertaining.

5. What are the most important open problems in this field and what are the prospects for progress?

One important question that divides people in semiotics is the question often referred to as the 'semiotic threshold,' i.e. the problem of defining the simplest system capable of semiosic activity. Personally I have suggested the living cell as the simplest existing semiotic entity on the grounds that the cell is the simplest system possessing the twin properties of self-referential activity (based on DNA) and other-referential activity (based on surface receptors coupled to mechanisms for intra-cellular signal-transduction) (Hoffmeyer 1995). This essentially agrees with Sebeok's claim for semiosis and life to be co-existents (Sebeok 1985). T. L. Short opposes this conception since semiosis or interpretation presupposes an ability for purposeful action and thus for making mistakes, a capacity that, in his view, limits interpretative activity to animals (Short 2007). An evolutionary counterargument to Short's view might address the question of scales and levels here. Since evolution, as I hold, has an inherent trend toward the production of systems with an ever-increasing capacity for semiotic freedom, one might suggest that the 'semiotic subject,' i.e. the living system responsible for doing the interpretations (and thus possibly misinterpretations) has not always been the individual organism. At earlier stages of the evolutionary process semiotic agency should more accurately be ascribed to the lineage, i.e., the evolving species. While individual organisms at this stage of evolution might yet not have acquired the full capacity for purposeful intentional activity, the lineage as such does indeed exhibit a capacity for making mistakes (followed often by extinction in this case). Only in later stages of evolution, when bigger brains had evolved, was this capacity taken over by individual organisms capable of coping with the world in much more fallible ways than e.g. individual insects or plants.

These are matters for future clarifications as are the merits of a more radical position such as John Deely's claim for a general physiosemiosis (Deely 1990; Salthe 1999). But it seems more and more urgent for biosemiotics to address the question of thresholds in a more nuanced way. For all we know, organic evolution presupposes some sort of continuity–simply because organisms in one generation necessarily must be very much like the organisms in the preceding generation–all the way back to the first organisms in the world. So-called hopeful monsters–saltatory creations of radically different organisms/species–do not seem to occur, and neither has any credible mechanism for such events been suggested. And yet, entirely new properties have certainly emerged in the course of evolution. To mention just a few of the more pronounced cases: Photosynthesis, multicellularity, sexual reproduction, appearance of immune systems, nervous systems and, of course, of consciousness. In all such cases the threshold problem poses itself, and yet it might be more fruitful to circumvent this recurring problem and instead search for or define the graded series of emergent events that supposedly have led from the most simple forms of sentience or irritability in living systems to more and more advanced expressions of life's agency or 'striving' (to use Darwin's own term) such as, e.g., intentionality, possession of emotional tones, of experiential world, or of consciousness.

9
Patrick Colm Hogan

Professor

Department of English

Program in Comparative Literature and Cultural Studies

Program in Cognitive Science

University of Connecticut, Storrs

---

1. Why were you initially drawn to the theory of signs and meaning?

I suspect that most people are drawn to any topic by a confluence of circumstances, some personal, some educational, some more broadly social. That's true in my case. These factors affected my subsequent interests in the philosophy, psychology, and politics of meaning.

Personally, my experiences of language were initially highly, if complexly or ambivalently, political. I was born in St. Louis in 1957 and grew up in a family where language was at least some sort of political topic. My father is Irish. His father had been involved in the independence struggle and was a member of parliament. The status of the Irish language was an important topic in Irish nationalism. My father used to give little benedictions in Irish at festive occasions and, despite the exasperated grimaces of his children, would occasionally talk to us in Irish. On the other hand, my grandfather was a socialist, more interested in the advancement of the working class than in the revival of a language that was, by this point, more associated with petit bourgeois intellectuals than farmers or wage laborers. It is perhaps unsurprising, then, that I have been concerned with the politics of categorization, but have been opposed to the more narrowly language-based (rather than materially-based) politics found in certain strands of post-structuralism.

Educationally, I was influenced by a perhaps unusually diverse range of teachers who treated the philosophy and psychology of language. In high school, I met Walter Ong and began reading his work on orality and literacy. I later took courses with him (at St. Louis University), as well as Marshall McLuhan (at the University of Toronto). As an undergraduate (at the University of Santa Clara), one of the teachers I worked with most closely was a Wittgensteinian who did his Ph.D. with Elizabeth Anscombe, probably Wittgenstein's most famous student. In graduate school (at the University of Chicago), I took courses simultaneously with Paul Ricoeur and Donald Davidson. Later, I sat in on lectures by Jim McCawley and, more importantly, Noam Chomsky.

Something that is perhaps worth stressing about this background is that it includes both Anglo-American and Continental traditions–subsequently, South Asian and other non-European traditions as well, particularly after meeting my wife, Lalita Pandit–a student of Sanskrit and daughter of a prominent philosopher, B. N. Pandit–in 1980. It also includes empirical and theoretical work from very different orientations. A somewhat unusual aspect of my background is that I do not closely identify with Anglo-American as opposed to Continental thought or with philosophical as opposed to psychological approaches. There are several reasons for this. One is that I am not much of a joiner (put negatively, I don't have much group loyalty). Thus I couldn't see myself as a follower of one or another school of philosophy or linguistics. A second is that I tend to see many elements of theories as open to revision and incorporation into other theories. Thus one may find valuable concepts in a range of sources without thereby committing oneself to the initial theories. Finally, I find many ideas stimulating and challenging even when I do not accept them. Of course, in formulating one's own views, it is important not to incorporate an incoherent mix of mutually contradictory ideas. But it is also important to recognize that the personal or other antagonism of two theorists does not mean that their theories are incompatible in their entirety.

Finally, related to these educational experiences, there was a broader academic orientation toward language at the time (I began college in 1976 and received my Ph.D., from SUNY/Buffalo, in 1983). Philosophy had undergone its "linguistic turn" and many other areas in the Humanities were strongly influenced by Structuralism and Post-Structuralism.

2. What do you consider your contribution to the field?

I can say what my interests are, what I have worked on. These are contributions in the sense that I have put forth ideas and arguments. Whether they are valuable contributions or not—that's obviously for other people to decide.

In answering the previous question, I made reference to philosophical, psychological, and political interests. This provides a useful organizational structure. I have addressed some issues that are fairly mainstream in the philosophy of language, taken up some issues in the psychology of meaning (particularly in relation to literature), and been concerned with some political issues in this area—what might broadly be categorized as the "politics of categories," particularly in relation to identity and stereotyping.

In the philosophy of language, I might isolate two arguments as representative of my approach (see Hogan 1996/2008). The first addresses the nature of meaning. It is unfortunately common for philosophers, literary critics, legal scholars, and others to argue about what meaning "really is." Though the issue is not always phrased in this way, the idea is that there is a fact about just what meaning is generally and thus what meaning is in specific cases. My argument here is simple. The definition of any term may be judged correct or incorrect only relative to an extension (a set of objects to which the term refers). An extension, however, may be judged correct or incorrect only relative to a definition. Clearly, then, the two cannot be judged correct or incorrect simultaneously. One or the other has to be stipulated. The point holds for "meaning" like any other term. Thus there is no answer to the question "What is meaning?" We must stipulate a definition or an extension–or some criterion for generating a definition or extension (e.g., one may stipulate a criterion such as "The definition of this term will be given by the chemical make-up of the following substance" or "The extension of this term is whatever all speakers of the language would agree is part of the extension.")

This leads to the second issue—just what is there to stipulate? Several types of entity are ordinary candidates for "meaning," the usual ones being ideal or Platonic, social, and psychological. Here I argue that there are only psychological meanings (and there are many types of psychological meaning; I will return to this in responding to the next question). The gist of the argument is as follows: We cannot have meaning without intention of some sort. So the psychological sense of meaning cannot be eliminated. Two questions arise with respect to Platonic and social entities.

First, are there any data that are left unexplained by a capacious psychologism? Second, do Platonic and social accounts offer an alternative anyway? I argue that the answer to both questions is "no." Consider the first question in relation to social accounts. A common argument for social accounts is that we "offload" meanings to experts. For example, I may know that oaks and elms are different, but not know which is which. I take it, however, that there are other people who have precise meanings for "oak" and "elm" and that their knowledge has normative force (thus I could get the meanings right or wrong). But what is striking about this account is that it is thoroughly psychological. It is not individualist or private. But it doesn't posit any meanings that are non-psychological.

One limitation of philosophy of language is that it tends to ignore the precise operation of meaning in the human mind. If meanings are indeed mentalistic, it is important to say just how they are stored, processed, etc. This brings us to the second, psychological area. Here, too, I will give two examples, in this case drawn from literary study. Perhaps the two topics that have been given the greatest attention in the psychology of literary meaning are metaphor and narrative.

The standard account of metaphor is the conceptual metaphor theory of Lakoff, Johnson, and others. My treatment of metaphor (see Hogan 2002 and 2003a) follows from the related, but distinct tradition of Tversky and Ortony. Conceptual metaphor theorists tend to see metaphor as operating fairly globally and providing human thought with structure. The approach advocated by Tversky, et al., sees metaphor as operating more locally. My argument might be summarized briefly as follows. Take a simple model of speech in which we understand certain topics by reference to certain predicates. Whenever we interpret, we select aspects of the predicates to map onto the topic. I select different aspects of "Republican" from "John is a Republican" when talking about war and when talking about taxes. ("Aspects" in these cases include procedural schemas, emotional associations, and so on.) This process of interpretation is constant across literal and metaphorical interpretation. The difference between literal and metaphorical interpretation is simply that, in literal interpretation, I assume all default properties apply from the predicate to the topic (e.g., I assume that John has Republican views on foreign policy even when the discussion concerns fiscal policy), unless I am given information to the contrary. However, in metaphorical interpretation, I do not assume this. There are cases of both metaphorical and literal interpretation which involve the addition of "structure" to the target, but other cases which involve only the addition of properties or relations, an increase in salience of already known properties, etc. Among other things, this account suggests why it is easy to produce and understand mixed metaphors; with the addition of priming, it also predicts that there will be complexes of metaphorical patterns, as stressed by conceptual metaphor theorists.

My discussion of meaning and narrative is somewhat more removed from the philosophy of language, connecting rather with my interest in emotion and narrative universals (see Hogan 2003b). Here, the basic semantic point is a straightforward one. I follow Rosch and subsequent theorists in understanding meaning as first of all a matter of prototypes. I argue rather simply that the point holds not only for birds, but for such mentalistic objects as stories. Specifically, there are stories that are widely perceived to be good cases of stories and stories that are not seen as such. Moreover, I argue that prototypes for stories are context-dependent just as other prototypes are context-dependent (e.g., the prototypical bird in an American Midwest backyard is not the same as the prototypical bird on a yacht at sea).

Thus far, the point is somewhat banal, given the semantic research done by Rosch and others. However, it suggests several things. First, it suggests that writers and readers are likely to have prototypes in mind when creating and responding to stories. Second, it suggests that these prototypes are likely to be different in different social and temporal contexts (e.g., a story told for dissemination over a long period of time to a general community has a different context from a story told for a small, familiar group at a particular moment). Finally, it suggests that the prototypes may differ depending on the, so to speak, "internal" context of the story (e.g., if the story concerns personal relations or political structures).

More importantly, it turns out that understanding narratives as based in prototypes allows us a fruitful way of examining stories across traditions. Indeed, it allows us to isolate some surprising patterns in story structure cross-culturally. Specifically, we may look at what stories are highly prototypical in the public sphere in different cultural traditions. One might expect that necessary and sufficient conditions for categories might be cross-cultural, but that prototypicality would vary culturally. In fact, this is often not the case. For example, central cases of color terms, parallel to prototypes, are far less likely to vary across languages than are marginal cases, which would be decided by necessary and sufficient conditions (see Comrie 1989, 36-8). As it turns out, examining highly prototypical stories across cultures reveals striking patterns. Specifically, three fairly detailed patterns tend to recur—a romantic narrative, a heroic narrative, and a sacrificial narrative. The details of specific stories necessarily vary, but sets of specific stories often converge on one or another prototypical form, suggesting both production and reception of stories that are based on context-selected prototypes. (I should note that not all public stories—not even all successful and enduring public stories told for entertainment–fall into one of these categories, though a great many do.)

Here, the question arises as to how one might account for this pattern. To do this, I turned to emotions. My first argument here is that emotion terms are prototype-based also, with all that this entails. Stories commonly involve a hero seeking some goal. He or she seeks the goal on the expectation that it will produce happiness. As the audience for a particular story becomes broader, the choice of the happiness goal must rely less and less on idiosyncrasies of the storyteller (which may be of interest to family or close friends). The result is that storytellers come to rely on happiness prototypes. From here, I argue that a range of factors—from human emotional biology to developmental experiences to group dynamics—make certain contexts and certain prototypes for those contexts highly likely. These contexts (physical, interpersonal, social) and associated happiness prototypes (plenty and health, enduring union combining sexual desire and attachment, individual prestige plus in-group authority) yield the three cross-cultural narrative prototypes.

An understanding of prototypes has consequences for the function of social categories as well, unsurprisingly as stereotypes are a form of prototypes. This brings us to politics and meaning. Here too I will give two examples, one bearing on identity, the other bearing on ideology—particularly racism—and the mental lexicon.

Identity is one of the most widely discussed topics in politically engaged social theory today. Identity politics based on one's ethnicity, race, sex, national origin, and so on, have been an important feature, not only of practical politics, but of political theory. Consider, for example, the influential work of Judith Butler, who argues that there is no essential sex or gender identity, but that what we take to be an essential identity is a product of performance. I am very sympathetic with Butler's theoretical opposition to identity—and her simultaneous acceptance of the importance of political activity related to identity categories. However, I often cannot make out just what she is arguing and I am often not convinced by her particular arguments when I do follow them.

One problem with theories of identity, in my view, is that they tend to confuse distinct topics. Specifically, there are two sorts of identity that it is particularly important to differentiate (see Hogan 2000a and 2004). One is *practical identity*. It is the entire complex of our attitudes, interests, skills, habits, propensities, and so forth. It comprises what we can do, desire to do, expect others to do. It is crucially a matter of the way in which our own modes of action fit with those of others around us. It of course includes verbal action and the cognitive structures that enable it—for example, our mental lexicon.

This is crucially different from *categorial identity*. Categorial identity is simply one's classification of oneself in one or more categories that one takes to be in some sense definitive of oneself.

As many writers have noted, the semantics of our mental lexicon are hierarchized. In other words, we consider some properties and relations more important than others for a particular class of objects. For example, having a flat upper surface is almost certainly more definitive for "table" than being wooden or metallic. My first point is simply that the same hierarchization applies to our conception of ourselves. Various properties and relations may characterize Jones's understanding of himself, thus forming part of his lexical entry for himself. For instance, two features of his self-concept may be "male" and "watches Hindi movies." However, it is unlikely that the two will be equal in importance. He will probably consider "male" to be very nearly definitive (i.e., if it changes, then his identity changes), while considering "watches Hindi movies" to be peripheral (i.e., it can change without his identity changing). Individually, a wide range of category types may be considered definitive. However, a small number of category types tend to recur frequently—sex, sexual orientation, race, ethnicity, religion, nationality, class, and a few others.

One's categorial identity, then, is a graded list of such (putatively) definitive categories. Each such category defines one as a member of an in-group and, correspondingly, sets that in-group against an out-group. Individual categories become socially consequential insofar as they converge with the categorial identities of others. What is perhaps most remarkable about categorial identity is that it is distinct from practical identity and more consequential for one's social attitudes. Specifically, in-group/out-group divisions carry with them a wide range of evaluative and actional biases. Moreover, research demonstrates that in-group/out-group effects occur with the most minimal stipulation of a partial extension for the group (i.e., a mere stipulation of who belongs to what group). Specifically, when test subjects are arbitrarily assigned to different groups and do not interact, they still exhibit group biases (see Duckitt 1992, 68-69).

While the basic forms of in-group/out-group bias are constant, particulars vary, and they vary in extremely consequential ways. For example, the "Aryan" out-grouping of Jews during the Nazi period was quite different from the U.S. out-grouping of, say, the French during the lead-up to the invasion of Iraq. This brings us to the second topic. I have argued that, once an out-group is formed, various aspects of our mental lexicon enter into our further conceptualization of that group. The problem in thinking about out-groups is roughly this. One obvious way of understanding other people is by modeling them on ourselves, just as one obvious way of understanding ourselves is by drawing on what we know about other people. However, this identification is precisely what is generalized to the in-group in categorial identification. As such, it can hardly be extended to the out-group. To understand out-group members, then, we search for other models. Commonly, searches of this sort—searches within the mental lexicon–begin with closely related concepts. This is simply because of the way our mental lexicons are set up, with multiple connections among related items. (If I say that something in my garage is not a wrench, you might wonder if it is a hammer. But you probably won't wonder if it is a kangaroo.) Moreover, the "search space" is constrained by the initial hierarchization of in-group over out-group, which points us toward closely related lexical items that allow for this hierarcization.

There are two common lexical domains for our modeling of out-groups: age and animacy (see Hogan 2001). (Sex/gender is another important domain of this sort, but I will not consider it here.) The age model assimilates the in-group to the normative adult, while conceptualizing out-groups by reference to children, adolescents, and the aged. The animacy model assimilates the in-group to the normative human category, while conceiving of the out-group in terms of sub-human (animalistic) or super-human (angelic or demonic) categories. These models may be mixed or may alternate even for individuals, but the development of enduring attitudes and policies is often bound up with the particular prominence of one model (or of two models with convergent consequences). For example, the demonic model was prominent in Nazi anti-Semitic propaganda.

3. What is the proper role of a theory of signs and meaning in relation to other academic disciplines?

There isn't really *one* role. It depends on the discipline. But there is certainly a wide range of disciplines in which philosophy of language, psychology of meaning, and/or politics of categorization are of key importance. We might consider them briefly in turn. Since my claims here are particular to disciplines, I will consider one particular discipline in each case.

Whenever a discipline is involved with interpretation, it is likely to benefit from a clear analytic of the types of meaning that may be relevant to its purpose. A great deal of conceptual confusion, thus theoretical and practical error, results from an imprecise use of the word "meaning." An obvious case of this is law (see Hogan 1996 and 2007). Positions on constitutional interpretation are often divided into two groups—advocates of "original intent" and advocates of the view that the constitution "evolves." The debate is often framed as if it concerns some interpretive fact, specifically whether the meaning of the text changes historically or was fixed at the time of writing (or perhaps ratification). But this is a false debate. There is no fact about what "the meaning of the text" is. Rather, there are different ways of stipulating criteria for that meaning. Most fundamentally, considering written law, one may distinguish between intended meanings and intended extensions of those drafting the legislation. Beyond this, one may distinguish the interpretive meanings or extensions shared by those who passed the legislation, those shared by particular courts in important decisions regarding the legislation, those shared by people generally at different periods, those shared by experts in relevant fields at different times, and so forth. Moreover, interpretation involves not only definitions and extensions, but moral, policy, and other goals, which also may be isolated and stipulated.

The possibility of stipulating different sorts of meaning does not imply that any and all stipulations are of equal value, given the purposes of law. Indeed, the main reason for being clear about the varieties and objects of psychological meaning (definitions, extensions, moral aims, etc.) is to allow clearer and more productive debate about just what sort of meaning we should favor. Moreover, none of this implies that we must prefer one sort of meaning in all cases. In fact, we almost certainly will favor different sorts of meaning for different legal topics. Consider, for example, a statute stating that schoolchildren must be provided with healthful diets. We are likely to wish to interpret the initial legislators' definitional intention for "diet" ("provision of food," not "method of slimming"). However, we are likely to prefer current nutritionists' understanding of the extension of "healthful" (i.e., we are likely to rely on relevant experts today when determining precisely what food is healthful, rather than relying on what the original legislators took to be healthful).

As to the psychology of meaning, work in this area has consequences for any discipline that considers, not mere physical facts, but the construal of facts, the significance different construals have for people, and the ways in which that significance changes personal experience as well as social practices and interpersonal relations. A rough and intuitive understanding of the psychology of meaning will almost certainly have deleterious consequences for work in such fields as anthropology, sociology, and political science. Consider, for example, the case of nationalism—a phenomenon of central importance in political science particularly. (By "nationalism" here, I am referring to the sets of ideas and feelings connected with devotion to a nation. I am not referring to the legal or economic system of nation-states.) When political scientists talk about nationalism, they must have some way of treating just how nationalists (and non-nationalists) conceptualize the nation. If their (tacit) theory of meaning is a matter of necessary and sufficient conditions, they may view conceptions of the nation as fundamentally formal, fixed, and explicit. Work in the psychology of meaning suggests it is much more likely that we conceive of nations in complex, contextually shifting, prototypical forms, forms that include a wide range of explicit and implicit information—representational, procedural, affective, and so on. Moreover, since nations exist in historical time, it is likely that we understand them in part by way of specifically narrative prototypes. Indeed, one may argue that different types of nationalism may be distinguished in part on the basis of whether they emplot the nation in heroic, sacrificial, or romantic terms. Nor are these emplotments arbitrary. Sacrificial emplotments become particularly likely in conditions of scarcity and despair. Romantic emplotments become particularly likely in conditions where the nation is divided. (For example, romantic emplotments of the nation often involve lovers from the different communities trying to be united despite social impediments; cf. Sommer 1990.) These emplotments are, as always, bound up with emotion prototypes, which themselves are, in turn, intertwined with nationalism

Finally, the politics of categorization obviously has bearing on any form of study that addresses group relations or identity. Consider gender studies. Personally, I find much work in this field to be enormously intellectually insightful and politically productive. However, when it is unclear about the politics of categorization, it necessarily suffers. For example, Judith Butler's anti-identitarian conclusions are rightly influential. However, it is often difficult to tell just what Butler thinks about an individual's feelings and preferences. At certain points, she seems to be saying that we are all simply determined by a sort of Foucauldian discourse. At other points, she seems to suggest that we have preferences and feelings that are not simply a function of discourse. To use her term, sometimes it appears that "I" am merely an effect of my performance (in the way that the apparent personality of the puppet is simply the effect of its performance, not its cause). But, at other times, she seems to say that we can initiate performance in ways that disrupt dominant discourse.

A simple distinction between practical and categorial identity, along with a distinction between self and self-concept, would, I think, go a long way toward clarifying the point. Suppose that in my actual experience, I am differently affected by different sexual experiences. I am sometimes attracted to some physical features, sometimes to others; sometimes a certain personality intrigues me, but sometimes it leaves me cold; perhaps I am almost always attracted to women, but sometimes I am indifferent to attractive women and sometimes I have fleeting interests in men, perhaps interests of which I am not even aware. My self-concept will not simply be a reflection of all this fluidity and diversity. Insofar as I base my self-concept on introspection, I will likely form a sort of prototype of myself, averaging across various experiences of myself, with the experiences themselves weighted by salience. Moreover, I will combine this with what other people report to me about myself, and about the categories to which I belong. This categorial information will add features to my self-concept—for example, if I am a real man, I don't like quiche, to take a silly example from a few years ago. I will also implicitly hierarchize my self-concept, as already noted. In short, my self-concept will, on the one hand, radically simplify my self and, on the other hand, it will add properties that I do not actually have. Moreover, this self-concept will foster certain sorts of behavior. In some cases, the behavior will reflect genuine preferences. But in other cases it will not. If I consider myself a real man, perhaps I will never eat quiche. My manly distaste for quiche will then seem like the cause of my "performance," when it is only an implication of that performance—performance that itself results from categorial identifications. In keeping with this, we might say that we do indeed "perform" or act on feelings and ideas that are not merely created by discourse. However, our practical identity—which is manifest in "performance"–is not a simple expression of spontaneous feelings and ideas. It is crucially shaped by discourse, both long-term and moment-to-moment, prominently on the basis of categorial identity.

4. What do you consider the most important topics and/or contributions in the theory of meaning and signs?

Before answering this question, I need to say something about the different levels at which one can—and should—discuss meaning and related areas. I understand descriptive and explanatory principles as applying to different levels of emergent structure in the study of meaning just in the way that we commonly understand such principles as applying to different levels of emergent structure in the physical sciences. Physics gives us one set of theories; chemistry another; biology another. These different levels of analysis address different levels of emergent, patterned complexity. In the case of meaning, I would distinguish three primary levels of analysis: biological, mental, and social. Within the "mental" stratum, I would distinguish the study of experiential intentionality from the objectifying study of mental representations (see Hogan forthcoming). (I should perhaps note that, within this scheme, the social level of analysis is not a non-mentalistic level, but a level at which patterns emerge through configurations of minds. Thus meanings analyzed at the social level remain psychological in the above sense.)

Within the social analysis of meaning, I feel that the foremost contribution has come from the Marxist tradition of ideological critique, particularly as expanded beyond class analysis to include the critique of gender ideology, colonial ideology, and so forth. This has been importantly supplemented by Foucauldian and related treatments of discourse—the establishment of authority, the canonization of ways of speaking, the authorization of particular concepts, the interleaving of discourse and institutional power, etc. (On this and some of the following topics, see Hogan 2000b.)

At the intentional level, Phenomenology, both the work of Husserl and that of Heidegger, is primary. I am not so much referring to what Phenomenologists had to say about meaning as such. Rather, I am referring to their more general treatment of intentionality (Husserl) and worldly action (Heidegger). These analyses provided extremely valuable backgrounds for our understanding of the intentionality of meaning and the enactment of meaning through our practical relation to the world. The latter connection was valuably elaborated (in a non-Heideggerian context) by Grice in his treatment of conversational cooperation and by Wittgenstein in his idea of language games. Finally, I would say that some of Donald Davidson's work has also significantly furthered our understanding of language practice in the world.

Regarding mental representations, I would first of all point to the importance of the early Analytic school. Though I agree with Quine's critique of the analytic/synthetic distinction, I believe that such pioneering theorists as Carnap, Russell, and Ayer presented us with models of conceptual clarity and precision. The other truly path-breaking theorists of mental representations, in my view, have been Rosch, Chomsky, and Rumelhart and McClelland. Rosch shifted our understanding of meaning from necessary and sufficient conditions to prototypes, and thus revolutionized semantics. Chomsky is famous for many aspects of his linguistic work—the competence/performance distinction, the division between observational, descriptive, and explanatory adequacy, and so forth. However, to my mind, his truly remarkable achievements come much later, with the development of principles and parameters theory. Though principles and parameters theory is first of all syntactic, it presents us a way of thinking about cross-cultural patterns and variations, language acquisition, and other matters that are not confined to syntax. Finally, Rumelhart and McClelland developed sub-symbolic neural networks which model meanings in ways that capture the contextually shifting aspects of meaning better than other models. They also provide a sort of transition between more traditional representational accounts of meaning and neurobiology, a transition that may help us to understand the relation between the two.

In the neuroscience of language, I cannot name any theorists or schools that are predominant. That is a testimony to the depth and rigor of the research in this field. There are countless papers on the storage, activation, synthesis of meaning in the brain. The results and interpretations of the results are constantly changing. This is because it is the most scientifically advanced of all the levels of semantic research—though it is still in its infancy as a science, which leads us to the final question.

5. What are the most important open problems in this field and what are the prospects for progress?

Of course, all the preceding levels remain important. Moreover, it is critical that we map the relations among these levels. One might conceive of the relation between the levels as roughly of the following sort: lower levels map onto higher levels–thus neurobiology maps onto psychology and psychology maps onto society—as (partial) explanations; higher levels map onto lower levels—thus society maps onto psychology and psychology maps onto neurobiology—as (partial) understandings or interpretations. For example, activation of distributed areas in the brain during the utterance of a particular word serves to explain the psychology of meaning for that word. But, at the same time, we are only able to understand or interpret that distributed activation pattern as semantic because we have a distinct psychological experience of a particular sound as being a word with a particular meaning. Such mappings define an extremely important field for future research and theorization.

However, while all levels and all mapping relations should be researched vigorously, not all hold equal promise for greatly advancing our knowledge of meaning in the near future. It is commonplace to remark on the rapid developments in our understanding of the brain. But, to paraphrase the great Joycean critic, Fritz Senn, just because everybody says it, doesn't mean it's wrong. Indeed, it seems clear that changes in our understanding of meaning in the brain have consequences at every descriptive and explanatory level. Consider, for example, the relation between circuits for physical manipulation and the neurological substrate of meaning for instrument words (see, for example, chapter four of Pulvermüller 2002). Research isolating this not only maps onto and helps to explain the existential psychology of meaning as developed by, for example, Heidegger. It also inflects the way we articulate that psychology, suggests different areas for future research, and so on. Similarly, research in social neuroscience has enriched our understanding of the politics of categorization. Thus work in the neurosciences seems not only the most promising area of research for advancing our knowledge, but the most crucial for work in all areas of the study of meaning.

Yet, I must immediately qualify this by pointing to an obvious fact about scientific innovations. As Karl Popper stressed, we cannot predict discoveries. We may be able to conjecture that a problem will be solved in the future. But we cannot say how—for to say how would amount to solving the problem. The result is that we cannot say what will be the most productive area for research and theorization. Tomorrow a psychological or social theory might be published that radically transforms our understanding of meaning. We don't know now. We can't.

10
Robert E. Innis

Professor
Department of Philosophy
University of Massachusetts Lowell

My Way through Signs

I came to engage myself with the theoretical issues surrounding the realms of 'signs and meanings' by a rather circuitous route. I was originally trained, both in high school and in college, in classical languages and in a mixed curriculum of a kind of updated version of scholastic philosophy, that took its inspiration from Aquinas, and of a large dose of the history of philosophy. One of the most important things I took away from this was the historicity and variability of conceptual and interpretive frameworks. This 'lesson' was reinforced by three postgraduate years (1963-1966) in Rome, where I was engaged in the study of theology at the Gregorian University and where all the lectures and examinations were conducted in Latin, even if we were dealing with texts in Hebrew or Greek, or whatever, and where the multinational student body spoke, and communicated with one another in, a multitude of languages. It became very clear to me that theology, in its multiple formats and historical variations, was fundamentally dependent upon interpretive procedures at every level. It was an essentially hermeneutical enterprise, its subject matters embodied in vast systems of signs, symbols, images, and rituals (and the 'spaces' in which they took place).

During that time in Rome, in 1964, I purchased at the Red Lion Bookstore, and still have the copy, Susanne Langer's *Philosophy in a New Key*. I read it with great avidity. It bore directly upon major themes in my theological studies, but it was not written as a prolegomenon to theological hermeneutics, although it bore upon it in the deepest of ways. Indeed, the author's own substantive commitments were then, and remained, resolutely naturalistic, without being reductive—as mine, too, ultimately became. But the range of topics treated in that book, indicated in its subtitle, 'A Study in the Symbolism of Reason, Rite, and Art,' were an anticipation of my more formal involvement in explicitly 'semiotic' concerns. Also in 1964 I bought a copy of Michael Polanyi's great book, *Personal Knowledge*, with its pivotal chapter on 'Articulation.' Both Langer and Polanyi referred to the work of Karl Bühler, the German psychologist and language theorist. This link, and a number of others, specifically references to the work of Alan Gardiner and Philipp Wegener, turned out to be fateful for my further studies and approaches to the theory of signs and meanings, since in 1966 I abandoned the formal study of theology and returned to the States to take my doctorate in Philosophy, writing my dissertation on 'the logic of consciousness' in Michael Polanyi's work. Polanyi's emphasis, relying on a plethora of non-philosophical sources, on the paradigmatic role of perception in world-building, on the tacit matrices of meaning, including linguistic meaning, and his assimilation of 'wholes' and 'meanings' opened up a distinctive position in philosophical reflection for me and, looking back now, has informed the types of issues in the theory of signs and meaning that has most drawn my attention.

Early in my teaching career I started to teach a course on the 'Philosophy of Language' which later evolved into a course called 'Language, Signs, and Symbols.' But the topics and frameworks belonging to that course soon infiltrated my courses in epistemology and aesthetics and further in the philosophy of religion and even in the philosophy of technology. The epistemology course moved from being called 'Theory of Knowledge' to 'Ways of Knowing,' with the 'ways' being thought of as sign- or symbol-defined mediating structures. And the aesthetics course more and more focussed on 'meaning structures' and 'image fields' rather than strictly speaking on traditional notions of 'art' and 'beauty,' which, to be sure, were not neglected but rather reformulated or reframed. The philosophy of religion course became a more broadly focussed course on the historicity and conceptual variability of the 'God symbol' or 'images of the Absolute' or 'images of the Ultimate.' And, I found, technology itself could be seen from a distinctively semiotic (as well as aesthetic) point of view. 'Signs, tools, and models' become the leitmotiv of this course.

From the scholarly point of view, as opposed to the pedagogical concerns which have continued and developed to the present day, I have been more and more involved in studying the most fruitful points of intersection between semiotics and philosophy, both historically and systematically, two orientations that, as a philosophy professor, are perforce intertwined in my work. I have been concerned to investigate the philosophical implications of semiotics and the semiotic implications of certain philosophical traditions and standpoints. Among my first published works, going back to the early 1970's, are articles on the centrality of language in Polanyi's epistemology, on Gadamer's hermeneutics, on the role of analogy in religious language, on semiotic approaches to art, specifically Susanne Langer's and Nelson Goodman's, and on Wittgenstein and Habermas. The really effective turning point for me, however, came with the publication of Umberto Eco's *A Theory of Semiotics* and with the meeting of the International Association of Semiotic Studies in Vienna in 1979, where I presented a paper on Karl Bühler, whose work more and more engaged me, ultimately culminating, in 1981, in a small book, *Karl Bühler: Semiotic Foundations of Language Theory*, which also contained a translation of his 'Axiomatization of the Language Sciences. In that period I published a review article on Eco's book in *International Philosophical Quarterly*. In a sense that review and that book, and the range of topics treated in those early papers, set the systematic point of entry to all my later work that make up what I hope to have contributed to the theory of signs and meanings. My initial 'being drawn' to the study of signs and meanings turned into a full-fledged absorption into 'all things semiotic.'

What, then, do I think I have contributed to the field? Answering this question will also outline what I consider, from my standpoint as a philosopher, which is my 'home discipline,' the most important topics in the field and what types of open questions still remain to be dealt with.

I have been mainly concerned to practice a kind of method that I have called 'retrievals and continuations,' or, in another formulation taken from Wittgenstein, 'seeing connections.' Semiotics has had a tendency to develop in polarized, or sometimes monolithic, fashion, depending on which point of origin a research tradition has taken off from and which is 'in' for the moment. The two major traditions, the Saussurean and the Peircean, have been, with a wide range of variations within these two frames, the defining poles. I have tried to broaden the terms of the discussion and to try to avoid at all costs the 'fallacy of false alternatives' in the study of signs and meanings. As a matter of fact, from the philosophical side, there are multiple points of entry into the study of signs and meanings and important interlocutors in the discussion can also be found outside the defining contours of these two conceptual frameworks, although I think that, if one had to choose, one would be better served by the Peircean framework by reason of its comprehensiveness, its essential openness, and its repudiation of linguocentrism.

Accordingly, I have spent a large part of my scholarly time exploring the heuristic fertility of various non-standard approaches to sign theory and their relationships to other currents, including substantial overlappings and enrichings. I have clearly been most sensitive to the philosophical side of these approaches and to the ability of semiotics to throw powerful light on central philosophical issues such as the nature of abstraction, the relations between perception and semiosis and between perception and metaphor, the relations between perceptual, hermeneutical, and semiotic approaches to art, the nature of the semiotic self, and the analysis of technological embodiment from the semiotic point of view.

For example, Karl Bühler, recognizing the twin importance of both Saussure and Husserl, saw the analytical importance for a variety of disciplines of the great distinction between phonology and phonetics. He argued that semiotics, *sensu stricto*, was not a 'material science,' even if all sign systems had to be materially embodied in a medium of some sort. Bühler was one of the first to see how the theoretical principles of phonology, which were based on attending to the differential formal and functional features of the sound systems undergirding languages, illuminated central features of the traditional philosophical problem of abstraction. Abstraction is governed by the 'principle of pertinence' and the language sciences by the 'principle of abstractive relevance.' Bühler saw in the apprehension of the sound system of languages a strong model for understanding the grasp of pertinence in the experiential continuum, which was 'cut' by various acts of abstraction. Generalizing Bühler's insight would allow us to see how different systems of pertinence could be either constituted or discovered in the flow of experience, which becomes the locus for 'multiple realities.' I found such a notion extremely helpful in bringing semiotic analyses into close contact with the types of analyses carried out by phenomenology of both the Husserlian and the Jamesian pragmatist sorts, though its value extends way beyond them to such domains as the aesthetic, as Bühler's influence on the Prague School showed.

One of Bühler's other permanently valuable insights was that the speech event itself, as a meaningful utterance, could be seen as accomplishing three different semantic functions, depending on the relations one considered determinative: the representational, the expressive, or the appellative or steering. Bühler's main point, for which he did not claim any originality, was not that speech allows us to perform different functions—this was known by all in the rhetorical tradition—but that one could specify and systematize the distinctive features and the precise relations involved in each semantic function. Roman Jakobson, from the linguistics side, potentiated, as it well known, these three functions into six, while Karl Popper, who had studied with Bühler in Vienna, added a 'critical' function, which he thought belonged essentially to philosophical analysis. But these functions also allowed Bühler to schematize psychology in terms of focussing on objective structures, focussing on expressive acts, or focussing on behavior, each type of concern being represented by a distinctive type of psychology and research tradition. The semiotic pivot is for Bühler the distinction between symbols, symptoms, and signals, a kind of semiotic triad that functions as the basis of the other types of semantic functions. While the basis functions for Bühler are representation, expression, appellation (which Jakobson dubbed 'conation'), Bühler opened the path to a thorough investigation of distinct yet systematically interrelated semantic functions of any semiosic event. Anticipating later work in the cognitive neurosciences Bühler also foregrounded the distinctiveness, indeed uniqueness, of symbolization, or the systematic and open-ended use of symbols, as the mark of the human. Bühler's insights were taken up into an updated concrete research program by the German psycholinguist Hans Hörmann whose *Einführung in die Psycholinguistik* I edited and published in English in 1986 under the title of *Meaning and Context: An Introduction to the Psychology of Language.*

Bühler had been influenced deeply by the logical writings of Edmund Husserl. I, too, had deep interests in phenomenology, both in its 'orthodox' Husserlian and later 'derivative' modes, principally as represented by the early hermeneutic orientation of Heidegger and by Merleau-Ponty's thick, multimodal descriptions of the primacy of perception, as well as 'parallel' modes that are not just variations on Husserlian themes, such as that practiced by William James with sovereign mastery in his *Principles of Psychology* and exploited later by Alfred Schutz under the rubric of 'multiple realities.' I saw that semiotics, with its analytical tools of divers provenance, and phenomenology, with its sensitivity to the particular, were mutually enriching approaches to the realm of signs and meanings. Semiotics, in its purest, most abstract, forms, focuses on the formal features of sign systems, while phenomenology, at times expanding out into an explicit hermeneutics, as in the work of Paul Ricoeur and Hans-Georg Gadamer, focuses on the contents of lived through and experienced meanings. I see the theory of signs and meanings as located between these two poles. And my subsequent work after the little book on Karl Bühler has tried to exemplify what such a framing of issues between these two poles would look like in a number of different ways and formats.

I have carried this work out both in a long series of articles and papers, dealing with a number of issues either directly or tangentially connected with semiotics, and principally in four books.

First of all, in 1985 when I published *Semiotics: An Introductory Anthology*, the goal was not just to select 'classic' statements of various semiotic approaches and analyses but by means of the introductions to each selection to stitch them together in a deep and consistent way. The interpretive thread that ran through them was the intersections between the analysis of signs and the analysis of subjectivity. While Roland Barthes, echoing Jacques Lacan, opined that the psyche was structured like a language, I pointed out that this was only part of the story. In fact the psyche, the self in its total range, both individually and socially, is structured as a matrix or locus of sign actions, of semioses. It relies on all those semiotic instruments and formed contents that make up the web of meaning in which we are embodied and live out our lives. My comments in the introductions, and the mix of texts selected, tried to give a taste of what semiotics had to offer not just *to* but also *from* the various disciplines which were represented in the collection: linguistics, philosophy, literary theory, anthropology, art theory, communication theory, ethology, and various intellectual stations in between. Rather than treating 'semiotics' as some superscience standing on its own, I wanted to show how it was more a framework of analysis that could inform the other discplines, helping them reformulate and make more precise some of their central theses and conclusions. But I also wanted to show that, no matter how rich were the theoretical resources of the twin founts of semiotics, Saussure and Peirce, they did not exhaust its scope or conceptual frameworks nor did they constitute an ultimate or complete set of conceptual options between which we were forced to choose. There were many rooms in the semiotic mansion and a vast system of hallways that allowed one to go from place to place, depending on what type of views one wanted to have along the way and out the windows.

Secondly, coming as I did from philosophy, with my systematic and historical interests, and also wanting to avoid the 'fallacy of false novelty,' I continued to pursue and to deepen my studies in the variety of ways central issues in semiotics could be treated by different philosophical traditions and approaches, including approaches that did not belong to either of the two 'official' poles: American pragmatism, Polanyi's model of personal and tacit knowledge, Bühler's language theoretical approach, Cassirer's marvelous philosophy of symbolic forms, and the monumental work of Susanne Langer. I most wanted to follow up the theme of the relationships between 'perception' and 'semiosis,' that is, how philosophical accounts that took their stand on 'the primacy of perception' intersected with accounts that acknowledged the primacy and distinctiveness of 'higher level' symbolic and meaning-making processes. My goal was to see how far we could 'push meaning down' into the perceptual and actional stratum and how much meaning-making at the 'upper levels' was itself characterized and conditioned by structures of embodiment already limned on the lower levels. More generally, I wanted to follow up the descriptive and analytical adequacy of Peirce's contention that the 'bottomless lake of consciousness' was ultimately to be thought of in terms of levels and types of sign processes. The problem that I set out to explore was how a number of other approaches allowed us to broaden the terms in which semiotic processes were normally discussed and to bring quite different voices into a common discussion, always with an eye on 'the thing itself,' that is, the ultimate contours and dimensions of sign and symbol systems and their bearing on the lived dimensions of human experience.

These studies have culminated in three books: *Consciousness and the Play of Signs*, *Pragmatism and the Forms of Sense: Language, Perception, Technics*, and *Susanne Langer in Focus: The Symbolic Mind*. In these three books I have striven to throw light from a number of different angles on the ultimate matrices of human meaning-making and to show the ultimate complementarity of different starting points and analytical procedures. The sources upon which I relied in the first two books were various but in my opinion substantial. But they were selected for their fundamental philosophical power and rigor as well as their openness to supplementation, expansion, and application. While acknowledging the great comprehensive scope of Peirce's phenomenological semiotics, I thought that he did not supply all, or at least the most completely explicitly balanced, of the analytical tools needed for tackling the host of philosophical problems that semiotics raised, though his range of interests overlapped other approaches in multiple ways. But it was his formulation of the types of problems that set the stage, for me at least, for a search for alternative descriptive and analytical approaches.

In *Consciousness and the Play of Signs* I tried to show how, in addition to Peirce, intellectual resources from Michael Polanyi, John Dewey, Karl Bühler, and Ernst Cassirer could be used to 'rotate' the problems of how to thematize 'consciousness' in terms of various forms of 'meaning' and 'meaning-making' embodied in the 'play of signs,' which was by no means a 'free play' nor a 'prison house.' From Polanyi I took and exploited principally the relevance of two key concepts based on his fundamental distinction between *focal* and *subsidiary* awareness. I pointed out that, if we followed up the implications of this distinction, we could see that we attend *from* sign configurations, as subsidiaries, *to* the 'spheres' they bear upon, the semiotic focal wholes, and by reason of this 'attending from' we *indwell* the sign configurations, extend ourselves into them, whereby they become part of our 'semiotic bodies.' Sign configurations, I argued, are embodied forms of meaning-making, complementing as exosomatic organs our endosomatically defined body. The *from-to* structure of consciousness, with the varieties of what Polanyi called 'subsidiaries' and 'focal wholes,' engenders various forms of *embodiment* relations because the various sign types have different *qualitative feels*.

From Dewey's pragmatist approach, in light of Polanyi, I took the notion of the *qualitative matrices of meaning*. Dewey had followed up Peirce's crucial hints about the semiotic implications of 'firstness' or 'quality.' His major contribution to semiotic issues was the development of the insight that there was a grasp of significance prior to all forms of explicit sign-reading and that indeed sign-action was truly a form of *action* in which the inquiring organism intervened *into* the environing field, in a continuous circuit of constructive responses. Dewey's great insight was identical in substance, on the human level, to Jakob von Uexküll's widely discussed 'functional circle.' Both Polanyi and Dewey formulated aesthetic theories with great semiotic relevance, but with an important foregrounding of analytical schemata that emphasize perceptual structures. They showed how apparently radically different starting points of philosophical reflection intersect at crucial points, principally the relations between 'perception' and 'semiosis.' Perception, they show, is intrinsically defined in terms of 'meaning' and 'meaning spaces' while semiosis, as sign action, is ineluctably materially embodied in sign configurations that themselves have distinctive, and determining, *feels* and that function as both enabling and constraining conditions of accessing the world.

I have also continued to argue that the work of Karl Bühler and Ernst Cassirer are permanently valuable resources for semiotic reflection quite generally. Of especial value is the *model of philosophizing* exemplified in their work, although Bühler was predominantly a psychologist with deep philosophical roots, while Cassirer was the historically informed philosopher *par excellence*. In separate chapters in *Consciousness and the Play of Signs* I explored the power of their projects to illuminate the core theme of 'between perception and semiosis.' What I have been looking for are ways to eradicate all temptations to force the descriptive and analytical procedures of semiotics into a procrustean bed or to commit the fallacy of false alternatives. I have been most interested in finding out and exploring the value of alternative descriptions and analytical frameworks. The different descriptions clearly do not give the same weight to the various dimensions of semiosis—but this is fully acceptable. Peirce's triadic schematization of consciousness in terms of iconicity, indexicality, and symbolicity, corresponding to the notion of quality, reaction, and law, or firstness, secondness, and thirdness has a rather different 'torquing' of consciousness than Cassirer's schematization in terms of expression, representation, and signification, where the basis is not, as with Peirce, how the sign is 'joined' to or 'refers' to its object, but to the gradual separation of the sign from its 'sign-bearing matter,' as we gradually move away from the 'thickness' of 'physiognomic' or expressive meanings to the 'transparency' of mathematical and relational signs. There is, however, no need to 'translate' Peirce's schema into Cassirer's. They are asking rather different questions and offer rather different answers, although we can clearly see where they complement one another *phenomenologically*. But the point is to see that we can ask quite different questions about semiosis from a philosophical point of view. I consider the defence of this position to be one of my strongest theses and contributions to semotic theory. The task is to integrate, in light of the thing itself, not to contrast in irreducible fashion.

In *Pragmatism and the Forms of Sense* I expanded the framework worked out in *Consciousness and the Play of Signs* to examine different aspects of the phenomenon of semiotic embodiment, which I consider one of the most important linkages between a phenomenologically adequate philosophy and a philosophically adequate semiotics. It is this notion of embodiment that I wanted to explore from rather untraditional angles. This notion plays a central role in the phenomenological tradition of philosophy, which also was committed to an exploration of experience prior to explicit or thematic forms of objectification, without, however, denying the great benefits of such objectification, both in symbolic and technologically oriented systems. I thought we could draw a parallel between 'semiotic embodiment,' exemplified paradigmatically in our embodiment in language and its transformation of our subjectivity, and 'technological embodiment,' our embodiment in tools, instruments, machines, and technological processes. As the subtitle of that book indicated—'Language, Perception, Technics'—perception was the middle, pivotal, term in the analysis. Language and technics were, I argued, following Cassirer, the two 'forms of sense' that defined the ultimate contours of world-building. Moreover, it was possible to analyze both of these forms of sense in terms of the oscillation between perceptual and semiotic categories, using many of the same intellectual resources that I availed myself of in *Consciousness and the Play of Signs*, but with significant additions that 'retrieved and continued' other important, but relatively neglected, positions.

In this book I showed how Peirce and Polanyi threw a powerful light on the perceptual roots of linguistic meaning, how the work of Karl Bühler and Alan Gardiner, themselves relying on the Philipp Wegener, charted in novel ways the movement from indication to predication by their development of an account of 'fields' and 'situations,' and how the Italian pragmatist, Giovanni Vailati, developed a fundamentally pragmatist 'linguistic turn' prior to the recognized linguistic turn of later 20th century philosophy. Further, relying on Polanyi's model of the from-to structure of consciousness, which made up a kind of 'tacit logic' or logic of 'tacit knowing,' I explored its relevance for the tacit logic of the meanings and structures embodied in technological artifacts and processes and their tendencies, both positive and negative, to 'bias' perception. Deweyan aesthetic theory, which weds experiencing to the apprehension and creation of 'qualitative meanings,' also, I showed, allows us both to describe and to criticize forms of technological embodiment. Finally, Cassirer's schematization of the vortices of consciousness in terms of 'ascending' levels of sense-functions was used as an analytical tool by Cassirer himself for taking the measure of the type of 'work' and the types of meanings engendered by technics, a further proof, in my opinion, of the flexibility and comprehensiveness of semiotic frameworks beyond the 'normal' domains.

Finally, in *Susanne Langer in Focus: The Symbolic Mind*, I have tried to point out how the many points of intersection and complementarity between her intellectual project and parallel ones can be more fruitfully accessed and her substantial insights applied. In particular, I think that her non-reductive naturalist semiotic account of symbolic transformation, of the various non-discursive forms of symbolization, especially art and myth, and of the biological and psychological preconditions for the rise of symbolization are permanent and substantial contributions to the study of cognitive processes from a semiotic point of view. More specifically, Langer helps us situate in a nuanced and open way the types of researches represented by such thinkers as Antonio Damasio, Gerald Edelman, Terrence Deacon, and a host of others who have occupied themselves with the biological foundations of mind, symbolization, and emotions, relying on both empirical investigations and conceptual reconstruction.

In conclusion, speaking as a philosopher, I consider the most important topics and/or contributions to the theory of meaning and signs to be centered around the impact of semiotics on the methods of philosophy and the objects of philosophical analysis. In this I agree with Susanne Langer that philosophy has first and foremost to do with the analysis of meanings, with interpretations, and not with the discovery of facts. I agree with Peirce that the theory of knowledge is transformed completely by the semiotic turn. Cognitional processes are structured as semiosic events or processes and are to be situated within the matrices of a comprehensive typology of signs. Perception itself, the 'lower threshold' of worldmaking, is to be included under the notion of abductive processes and is an essentially semiosic event. The work of Karl Bühler shows the fusion of semiotics, psychology, and the philosophical theme of abstraction and metaphor. Semiotics itself can be enriched by positions developed without explicit reference to thematically semiotic concerns: Michael Polanyi's theory of tacit knowing is permeated by the thesis of the identity of wholes and meanings and of the phenomenon of indwelling or embodiment and John Dewey's analyses of the pragmatic matrices of inquiry and of the structures of experiencing foreground the role of 'qualitative meanings' at every level of our encounter with the world. The theme of the 'ascension' of consciousness to 'higher' levels is treated with phenomenological and historical acumen by Ernst Cassirer in ways that are not superseded by the Peircean analytical framework. Susanne Langer has pointed the way to all the ranges of topics that a comprehensive and philosophically astute semiotic theory must deal with when we take a non-reductive naturalism focussed on the category of 'feeling' with all seriousness.

As to the most important open problems, I have the sense that we must at all costs avoid the appearance of rearranging the deck chairs on the *Titanic*. Semiotics for me is not so much a separate discipline that must be cultivated on its own, a kind of superscience, but a dimension or point of view, with distinct angles of vision upon the whole realm of cultural phenomena. It does not so much supplant as supplement, integrate, connect. There is a semiotic dimension to philosophy, to aesthetics, to anthropology, to psychology, to sociology, and so forth. But I look upon semiotics as an interpretive tool, rather than something to be always cultivated at the theoretical level. So, in one sense, I think the 'open questions' are not so much theoretical as applied. What is the cash value of the various semiotic notions when we want to put them to work? The job of semioticians is, it seems to me, to work closely with the 'substantive' disciplines—psychology, musicology, sociology, anthropology, the history of religions, and so forth—both to help refocus aspects of their analyses and to learn how the 'categories may be filled with content.' We want to avoid at all costs the great semiotic night in which all the cows are black, to echo Hegel's biting comments about the role of the 'absolute' in Schelling's philosophy of identity. While it is true that we can see signs and sign functions everywhere, semiotics is not a purely formal discipline, but must be filled with content. Here semiotics goes over into hermeneutics. The ultimate theoretical lesson of semiotics is that it ends in a concrete hermeneutics.

On the practical plane, then, I would propose that semioticians, whether they call themselves that or not, pay close attention to the 'content' disciplines. But I would also say that for those of us in the university world it is essential to find ways of bringing semiotic insights to bear on our teaching, to give our students a kind of semiotic x-ray vision, so that semiotic categories and concerns will permeate their approaches not just to their studies but to their lives. Semiotics is not 'about semiotics' but about what semiotics is itself about. This, I think, will be the crucial test of how theories of signs and meaning will have what William James called a 'cash value.' This cash value will be measured by the degree to which our theories and theoretical investigations enrich, illuminate, and transform our own meaning-making activities, including the activity of theorizing.

11
Mark Johnson

Knight Professor of Liberal Arts and Sciences
Department of Philosophy
University of Oregon

---

1. Why were you initially drawn to the theory of signs and meaning?

As an undergraduate at the University of Kansas in the late 1960's, I was attracted to philosophy because I believed it was about the human quest for meaning and significance in life. I thought about meaning from the perspective of courses I was taking in English literature, existentialism, philosophy of religion, and ethics. I was in for a big shock when I entered graduate study in philosophy at the University of Chicago, which had a heavy orientation toward analytic philosophy of mind and language. There I learned that meaning was something that concepts and propositions had. It was implied that semantics had virtually nothing to do with how things, people, and events could be meaningful to someone. I have never gotten over my dissatisfaction with views of meaning as purely linguistic and lacking any real connection to how experiences are meaningful to human beings. Not surprisingly, in graduate school I was attracted to Paul Ricoeur's courses on hermeneutics, religious language, and metaphor. This eventually led to my doctoral dissertation, in which I argued that metaphor was central to human meaning and that it could not be reduced to literal propositions. In short, there was more to meaning that was dreamt of in analytic philosophy.

As a young assistant professor in philosophy, I was invited in 1979 to the University of California, Berkeley, for a visiting appointment in the Philosophy Department. I was compiling an anthology on metaphor theory and I contacted Berkeley linguist and cognitive scientist George Lakoff to ask him to contribute an essay to my volume. From the day we met in early January, we realized that we held very similar views about the central role of metaphor in human conceptualization and reasoning. Moreover, we both lamented the fact that mainstream work in each of our respective disciplines—philosophy and linguistics—did not give us the theoretical resources to explain metaphor or other deep dimensions of meaning. In *Metaphors We Live By* (1980) we set forth our account of the pervasiveness of conceptual metaphor in ordinary thought and language, and we suggested that taking metaphor seriously would require the rethinking of several widely accepted philosophical ideas and views.

One of the more important implications of this work was that metaphors are grounded in aspects of our bodily experience, especially our sensory-motor experience. Metaphors typically involve a systematic mapping of entities, relations, and structures from a sensory-motor source domain to a more abstract target domain. For example, in the metaphor Understanding Is Seeing, we conceptualize and reason about acts of abstract thought by means of the structure and logic of our visual experience, such as "I see what you mean," "Could you shed more light on that hypothesis," and "His arguments are murky."

Our early explorations into the bodily origins of conceptual metaphor soon revealed vast reaches of preconceptual, nonconscious meaning, conceptualization, and reasoning. Eventually, this led us to identify "image schemas"—recurring patterns of sensory-motor experience that structure our prereflective meaning and also provide the basis for abstract conceptualization and rational inference.

2. What do you consider your contribution to the field?

My most significant contributions center around three topics: (1) embodied image schemas, (2) conceptual metaphor, and (3) deep sources of meaning in emotions, patterns of feeling, and sensory-motor processes.

(1) Image Schemas

Consider the question, "Where does meaning come from?" My answer is that it comes, first and foremost, from our bodily experience. The meaning of any object, event, or experience is its relation to, and significance for, some past, present, or future possible experience. From the perspective of embodied cognition, one must look for the emergence of meaning in the ongoing interactions of an organism with its environments. Image schemas are the most basic recurring patterns of those interactions, and so they will depend on the nature of the organism (its perceptual, motor, and cognitive capacities and makeup) and equally on the nature of the environments inhabited by the organism. For humans, they will include, for example, containment, verticality, balance, forced motion, center-periphery, front-back, right-left, near-far, source-path-goal, and scores of other basic structures of our daily experience (Johnson 1987; Hampe 2005).

Besides carrying its own body-based meaning, each image schema will also support a set of spatial or bodily inferences. For example, a Container schema has a minimal structure (boundary, interior, exterior) and generates its own spatial or bodily logic (e.g., If object O is in container A, and container A is in container B, then object O is in container B). Humans learn the meaning and implications of containment naturally and unconsciously through hundreds of interactions with containers every day of their lives. This "logic" is realized neurally as weighted synaptic connections in sensory-motor areas of the brain (Rohrer 2005; Dodge and Lakoff 2005).

(2) Conceptual Metaphor

It is not surprising that our perceptual, spatial, and action concepts would be structured by universally shared body-based image schemas, but how is abstract thought possible, and how can it be tied to our embodiment? Lakoff and I (1980, 1999) gave evidence that what we named Conceptual Metaphor is one of the principal devices for appropriating the meaning and logic of various bodily source domains (e.g., seeing, touching, tasting, walking) to structure our understanding of abstract entities and processes (e.g., our conceptions of understanding, mind, knowledge, and self-identity). A conceptual metaphor exists, not merely in the language or symbol system that might express it, but more fundamentally as a structure of human understanding, conceptualization, and reasoning. It is a mapping of entities, events, and relations from a sensory-motor source domain onto a target domain that involves some abstract notion. For example, in the conceptual metaphor Ideas Are Objects concepts are conceived to be quasi entities that can be grasped, manipulated, placed in word-containers, transferred to another person, and analyzed into their component parts. This "primary metaphor" (Grady 1997) [Ideas Are Objects] is part of more complex systematic metaphors by which we conceptualize understanding, thinking, creativity, and imagination. In Thinking Is Object Manipulation, for instance, the source domain consists of our experience of perceiving, handling, retrieving, and exploring the properties of concrete objects, which we then use to understand processes of thinking. The conceptual mapping would include:

- The Mind Is A Body
- Thinking Is Object Manipulation
- Ideas Are Manipulable Objects
- Communicating Is Sending
- Understanding Is Grasping
- Remembering Is Retrieval (or Recall)
- Memory Is A Storehouse
- The Structure Of An Idea Is The Structure Of An Object
- Analyzing Ideas Is Taking Objects Apart

In this metaphor, ideas are objects that you can play with, toss around, or turn over in your mind. Just as objects have physical structures, likewise ideas have parts with structural relations. One can put ideas together, break them down into their components, inspect them, and hold them up for scrutiny. Complex ideas can be crafted, fashioned, shaped, and reshaped. There can be many facets to a complex idea. Analyzing ideas is taking them apart into their elementary components.

Lakoff and I (1999) have argued that virtually all of our abstract concepts are defined by multiple conceptual metaphors and that, consequently, we reason on the basis of the details of the mapping that constitute the metaphor. For example, if Ideas Are Objects then complex ideas are complex (metaphorical) objects that can be analyzed into their component parts. Such a metaphor should therefore support a compositional view of meaning, which is exactly what we find in many objectivist theories of meaning and thought.

(3) Deep Meaning

Most theories of meaning, concepts, and reasoning focus on the structural dimensions of mind. Current theories of image schemas and conceptual metaphor are no exception—they, too, identify the underlying structural features that make up the schemas and define the source domains of metaphors. However, there is much more to meaning than structural aspects, although previously we have not had the theoretical resources to explore these deeper dimensions, such as qualities, emotions, and feeling contours. In *The Meaning of the Body: Aesthetics of Human Understanding* (2007) I have attempted to show how meaning emerges in the deepest reaches of our bodily engagement with our world, through our felt coupling with aspects of our physical, social, and cultural environments. Such an argument requires use of recent cognitive neuroscience of perception, emotion, and action. Antonio Damasio (1999) has argued that emotions are our most primordial way of assessing how we are doing in our ongoing interaction with our world. Don Tucker (2007) has attempted to sketch a theory of embodied cognition that gives a central role to the emotional, feeling, and motivational aspects of our limbic system in our construction of meaning and in our abstract thought. Tucker shows how brain structures deep in the limbic core, in reciprocal interactions with higher cortical areas responsible for perception and action, generate the feeling-infused world that we experience, both reflectively and pre-reflectively, from which our thought and expression emerge.

The key problem is to relate these accounts of felt meaning to natural languages and other forms of symbolic interaction in a way that gives direction for serious explanations of the phenomena. The wing of Cognitive Linguistics that I favor pursues the very bold hypothesis that the syntax, semantics, and pragmatics of natural languages (and all forms of symbolic interaction) are grounded in these deepest sources of bodily meaning (Feldman 2006). In other words, the forms and formal relations we employ in natural languages are meaningfully tied to the nature of our bodies, the structural characteristics of our brains, and the patterns of interaction we routinely have with our environments. The semantic content also arises from image schemas, emotional patterns, and various ways we imaginatively recruit bodily meaning for abstract thinking. Moreover, all of this syntactic and semantic structure is intimately tied to the pragmatics of the various purposes served by our language and other forms of symbolic interaction.

3. What is the proper role of a theory of signs and meaning in relation to other academic disciplines?

Because all academic fields and disciplines use the general resources of shared human cognition, there can be no field left unaffected by research on embodied and imaginative cognition. To cite just one example—the case of Conceptual Metaphor—we must realize that all of our greatest theoretical achievements, in every conceivable field, are framed in terms of some particular set of image schemas, conceptual metaphors, and other types of imaginative structure. In every science, how we identify the relevant phenomena, what counts as evidence for a theory, what the foundational concepts are, and how we reason about and communicate those concepts is directly dependent on the defining metaphors of the theories. This holds equally for linguistics and semiotics, too. Most of their fundamental concepts will be metaphorically defined. To give just one example, any theoretical understanding of metaphor will itself be framed by a particular metaphor (such as: mapping, projection, or interaction). Our philosophical theories, like our religious views, are vast perspectives built on metaphors, even though most of us have forgotten that they are irreducible metaphors and not literal, foundational truths (Lakoff and Johnson 1999).

George Lakoff (1996; 2008) has recently applied some of this new research from cognitive science to the nature of moral and political reasoning. The metaphors by which an ethical or political view are framed will profoundly shape how we are able to think about our deepest political views of freedom, equality, democracy, justice, selfhood, society, state, war, and government. Our various moral systems (and the theories that support them) are built from metaphors for will, action, freedom, causation, reason, justice, good, evil, and harm, which are bound into moral systems via models of the family, in particular, strict father and nurturant parent conceptions of family structure (Johnson 1993; Lakoff and Johnson 1999). Strict Father models emphasize metaphors tied to authority, obedience, strength, and discipline, whereas Nurturant Parent models give priority to metaphorically defined notions of care, empathy, responsibility, and earned respect. These family models of morality are then developed into traditional conservative and progressive political perspectives. Prototypical conservative views are based on strict father models, whereas classic progressive views are built on nurturant parent models.

Another important consequence of this type of research is its application, not just to linguistic meaning, but more broadly to all types of human symbolic interaction. To the extent that we are describing the bodily basis of human understanding, these structures should show up in any type of symbolic expression, including, besides written and spoken language: sign language (Taub 2001), spontaneous gesture (McNeill 1992), art (Johnson 2007), music (Zbikowski 2002; Johnson & Larson 2003), visual cartoons and advertising (Forceville 1996), architecture, dance, and ritual practice. In sum, the types of research described above are just a few examples of conceptual tools that can be used to analyze virtually any aspect of human inquiry, understanding, and action. Proponents of objectivist and literalist theories of mind and language tend to find such results about human cognition disturbing and even dangerous, but I would submit that these results make it possible for us to understand how any thing or event can be meaningful to us and how we are able to make sense of and reason about it, both with and without language.

4. What do you consider the most important topic and/or contributions in the theory of meaning and signs?

Obviously, I believe that the most dramatic events are those surrounding embodied accounts of meaning and thought. In the western world we have inherited profoundly dualistic views of the self, founded on a sharp mind vs. body dichotomy that places all thought and "higher" cognition in "mind" and relegates all sensing, feeling, and even imagining to the body. Overcoming mind-body dualism and all of its manifestations in virtually every aspect of our lives, is a daunting task for humankind, but it is a task that must be undertaken, if we hope to understand mind, thought, and language.

Consequently, the greatest contributions, in my view, are those that explain how meaning and thought emerge from ongoing organism–environment interactions without presupposing disembodied mind, and without introducing any external causes allegedly entering the flow of experience from without. Cognitive neuroscience is still in its nascent stages, but it promises dramatic revelations about how we make sense and how we communicate meaning. Neuroscience by itself cannot give a fully adequate account of mind and language. In addition, we need multiple levels of explanation based on multiple methodologies, as employed in cognitive linguistics, philosophy, psychology, and various sciences. Finally, we need philosophical reflection on the limiting assumptions of any science and also on its implications for virtually every field of human endeavor. In my wildest moments of wishful thinking, I envision a future in which Cognitive Linguistics will proceed in dialogue with the best work in neuroscience and psychology, towards a theory of embodied meaning that will someday supplant what I regard as impoverished universalistic, disembodied, and scientifically inadequate theories.

5. What are the most important open problems in this field and what are the prospects for progress?

Broadly speaking, the deepest problem is how to account for abstract conceptualization and reasoning for creatures like us, who are inextricably bound to and shaped by our embodiment. Our brains evolved first for complex sensory-motor processing geared to survival and flourishing within our environment, with deep affective and motivational circuits at the heart of this process. But the emergence of language and other forms of symbolic interaction opened up possibilities for abstraction. At present, we do not have the full story on how this works, although we have some promising speculations.

It seems to me that the best prospects for real progress on this issue must come from cognitive neuroscience (in dialogue with Cognitive Linguistics) in the form of neural theories of language and symbolic interaction. Cognitive linguistics will continue to play a crucial role, but at some point we will need to understand how our bodies and brains make possible the syntax, semantics, and pragmatics of human symbolic interaction. There are currently some promising accounts of the neural bases of various spatial, perceptual, and motor concepts, but we have only the most sketchy ideas of how these sensory-motor capacities are recruited for abstract thought (Gallese and Lakoff 2005; Feldman 2006, Edelman and Tononi 2000). For example, if conceptual metaphor is a real phenomenon, then there must be re-entrant circuits connecting areas of the brain responsible for sensory-motor processing and emotion with higher cortical areas responsible for planning, reasoning, and abstract thinking. At present, there is some scant evidence for this (Rohrer 2005), but we are only beginning to explore these processes. The next two or three decades promise dramatic developments in our understanding of how human meaning, conceptualization, reasoning, and communication work.

12
John Michael Krois

Professor
Department of Philosophy
Humboldt-Universität zu Berlin

The Five Questions

1. Why were you initially drawn to the theory of signs and meaning?

In the 1960s and early 1970s, when I was a student, the philosophy of language was supremely dominant. Even the philosophy of science was slanted towards the notion of representation in terms of language. It seemed obvious to me that meaning did not come into the world with language. The linguistic turn in philosophy, I thought, went only halfway. The theory of signs promised to accomplish what phenomenologists only claimed to do–to get beyond language–but without assuming any sort of intuition or reliance upon empiricist "givens". During my last year as an undergraduate I took a course on Modern Art by the art historian Frederick Leach. At the time I was dividing my time between Ohio University's departments of art history and philosophy. In Leach's introduction to the course he mentioned a book by Ernst Cassirer. I never heard that name before, yet I soon realized that he and the philosopher Charles Peirce had both developed a theory of signs and symbols as a way to avoid the limitations of the philosophy of language, without falling back into a philosophy of "ideas." At the time I could not have put things this simply, but the theory of signs and symbols had the potential to bring together what had become disconnected in philosophy: aesthetic and evaluative phenomena, cognition and the theory of reality. This persuaded me to spend 40 years following up this prospect.

2. What do you consider your contribution to the field?

For one thing, rescuing Cassirer's theory of symbolic form (most of which had remained unpublished) and, secondly, contributions to the development of the embodiment theory of imagery. Few people shared my interest in the work of Ernst Cassirer in the early 1970s. Like Peirce, Cassirer developed his entire philosophy around the theory of signs and symbols, but although Cassirer's philosophy once had a heyday in America, largely via Susanne Langer, his thought - like that of the Pragmatists - was off the philosophical agenda when I first learned about it. Today, Cassirer's approach to cultural theory is undergoing a renaissance. Three factors contributed to the resurrection of Cassirer's project of a philosophy of symbolic forms. I found someone else interested in Cassirer to work with (my dissertation director Donald Verene, then at Penn State), discovering that Cassirer's unpublished papers at Yale added previously unknown dimensions to Cassirer's work, and meeting Oswald Schwemmer in the early 1980s with whom it became possible to edit this corpus of unpublished writings. These unpublished papers, mostly from the last decades of Cassirer's career, outlined a biosemiotic approach to meaning. Cassirer was Jacob von Uexküll's close friend and associate at Hamburg. Cassirer's late philosophy combined a semiotic approach to meaning with a philosophical anthropology. The drafts for his incomplete 4th volume of his Philosophy of Symbolic Forms paved the way for an embodied approach to cognition decades before it emerged in the intellectual milieu of the 1980s.

I have argued that iconicity neither necessarily involves mimesis (similarity) nor that it can be sufficiently understood by means of a textual model of meaning (such as that of Goodman and his followers). Unlike most phenomenological approaches to iconic meaning I take visual perception to be only an illustration rather than the model of iconic form. The phenomenologically primary iconic forms derive from the body schema. The so-called "image schemas" deployed in cognitive science are actually the building blocks derived from the iconic form of the body schema. I have sought to demonstrate this in a series of essays. Working with others at the Humboldt University I plan to work out this theory in detail in conjunction with the theory of "image acts" developed by the art historian Horst Bredekamp. The embodiment theory of imagery combines the theory of embodied cognition with the theory of signs and meaning.

3. What is the proper role of a theory of signs and meaning in relation to other academic disciplines?

The theory of signs and meaning can provide the link between diverse disciplines. This is a commonplace among semioticians, but it has yet to be realized in a positive way among researchers in concrete fields of study, who often take this to be a kind of academic imperialism. This is especially true in cases where the "two cultures" syndrome comes into play. This results from the overemphasis upon conventionality in the Saussurean tradition of *semiologie*, which still pervades the work of many cultural theorists. The Peircean (pragmaticist) tradition has been demonstrably employed with greater success. One need only to mention the Copenhagen school of biosemiotics or the work of Terrence Deacon.

4. What do you consider the most important topics and/or contributions in the theory of meaning and signs?

Since Plato, the place of imagery and depiction in philosophy has been at the periphery. The introduction of "aesthetics" in the 18th century as a special field only served to cement this situation, so that those concerned with the study of images and depiction were per defintionem dealing with a topic outside the real interests of philosophy: the true, the good, the real. The fleeting and emotionally laden iconic forms that Plato put at the bottom of his divided line and which he portrayed as keeping humans literally in the dark are the outcasts in the history of philosophy. In practice, iconic forms are ubiquitous. Even language tokens have an iconic form. Thanks to the theory of speech acts, the concrete practice of communication was admitted to philosophy. The real task of the theory of signs and meaning is to complete what has been called the "iconic" or "pictorial" turn in philosophy. The new imaging technology utilized in medicine and science show that iconic forms do not need to copy something given in order to be true. Peirce's conception of semeiotic can help to show how philosophy has erred since Plato about the peripheral importance of imagery and depiction.

5. What are the most important open problems in this field and what are the prospects for progress?

Considered historically, the theory of signs and meaning has developed in two directions: one follows the traditional emphasis upon language (Saussure and most schools of philosophy of language), the other takes iconicity to be phenomenologically prior (Peirce and Cassirer). The former approach emphasizes syntax and semantics, the latter pragmatics and, hence, embodiment. The theory of embodied cognition that has revolutionized cognitive science needs to be understood in terms of the pragmatic approach to semeiotics and vice versa. Embodiment without signs is blind (mechanistic), sign theory without embodiment is idealism. Researchers in every field need to avoid these remnants of Cartesian dualism that continue to haunt every field of study.

13
Kalevi Kull

Professor in Biosemiotics
Department of Semiotics
Tartu University

Semiosic means alive: A Tartu view

1. Why were you initially drawn to the theory of signs and meaning?

The path to semiotics, and particularly to biosemiotics, has had for me at least three guides.

　A. *Theoretical biology* as accompanied with field studies.

These were beautiful places — diverse forests, the coast of the Baltic Sea, wooded meadows — where I started the search for a theory of living processes (or theoretical biology) that later turned out to be biosemiotics. Since my high school years, I have spent many summers working as a field biologist, together with scholars who are masters knowledgeable in the diverse life of local ecosystems. The summers from 1968 to 1973 I lived at the Puhtu Biological Station on the east coast of the Baltic Sea, where we studied the ontogenesis of the thermoregulatory behaviour in several species of birds. This included ethological studies (both diurnal and nocturnal), laboratory experiments, and telemetrical studies (registration of birds' physiological parameters during flight). Our discussions were focused on a general theory of behaviour — it was our intention to develop such a theory. Then I came across Jakob von Uexküll's work. This was followed by modelling work at a forest ecology station, and further, by studies on species coexistence mechanisms, which led to the discovery of the most species-rich plant communities in Europe.

Already during our student years (1970-75) at the University of Tartu, we established regular theoretical biology seminars, and in 1975, the annual Estonian Spring Schools in Theoretical Biology, which continues today (the 34rd took place in May 2008). These were influenced by C. H. Waddington's four-part symposia "Towards a Theoretical Biology", which saw general linguistics as a promising paradigm for the theory of general biology. Several of our Spring Schools were focused on the semiotic aspects of biology (for instance, 'Theory of Organism (dedicated to Jakob von Uexküll)' (1977), 'Theory of Recognition' (1995), 'Languages of Life' (1996), 'Theory of Communication' (2007), etc.

It appeared that similar groups of young biologists in theoretical biology were established at about the same time in St. Petersburg (led by Sergey Chebanov) and in Moscow (led by Alexander Levich and Alexei Sharov) — all three with an inclination to semiotic approaches. Thus we organised some joint meetings, among these a larger regional conference "Biology and Linguistics" in 1978 in Tartu — which we called biosemiotic. These regional meetings in the late 1970s also meant our study of non-Darwinian biology. This was a structuralist paradigm in biology (of Lev Berg, Alexander Lyubischew, Sergey Meyen, and others), which had been important to grasp as a step towards a truly semiotic, poststructuralist biology.

B. *Local intellectual traditions.*

The ecosystem, in which I live, on the East coast of Baltic Sea, is the country where Karl Ernst von Baer, Jakob von Uexküll, and Juri Lotman have lived and worked. This is one of few countries in the world where all intellectuals, at least since the 1970s, know the term *semiotic*. Either by chance, or due to a *genius loci*, or because they belong to the same line in the history of ideas, Baer's, Uexküll's and Lotman's approaches fit each other well, and on their basis, a rich and creative school has formed that has educated the contemporary semioticians in Tartu.

The *Geist* of Baer is in the air in Tartu. This means the strength of an epigenetic view in biology that survived here during its low period (from 1930s to 1990s), when genetic preformism dominated in Europe and America. Jakob von Uexküll was a major follower of Baer (see Uexküll 1928; 1940; 1982). My study of his works, and personal contacts with Juri Lotman, ended up with my joining the semiotics department in the 1990s. In 1992, I gave my first course in biosemiotics, which has turned into a regular course since then.

The Tartu School of semiotics, as it has developed since the 1960s under the leadership of Juri Lotman, has a particular feature that may probably explain its vitality. This is its interest in the mechanism of the creativity of culture in general (Lotman 1990; 2005; 2008; Torop 2000). The Department of Semiotics at the University of Tartu has grown into an international centre of semiotics that carries on the semiotic traditions of Jakob von Uexküll and Juri Lotman, thus bridging the concepts of umwelt and semiosphere.

C. *The biosemiotic circle.*

The history of biosemiotics can be traced quite far back (Favareau 2006; Kull 1999). However, an international biosemiotic circle has been formed quite recently, in early 1990s, mainly due to Thomas A. Sebeok and Thure von Uexküll who were able to build a network of people in this field. One can say that it emerged in Glottertal near Freiburg, Germany, where Thure Uexküll and his colleagues organised a workshop on Jakob von Uexküll and biosemiotics, in 1992, and where Jesper Hoffmeyer and myself first met (see Sebeok 2001a; Emmeche et al. 2002). Thomas Sebeok had just edited a volume *Biosemiotics* (Sebeok, Sebeok 1992 — the very first book with such title), and Thure Uexküll had visited biosemiotic workshops both in Tartu (1989) and in Copenhagen (1990). Soon after the Glottertal meeting, I took a bus to Copenhagen to visit Jesper Hoffmeyer, followed by Jesper's visit to Tartu. Thus the biosemiotic co-work between the Tartu and Copenhagen groups was established, and this turned out to be a very productive bridge. In 2001, we established the annual international *Gatherings in Biosemiotics* (see Emmeche 2001; Emmeche *et al.* 2002a), and in 2005, the *International Society for Biosemiotic Studies* (see Favareau 2005).

2. What do you consider your contribution to the field?

A methodological comment. Describing one's contribution to a field, a modernist view to science — science as anything that is progressing and cumulating, is still often used. The end of modernism in science would mean the acceptance of inquiry as primarily learning, understanding, reformulating, interpreting, and reordering work and activity. This is a shift from a linear and progressing to an ecological and (re)cycling behaviour. Semiotics proper is a field of knowledge that characterizes the non-modern, particularly after-modern culture (Deely 2001).

Thus, the question about one's contribution should be reformulated as a question about the key understandings one has arrived at, and about the focuses in one's semiotic work. There are two (central ones) in my case.

A. *On the nature of species, or the mechanism of categorisation.*

In biology, the problem of species has survived many generations of biologists. A way towards a semiotic solution has been indicated by the recognition concept of species (Paterson 1993). According to this approach, species is a communicative structure that emerges in communicating populations, assuming that for each individual there exists an individual recognition window that limits the difference between the partners in communication (Kull 1988; 1992). Emerging species is thus a natural category.

Categorisation is what all living beings do and what organises them; categorisation is based on recognition processes that are inevitable for organisms; speciation and perceptual categorisation are analogical in their mechanism. This is in the nature and origin of species — that species is a self-keeping category *per se*; that species occur because the continuous variability in a communicative population is unstable; that biological species is the same kind of category as any semiosic category (Kull 1992). Thus, what we have here is an explanation of the origin of qualitative differences, or a general mechanism that makes differences, or a process from which the relation of similarity emerges. This leads also to a general definition of semiotics as a study of qualitative diversity.

B. *On the reality and realities, or the nature of meaning.*

A study of the nature of semiosis that includes its inevitable attributes (recognition, memory, feed-forward, code, emergence of absence, etc.) leads to a general model of the life process, a model that explains the emergence of complementarity. A most compact conclusion from this understanding states that *semiosis multiplies reality*, that mind means plurality. Or, synonymously, that life is the local plurality. This means that this "discovery" is also the answer to the question about the nature of life. Life is the phenomenon of the occurrence of plurality in the world. What thus turns to be locally plural is the reality itself. And this IS life, life itself (Kull 2007).

Since nothing can be simultaneously true and original or new (i.e., only faults can be original), this understanding also takes much from predecessors, namely from Jakob von Uexküll's concept of umwelten, from Juri Lotman's concept of non-translatability in translation in semiospheres, from Robert Rosen's analysis of 'life itself', and from the Copenhagen concept of complementarity. However, this also uses the concept of semiosis as developed by Charles Peirce, and applies the concept of semiotic threshold via Umberto Eco, Thomas Sebeok, and Juri Lotman (i.e., accepting the existence of both the non-semiotic and the semiotic).

These two points (A, and B) appear for me as certain major insights, *heureka*-ideas, or understandings that have led to (or are connected with) many particular 'findings' in the interpretation of organic processes and phenomena, and are backed by (or based on) the study of the history and work of other biologists and semioticians.

Besides, there are two other fields I am working in.

C. *Semiosic basis of development and evolution.*

It occurs to me that the principal stages in the development of organic systems are semiosic by their nature. For instance, the development in the sequence of vegetative, animal, and human, can be understood as the jumps over the iconic-indexical and indexical-symbolic threshold (Kull 2000b). The biological evolution, approached this way, is non-Darwinian in its basic processes. Organic evolution may even not require much natural selection, because adaptation usually develops prior to its fixation in genetic memory (the latter taking place due to stochastic molecular-genetic processes) (Kull 2000a; Hoffmeyer, Kull 2003).

D. *Conceptualization of biosemiotics.*

I have been interested in the history of biosemiotics. No, this is not an explanation via history — the reason to study history should not be based on a historical explanation. Studying history is the same as studying a life process. Life's explanation should not lie in the past, it rather relies on something that reminds us future, i.e., in void or absence.

Thus I have tried to rethink the history of biology as something that is broader than its modernist account. This includes an analysis of the three major archetypes of biological thinking (ladder, tree, web) (Kull 2003); an account of Jakob von Uexküll's work (Kull 2001); the placement of particular works in the history of biosemiotic ideas (Kull 1999).

3. What is the proper role of a theory of signs and meaning in relation to other academic disciplines?

A. *Semiotics is complementary.*

A distinction made by John Locke is remarkable — the three main fields of knowledge are physics, semiotics, and ethics. This is, in a way, even beyond Peirce, because Peirce was not much interested in physics, or, more precisely, Peirce did not believe in the universality of physical laws, and thus deduced all methodology from life sciences, or logic. Thus the role and relatedness to other disciplines is still a problem.

Semiotics and physics can be seen as the two basic complementary methodologies, the first for qualitative, and the second for quantitative inquiry (Kull 2007). Semiotics deals with the pluralist and incommensurable, whereas physics is the approach for the convertible and monistic.

B. *Semiotics is fundamental.*

If the major advances in the understanding of the world (as both developmental and evolutionary biosemiotics aim to describe), and the principal steps in the history of philosophy (as John Deely has attempted to demonstrate, in Deely 2001) are directly related to the advancements in semiosis and its (self)understanding, then Sebeok's global semiotic approach (Sebeok 2001b) turns out to be fundamental indeed. Semiotics is fundamental also in the sense that it studies (and can explain) the principal processes of life, mind, and culture (Anderson *et al.* 1984).

C. *Semiotics is practically applicable.*

Semiotics is practically applicable in order to study and analyse particular cases. Any particular phenomenon of life or culture can serve as an object for a semiotic inquiry. Accordingly, there (should) exist practical methods of semiotic analysis. Different semiotic schools have already developed some versions of these methods.

4. What do you consider the most important topics and/or contributions in the theory of meaning and signs?

What occurs to me as the fundamental achievements and results of semiotics, include the following.

A. *The basic models of semiosis.*

There are several of these, particularly the triadic model by Charles S. Peirce, the dyadic one by Ferdinand de Saussure and his school, the cyclic (feed-forward) model by Jakob von Uexküll, the communicational one by Roman Jakobson, and the semiospheric conception by Juri Lotman. These are complementary models, each having its own separate value and applicability.

B. *The concept of semiotic thresholds.*

As a concept of lower semiotic threshold it has been introduced by U. Eco (1977), then developed and (re)placed by T. Sebeok and other biosemioticians (Anderson *et al.* 1984; Sebeok 2001b; Emmeche *et al.* 2002b), and further applied by T. Deacon (as the symbolic threshold, Deacon 1997). The lower semiotic threshold distinguishes between semiosic and non-semiosic, whereas the indexical and symbolic threshold may allow us to distinguish between the vegetative, animal, and human (propositional) semiosis.

C. *The development of biosemiotics, zoosemiotics, and semiotics of culture.*

The development of biosemiotics, zoosemiotics, and semiotics of culture, both as clearly separated fields, and as parts of the same semiotics (Hoffmeyer 1996; 2008). Very much due to these fields, it has been possible to overcome the superficial divides between mind and body, and culture and nature, and to view both organism and culture as semiosic processes.

D. *Turning semiotics into semiotics.*

This has been very much Thomas A. Sebeok's enterprise and his major achievement. This is why we have this field recognised as one (and as many).

5. What are the most important open problems in this field and what are the prospects for progress?

Let me point out just two that are, however, extensive.

A. *The biosemiotic project.*

This is indeed a pretty ambitious enterprise — to put biology on a semiotic basis. It will include rethinking much of biological theory, and a reworking of biological methodology. It means a reformulation and interpretation of biological knowledge on the basis of semiosis. And this is a full-scale introduction of qualitative methods into biological research. Particularly, this will include a deep inquiry into the modelling and analysis of the main attributes of life — activity, needs, intentions, memory, categorization, etc. As a result, it will give also a deeper understanding and description of semiotic thresholds, including the threshold that is responsible for being a human.

B. *The problem of semiotic balance.*

Stability/instability of semiosic processes includes a peculiar set of phenomena, and its importance stems from the importance of preserving diversity and humanity. The study of organic balance will be a guide and the basis here. This is because the balance of life (which is an assumption for an ecological balance) by its very nature is a semiosic balance. Which means that the problem of peace, of the balance of cultures, will converge with the problems of ecological balance and the problem of health; thus the protection of biodiversity and protection of cultural diversity turn out to be the same — the protection of diversity, or quality as such.

14
Jean Petitot

Professor

Centre de Recherches en Epistémologie Appliquée (CREA), Ecole Polytechnique, Paris

Ecoles de Hautes Etudes en Sciences Sociales, Paris

---

1. Why were you initially drawn to the theory of signs and meaning?

After graduation from Ecole Polytechnique in 1968, I started my scientific carrier in the research lab of pure mathematics the great mathematician Laurent Schwartz had just created. At that time, I was already interested in structuralism, though, and I attended Claude Lévi-Strauss' courses at the Collège de France. In 1971, I got employed at the Center for Mathematics at EHESS (Ecole des Hautes Etudes en Sciences Sociales). Charles Morazé, who had founded the EHESS together with Fernand Braudel (by then, the sixth section of the Ecole Pratique des Hautes Etudes), told me to contact the colleagues at the EHESS who shared my interest in structuralism. They were basically all members of A.J. Greimas' group. I then organized a seminar, grouping a series of very young scholars such as Jean-François Bordron, Frédéric Nef and Guy Le Gaufey, and I started participating actively in the activities of Greimas' Groupe de Recherches Sémiotiques. There I met colleagues who later on would become genuine alter egos, and who introduced me to other cognate groups. Here I'd particularly like to mention Per Aage Brandt, Paolo Fabbri, who introduced me to Umberto Eco, and the friends from the DAMS group in Bologna (Omar Calabrese, Patrizia Violi, and many others), Herman Parret and Jean-Claude Coquet.

2. What do you consider your contribution to the field?

In the field of pure mathematics, I worked with the theory of singularities, both in algebraic geometry (Grothendieck, Hironaka) and in differential geometry (Thom). This is the reason why I was able to follow up immediately when René Thom in the late 60s introduced the revolutionary idea that this type of mathematics could be used to formalize structuralism. Thus, I became the first disciple of René Thom in semio-linguistics (later on I was joined by Wolfgang Wildgen from Bremen). I guess my most important contribution to this line of research consisted in reconsidering the theoretical foundations of semiotics with respect to this new mathematical framework, that is to say in providing morphodynamical models of the elementary structures of signification (from Greimas' semiotic square to Lévi-Strauss canonical formula of the myth) and in accurately accomodating structuralism within the history of theories of form (Leibniz, Kant, Goethe, Peirce, Husserl).

3. What is the proper role of a theory of signs and meaning in relation to other academic disciplines?

In my view semiotics would greatly benefit from establishing tight bounds with two very different types of disciplines:

1. The cognitive sciences, and particularly the cognitive neurosciences. It is at this level that the deepest and most fruitful theoretical hypotheses are likely to be validated and falsified.

2. Classical human sciences. I believe that after a long and intense period of conceptual development, general semiotics would also greatly benefit from representing technical scholarship in the arts and literature.

4. What do you consider the most important topic and/or contributions in the theory of meaning and signs? 5. What are the most important open problems in this field and what are the prospects for progress?

Both these questions are pretty hard to deal with since they can be answered in many and very different ways. Personally, I consider that one of the most promising new horizons for semiotics is the cognitive neurosciences (perceptual and conceptual mental contents, aesthetic values, emotions). It certainly still is possible to investigate social or cultural objects in the "depsychologized" way in which they have been studied so far within semiotics; yet, the possibility of examining the neurally implemented cognitive mechanisms underpinning the processes of semiotization is a radically new and fundamental possibility. I think it would be good to move toward a *neurosemiotics*.

15
Roland Posner

Director
Research Center for Semiotics
Berlin University of Technology

---

1. Why were you initially drawn to the theory of signs and meaning?

I had a broad high school education in classical philology (Latin and Greek) and in modern philology (two foreign languages) as well as in the sciences (physics and chemistry) and the arts (piano and organ at the conservatory). With this background, I went to the University of Bonn in the 1960's in order to study scientific methods for the investigation of cultural phenomena. But what I was offered there did not meet my expectations.

Culture was divided up into closed areas, such as society, technology, the arts, and religion, and treated in independent disciplines, which isolated their subject matter within separate fields. Philologists were proud not to be familiar with what goes on in society, technology, and nature; literary scholars claimed not to be interested in language, music, and the arts; and even within the field of literature germanists, romanists, slavists, sinologists, etc. hardly communicated with one another. Most academics tended to regard the subject matter of their own disciplines as unique, and it was not clear to them that they were asking parallel questions and developing similar types of methods to answer them. The result was that up to the 70's and 80's the majority of academics were convinced that human cultures could not be scientifically analyzed as such. Instead of trying to do what seemed impossible, they restricted their research efforts to the isolated study of some national literature or art or music, to the social history of some institution, or to the development of some technology.

Philosophy was mostly dealt with historically, and the question as to what was its source of knowledge compared with that of the empirically oriented human, social, and natural sciences was neglected.

In this situation I was happy to find other students who had similar doubts about the adequacy of academic teaching, and we formed working groups such as the "Initiative for the Comparative Study of Literature" at the University of Bonn (1963) and the "Circle for the Study of Methodological Questions in the Individual Sciences" at the University of Munich (1965).

Within this intellectual milieu I started reading Wittgenstein, whose *Philosophical Investigations* had become available in a preprint of the first volume of his works in 1963; I discovered the project of "Unified Science" initiated by Rudolf Carnap, Otto Neurath, and Charles W. Morris; and I translated Morris's *Foundations of the Theory of Signs* into German.

Reading this American text from the 1930's felt like coming home: It was written in the style of a classical piece of German philosophy, starting with a Latin motto from Leibniz claiming that it is the study of signs which leads us into the core of things, and culminating with a quote from Goethe pleading for tolerance in the choice of any form of representation, "provided, of course, that the form of representation does not masquerade as what it is not". In the last sentence of his treatise Morris states that the tradition characterized by these two century-old quotations "appears in a modern form in the identification of philosophy with the theory of signs and the unification of science", and this was the program I adopted for myself and wanted to test in my own studies.

As a first step, I undertook an investigation into the linguistic tools used by literary scholars in their interpretations of Goethe's poems, that is, I compared the sign structure of the interpreting text with the sign structure of the original and in each case tried to explain the differences by assuming the application of Harris-type transformation rules to the original text by the interpreter. The result of this analysis of 200 years of Goethe philology was that literary interpretation can indeed be explained as a complex linguistic operation performed on a given poetic text and that the transformations performed not only depended on the purpose of the interpretation (didactic, explicative, appreciative, etc.), but also on the dominant style of the respective historical epoch. Encouraged by this outcome, I continued this line of research in the late 60's and 70's by critically examining contemporary types of structuralist interpretation of art and music, where the semiotic procedures not only involved the transformation of complex signs, but also their transposition into another medium, combined with context change. In the 80's, I generalized this approach one step further and started analyzing non-aesthetic artifacts, the forms of which I described as indicating their function within civilization.

2. What do you consider to be your contribution to the field?

As a first point, let me mention my **theory of culture**. The irrational agnosticism concerning the scientific study of culture as a whole, which I had encountered in the university life of the 1960's and 1970's, was a strong motivation for me to design a theoretical approach to culture as a whole that could be acceptable as a conceptual framework for anthropologists and ethnologists as well as for scholars in the humanities and social sciences and for researchers in biology and ethology. I systematically read their textbooks and examined them with respect to the compatibility of their terminology and their theoretical claims and to the combinability of their methods of research. This reading experience, which took place mostly at the Netherlands Institute for Advanced Study in the Humanities and Social Sciences in the 1980's, confirmed my conviction that culture is a semiotic entity and that cultural studies must be based on a sign-theoretic approach. In my 1989 treatise on "What is Culture?" I showed that all subject matter classified as "cultural" by one or another academic discipline can be accommodated if one conceives of culture as a special type of complex sign system. Treated as such, every culture includes a SOCIETY consisting of individual and collective *sign users* (institutions); they develop a CIVILIZATION consisting of *texts* (in the broad sense of artifacts) of various genres; these are formed according to the MENTALITY of the sign users, i.e., according to conventional *codes*, and serve to convey *messages* that enable the sign users to solve their problems of life. This approach assigns all cultural matters a well-defined position within a structured whole and thereby provides a semiotic explication of the relationship between the traditional disciplines involved in cultural research. Controversies between ideologized directions of research in cultural matters fighting for supremacy become superfluous because each can reinterpret itself as a valuable contribution to the grand objective of jointly making cultural life scientifically transparent.

My conception of culture rests on key terms used in the theory of signs (which are italicized in the preceding paragraph). But it does not leave that theory unaltered. It requires distinguishing between various types of sign processes (such as indication, signification, and communication), types of sign users (intentional sign producers, addressees, bystanders), and types of codes (innate, artificially stipulated, and conventional ones) as well as describing them with respect to their function in culture. It also requires studying culture change as a result of the dynamics within the system of culture-specific codes and studying interaction between cultures as the adoption of extracultural codes and world views. The ultimate question to be answered is that of the raison d'être of cultures within the evolution of life. These are topics, which I address in the 2003 essay on "Basic Tasks of Cultural Semiotics".

While I was busy analyzing culture, the humanities and social sciences in Central Europe became involved in a paradigm change. They no longer interpreted themselves as investigating the mind ("Geisteswissenschaften") and society ("Gesellschaftswissenschaften"), but were reorganized in the form of cultural sciences ("Kulturwissenschaften"). I felt encouraged by this unexpected development and was happy to contribute to it by offering my version of cultural semiotics as a basic module in the newly designed curricula for the bachelor and master's programs.

As a second major achievement, I should mention my **theory of interdisciplinarity**. I am convinced that the important goal of empirical sciences investigating nature and studying human culture as part of nature can only be reached if the lack of cooperation between academic disciplines in general is overcome and adequately organized interdisciplinary research becomes a normal academic procedure. As I know from extended university experience in various countries on several continents, most attempts at interdisciplinary cooperation are hampered by unclear conceptions concerning the status of disciplines and the options of cooperation available to them.

My proposal here proceeds from the assumption that a discipline in the epistemological sense includes a homogeneous domain of research, a unified perspective, a central method, a core body of knowledge (theory), and specific means of presentation. However, the traditional disciplines differ in what constitutes their identity. This can be either the domain of research (as in astronomy), or the perspective (as in history), the central method (as in anatomy), the theory (as in physics), or the means of presentation (as in logic and statistics). Depending on whether a domain-based discipline meets another domain-based discipline or rather a perspective-based, method-based, theory-based, or presentation-based one, highly different configurations of interdisciplinarity will emerge.

A peculiar case is what one calls an "interdisciplinary approach". It is usually characterized by the fact that it lacks one or more components of a standard discipline. Thus semiotics is often called "sign theory", because it evidently has produced an elaborate terminology, some axioms, and many theorems, whereas its domain of research remains controversial and its methods are not regarded as specifically semiotic by many.

In this conception, the various configurations of interdisciplinary research can be clearly distinguished from multidisciplinarity and transdisciplinarity, and, in addition, a semiotically guided explication can be given of the differences between an academic discipline, an auxiliary discipline, an applied discipline, and a metadiscipline. These ideas are presented in Article 123 of *Semiotics–A Handbook on the Sign-theoretic Foundations of Nature and Culture*, and they determine the organization and layout of this collaborative work of 178 contributors (comprising 3878 pages in four volumes, published 1997-2004).

Further away from the tradition of sign theory, but nearer to its basic tasks, is my work in **cognitive semiotics**. It was motivated by the observation that from Plato and Aristotle to Peirce and Saussure two separate terminologies have been used to describe what happens in a semiosis (or, more specifically, in interaction between organisms).

On the one hand, there occur *extraorganismic* objects: sign vehicles, signals, sounds, pictures, words, etc. They appear to be endowed with a magic power that somehow makes them carry meanings, contain messages, or make sense. How does one study such objects? One classifies them into different types. Historically, this *object-oriented* approach has given access to a rich realm of sign types, but is now approaching stagnation due to the taxonomic methodology and continuing disagreement concerning suitable criteria of classification.

On the other hand, all European languages offer a rich terminology for the description of *intraorganismic* attitudes and processes such as thinking and knowing; hoping and fearing; believing, assuming, and hypothesizing; wanting, wishing, and intending; remembering, inferring, and concluding. These appear to happen inside an organism without a material basis. Someone who wants to study them seems bound to investigate the so-called "inner life" of a person or animal. Psychological introspection and logical analysis of rules of inference are methodological procedures usually applied in this *subject-oriented* approach.

A key to the connection between these two seemingly incompatible perspectives is the usual talk of "clues" or "evidence", on the basis of which one is supposed to think, believe, infer, or even wish and intend something. Logicians and psychologists have to realize that what they call "evidence" is exactly what is analyzed as a sign, i.e., an index, icon, or symbol in semiotics. And semioticians and information theorists have to realize that what they call a " message" does not exist without someone conceiving of it, someone wanting someone else to receive, accept, believe, or infer it, and someone making someone else do something by producing it.

Led by such considerations, I worked out a conceptual framework for the analysis of all possible types of extraorganismic signs with respect to the types of intraorganismic processes required for them to happen. It takes the form of a hierarchy of sign concepts based on three central concepts of intensional logic, namely 'believe', 'cause', and 'intend', and was published in 1993 in the volume *Signs, Search, and Communication: Semiotic Aspects of Artificial Intelligence*. Byproducts of this work are the definitions of various types of sign processes that are less complex than speech acts in the sense of John Searle and a proof of the universality and completeness of the speech act taxonomy proposed by Searle.

This systematization of sign process types is usable as a basis for the construction of systems of artificial intelligence that develop the complex capacity of communicating with humans and with one another in the strong (Gricean) sense of communication. One of the important consequences of this approach is the claim that communicative competence in the strong sense discussed here cannot be programmed into an information processing system. It must rather be trained. Further, full communicative competence cannot be reached by training restricted to the exchange of information within simple dialogue situations; it must include the ability to distinguish ratified communication partners from non-ratified participants, addressed ratified communication partners from non-addressed ones, eavesdropping non-ratified participants from bystanders, etc.

Regarded from a semiotic point of view, communication training for computers will eventually differ very little from the socialization of children, from therapeutic training for paranoid individuals, and from management reorganization in bureaucratic institutions, thus confirming my claim that the sign users involved can be (human) organisms as well as (social) organizations and information processing machines.

My latest contribution to the field of semiotics is still a work in progress. It is the establishment of a research group working at the **Berlin Dictionary of Everyday Gestures**–a project now 10 years old and based on the concept of speech-replacing emblems. This group has interviewed more than 1000 individuals so far, concerning the forms, meanings, and uses of their gestures, and has thereby identified about 200 solo gestures and about 100 duo gestures including their form and meaning variants. The majority of emblematic gestures emerge from body reflexes (as in blinking eyes expressing irritation) and from the simulation of handling culture-specific artifacts (as in playing an imaginary street organ to express monotony and boredom). They tend to be accompanied by interjections and verbal comments using body metaphors–which reveals the physical basis of culture. There is no human culture that is not gestural in this way. In the last years, parallel research groups preparing gesture dictionaries based on our principles of empirical work have been formed on three continents, so that we will, in due time, have a sound basis for comparative gesturology.

Last but not least, let me here refer to an achievement in the field of semiotics, which does not primarily consist in the presentation of my own research, but rather in the promotion of the work of others. I mean the scientific quarterly *Zeitschrift für Semiotik*, which is celebrating its thirtieth anniversary this year. This is an international journal written in German, which has so far published 15000 pages organized in 83 thematic issues, each covering a different topic of general or applied semiotics and presenting contributions by authors from all over the world.

3. What is the proper role of a theory of signs and meaning in relation to other academic fields?

Since Antiquity, semiotics has been geared towards solving everyday practical problems. Medical semiotics, named so by the Greeks, helped physicians recognize illnesses on the basis of their signs (symptoms). The art of divination practiced by the Romans aimed at the prediction of future events through the interpretation of omens. Medieval heraldry regulated the design of coats of arms to enable knights to recognize each other. The cryptanalysis of the Baroque period made great efforts to decipher texts written in unknown characters and languages. The Enlightenment investigated particular ways of presentation, which could be expected to achieve desired effects in the various genres of the arts.

All these are tasks of **applied semiotics**. They could be accomplished all the better, the more knowledge was available regarding the differences in the ways in which the various types of signs and semioses function. Thus, on the basis of precursors in Antiquity and the Middle Ages, a **descriptive** and **comparative** semiotics developed, which saw as its main goal the establishment of an increasingly comprehensive and differentiated classification of signs. Philosophy then systematized the criteria used for this classification, which eventually led to the development of **theoretical semiotics**. Its aim is to set up a system of operations for the analysis of signs as well as a system of terms and axioms from which theorems can be derived to explain and predict how the meaning of complex signs depends on their structure, on their domain of reference, and on the goals of their users.

Encouraged by the epochal development in modern logic and linguistics, early twentieth-century semiotics set out to provide general concepts for all relevant types of signs and semioses. This intention brought semiotics into competition with fields that had already established themselves as university disciplines and had developed their own independent approaches to the signs and semioses occurring in their subject matter; among the disciplines involved were biology, psychology, and medicine on the one hand and philology, musicology, and art history on the other. Semiotics responded to this challenge in two ways: (1) it concentrated on areas not systematically treated by the more established disciplines—a tendency which led to the constitution of **regional semiotics** such as theater semiotics, film semiotics, and the semiotics of nonverbal communication; (2) it made the subject areas of the individual disciplines accessible to a unified and precise description within its own conceptual framework. The advantages of the latter approach became particularly evident in the analysis of multi-media semioses in nature and culture. With regard to culture, it became possible—in opera, circus, and theater as well as in newspapers, magazines, films, and television—to identify the specific contribution of the various sign types to the overall effect, to weigh them against each other, and thus to create the preconditions for a rational choice of the most effective medium in each case.

The advantages of the semiotic approach appear not only in

its results but also in its methods. Since the disciplines which interpret cultural artifacts–among them anthropology, archaeology, philology, musicology, and art history–have, after a common beginning, developed their procedures of analysis and description independently of each other, their methods now seem to be quite dissimilar and incompatible (as I pointed out in my answer to question 1). In contrast, the semiotic approach explores the possibilities of applying the same procedures of analysis and description to artifacts of all kinds. In this way, semiotics has taken the role of an **object-science** and has as such been able to stimulate the sign-related disciplines to systematize their methods as well as their results and modes of presentation.

The influence of semiotics on the academic disciplines is not limited to those disciplines that study sign processes. The fact that all disciplines have to use certain methods of investigation and modes of presentation, and that both the investigation and the presentation of a subject involve sign processes, led to the claim that even the philosophy of science is essentially semiotics. Since the time when this claim was made (here I refer to my answer to question 1 again), epistemologists also became aware of the institutionalized communication that takes place among scholars and scientists, and this practice has become a further area of investigation for a semiotically designed philosophy of science. Consequently, one can say that semiotics is active not only as an object-science on the same level as the sign-related academic disciplines, but also as a **metascience** that takes all academic disciplines as its domain, regardless of whether they themselves study sign-processes (the humanities, the social sciences, biology and medicine) or not (physics, chemistry, and astronomy).

Its multidisciplinary subject matter brought semiotics into competition with other **interdisciplinary approaches** (compare my answer to question 2): hermeneutics, gestalt theory, information theory, systems theory, and others. Each of these approaches was forced to justify its claims with respect to the individual disciplines, and thus each has occasionally displayed a tendency to universalize its domain and to accuse competing approaches of being unscientific. This has been facilitated by the fact that most interdisciplinary approaches make implicit use of their mutual results, so that it is difficult to determine their systematic relationship to each other. Therefore, it remains to be clarified for each approach whether it is defined by a subject matter, a perspective, a method of investigation, a theory, or a mode of presentation, and how these relate to the subject matter, perspective, method of investigation, theory, and mode of presentation of semiotics.

In my opinion, hermeneutics, gestalt theory, information theory, and systems theory can all be combined with semiotics on the appropriate level of its various branches (pragmatics in the case of hermeneutics and systems theory, syntactics in the case of gestalt theory and information theory) to form an even more comprehensive and unified interdisciplinary approach. However, this proposal has not yet been worked out with the necessary precision.

As a conclusion for semiotics students and researchers active in the present situation, these considerations amount to requiring great flexibility. Semiotic expertise must be combined with scientific competence in at least one of the traditional sign-related disciplines, and in research one has to work partially by direct application of semiotic procedures, partially by making a detour via the application of the more specialized methods and theory fragments of one or more traditional disciplines, and then semiotically reinterpreting the results. This is a three-level approach:

1. direct investigation of the subject matter in question by means of the methods and theories of one or more traditional disciplines,

2. direct application of semiotic problem formulations, methods, and theory fragments to this subject wherever feasible, and

3. systematization and synthesis of the results from level 1 and 2 in a semiotic perspective (thus applying semiotic terminology, theory, and modes of presentation to them).

In favor of this complicated practice one can say that there are few other disciplines or interdisciplinary approaches which are both near enough to their subject matter (object-level) to be able to analyze it directly and distanced enough from it to be able to judge the results of traditional research (metalevel) about it. This explains why semiotics has become a rather popular approach in the analysis of experiences of human everyday life.

4. What do you consider to be the most important topics and/or contributions in the theory of meaning and signs?

Let me mention three topics and, accordingly, three achievements that I regard as the greatest steps towards a general theory of signs and meanings in the Western tradition.

The first has to do with the question of what is the relationship between the two separate meaning-related discourses which we find in ancient Greek philosophy. Their remnants are still noticeable today in old-fashioned twin formulas such as "semeion and logos" or "signs and symbols". The distinction made here is based on the separation between "nature" and "culture" ("natural signs" versus "cultural symbols", "natural meaning" versus "nonnatural meaning") and has given rise to the ontological opposition between the so-called realms of "real" versus "ideal" being. It was St. Augustine (354-430 A.D.) who eliminated this opposition by applying the Latin term "signum" both to natural signs and to cultural symbols. In his treatise on "Dialectics" he claims that "Loqui est articulata voce signum dare" ("to speak is to give a sign by means of an articulated voice"). For him, logos and symbol are just special cases of signum or sign. "Sign" is a general term which not only designates the track on the ground indicating an animal, and the bodily symptom indicating an illness, but also the gesture of pointing to someone or some place, and the words uttered to draw attention to some state of affairs. In the same way in which one takes a set of traces (e.g., paw prints) occurring at a certain place as indicating the movement of the animal that caused it, one takes an utterance of words as indicating some intention of the person that caused it. Of course, there is a great difference between unintended events and intentional actions, but this does not change the fact that both cases give rise to conclusions about states of affairs indicated by signs. The fact that humans and certain other animals (as well as institutions and certain types of machines) can produce events with the intention of causing a person to believe or do something–and with the expectation that a person taking this intention to be indicated through that event will in fact behave in the intended way –, is not more than an interesting complication.

Augustine's unifying approach set the challenging task of reconstructing the relationship between all sign types on a common conceptual basis. Until this task is accomplished, far reaching projects such as that of producing cognitive systems endowed with artificial intelligence will remain out of reach.

The second topic and achievement I regard as crucial for a successful semiotics is the invention of systems of propositional and predicate logic by Leibniz, Peirce, Frege, Russell, and others. They show the way towards a systematic explication of the meaning of a (verbal) text on the basis of the meanings of its constituents.

In the twentieth century, many further such systems (e.g., modal logic, intensional logic, and model theory) have been worked out and successfully applied. They mostly deal with the semantic values of special syntactic constructions and of fragments of the lexicon of natural languages. However, there are many other types of complex signs that pose similar problems. In order to cope with them, we need

- a logic of graphs
- a pictorial logic
- a logic of gestures
- a logic of human performances
- a logic of musical meaning
- a logic of architecture, etc.

It is to be expected that these projects will force new ideas upon us regarding the possible goals and limits of semantics as a branch of semiotics and thus will lead to considerable conceptual changes in the general theory of signs.

The third achievement, which has determined the profile of contemporary semiotics, is the development of systematic pragmatics by Charles W. Morris, John Searle, and H. Paul Grice in the middle of the twentieth century. It enables the semiotician to distinguish the coded meaning of a sign from a message that is created by applying a metaphor, a metonymy, or another type of implicature to a coded meaning. This approach spares us the blind alleys in which many information theorists found themselves caught when they tried to treat all sign-message couplings as being fully determined by an underlying code. The principles for the reconstruction of implicatures bring various aspects of the sign context into the explication of a sign process and take into account the ways of reasoning carried through by sign recipients and anticipated by sign producers.

Historically, pragmatics can be regarded as a systematization of the century-old lists of rhetorical figures. Here again, most efforts of analysis were directed towards the explanation of the messages of (verbal) texts. The coming decades will have to include pictorial, gestural, performative, musical, architectural, etc. messages and thereby make semiotics fulfil its promise to describe and explain signs and sign processes in all perceptual modalities, media, and codes.

5. What are the most important open problems in this field and what are its prospects for progress?

I have already sketched the most important problems in dealing with the central achievements of semiotics and I am confident that the bundle of theoretical paradigms which guide the work of contemporary semioticians (see *Semiotics–A Handbook on the Sign-theoretic Foundations of Nature and Culture*) is capable of carrying this work to success.

The main obstacles I can see are not directly connected with this work, but rather with its external circumstances: If the university systems in the globalized world offer nothing more than a mixture of commercialized research, backwards oriented academic teaching, and arbitrary post-modern entertainment projects, then the prospects for research in a field which is so highly dependent on a well-functioning system of academic disciplines and well-organized interdisciplinary cooperation, is doomed to failure.

16
François Rastier

Research Professor

CNRS, Paris

---

1. Why were you initially drawn to the theory of signs and meaning?

I have always been interested in texts that are difficult to understand, ever since the 1950es and my discovery of Ronsard and his *Hynmes*, and Maurice Scève's *Délie*, *La Divina Commedia*, Joyce's *Ulysses*. In my first research paper from 1966, I addressed the issue of signification in Mallarmé.[1] I now realize that all the texts we re-read, even those which seem limpid, like Primo Levi's works, are in fact difficult—and it is for this very reason that we read them again, and because we read them again they become classics.

All this will probably seem pretty literary to you, but as I see it the works of the past are our educators, and if we stopped reading them, they would become unreadable. Moreover, the very fact of being interested in things that are difficult to understand may very well go hand in hand with scientific curiosity. Texts that slow down our reading pace seem in and by themselves to give shape to the question of interpretation.

As you have surely already understood, the theory of signs and meaning depends in my view on the theory of texts and textuality. As such it is a tacit denial of current attempts to found the theory of signs and meaning on communication. It is also a refutation

---

[1] An echo of this can be found in Rastier 1974. These last years I have been working on authors such as Chamfort, Breton, Borges, Beckett, Primo Levi (cf. Rastier 2005). Writers have always been ahead of linguists: just as painters have understood vision, writers have acquired remarkable insight in semantic perception. I indeed started my carrier as a teacher of linguistics in an experimental department of French literature, but I keep thinking that linguists would profit a lot from courses on literature.

of the attempt at reducing languages to sheer "instruments" of communication. It is the paradigm of *transmission*, connected to writing, which has launched linguistic reflection: it makes clear why oral communication is not simply exchange of information.

I was lucky to have Algirdas Julien Greimas and Claude Hagège as my professors. I collaborated with Greimas for five years; just to mention one example: in our joint article *On the interaction of semiotic constraints* (Greimas and Rastier 1968) we introduce what later would be reified as the "semiotic square."

What I find so remarkable in Greimas' *Structural Semantics* is in fact something which still has not been sufficiently developed, and that is the attempt to *actually* combine the theory of signs and text theory. My doctoral thesis—corresponding to the German *Habilitationsschrift*—from 1985 is written in the vein of the above topic, but with specific focus on the concept of *isotopy*, dealt with in the first tome, while the second tome is devoted to concrete analyses of texts.

After my thesis I worked about ten years as a researcher in the "Laboratoire d'informatique et de mécanique pour les sciences de l'ingénieur", in Orsay: a research lab in computational linguistics. I was directly involved in the development of cognitive science in France—I was for example the chief editor of the first cognitive science journal in France, *Intellectica*. Computational linguistics is today about to fuse with corpus linguistics, which makes it possible to endow linguistics with an experimental method that enables the discovery of new data (cf. Rastier 2005).

Allow me now a little digression as regards cognition which occupies a preeminent position in the present book. The problem of gnoseology is a classical philosophical problem. Traditionally, language is considered to be a transparent veil or a surface manifestation of an external reality: therefore linguistics and, in its wake, semiotics strangely consider that what is real is something external with respect to their object. All too often people stick to an instrumental understanding of language, considered as a simple score representing a pure conceptual level, which is confused with the semantic level:[2] if so, people ignore Saussure's theoreti-

---

[2] Remember Jackendoff's slogan from 1983: to study language amouts to studying cognitive psychology. Thought and the semantic level of the languages are assimilated, hence the contents and the expression of the languages become the objects of two different disciplines: psychology and linguistics. Nothing is more traditional than this language/thought dualism. Charles Mongin, back in 1803, explained in his *Philosophie élémentaire* that

cal revolution which reintegrates the signified (*le signifié*) into the natural languages, to the extent that a concept is simply inseparable from its expression.

The problem of cognition is radically redefined when you take into consideration signs and semiotic performances. The aporetical circularity between objects and representations (which was a forerunner of Fodor's *methodological solipsism*) then becomes a simple complementary relation between the subjectifying moments and the objectifying moments of the same interpretative processes. The general problem concerning the relation to the environment is particularly interesting for the semiotic environment–however, this does not imply any external memory store (in Merlin Donald's sense).

In short, I prefer approaching knowledge from an epistemological point of view and thus leave gnoseology to philosophy. Knowledge is not in our heads, but in our texts, and that is where we constantly look for it and produce it; by the way, according to Ferdinand Gonseth the relation between investigation and textualization is dual and complementary. An important subset of our insights concern scientific texts, but knowledge does not boil down to this. In more general terms, you can say that knowledge is not an object which can be stocked, but a critical interpretive mode which is interested in each and every semiotic performance.

For this reason, there is no unity in cognition: human cognition is a result of its being coupled with the cultural objects. It is by and large an interpretative device. Even hallucinations have been shown to be highly culturalized. Cognitive Sciences have engaged in a vast program of naturalization of cultures, therefore they generally neglect the cultural factors of cognition. This is the consequence, not of a scientific program, but of a scientist ideology (inherited from logical positivism and perhaps even from the kind of positivism that had its heyday around the end of the 19th century). I have therefore defined my research program in inverse terms, namely as *the culturalization of the cognitive sciences* (cf. Rastier 1991), and in particular I would like Cognitive Linguistics to take an interest in languages, discourse types, genres, as well as styles and texts.

Let's take a simple example: we know since Liberman's discovery of categorical perception that linguistic sounds are not processed as noise or non-linuguistic sounds and more generally

---

the object of a general grammar is thought analyzed by means of signs.

that cultural objects are taken in charge by acquired and highly top-down perceptual strategies. This property of acoustic perception can be transposed to the perception of signifieds, and that is why I have proposed to study semantic perception and its variation in accordance with the context and the text (cf. Rastier 1991, chapter VIII). The regimes of semantic perception, which are induced by genres and styles, *constrain* the formation of mental images while we read.

2. What do you consider your contribution to the field?

The field of semiotics has not been established, and, probably luckily so, semiotics has not been capable of becoming a discipline proper. I myself have always been working in the domain of linguistics. By the way, I champion a federative conception of semiotics: linguistics is in this perspective *the semiotics of the languages* —often called *natural* languages although they are cultural through and through. It is difficult to highlight all what I owe to those scholars whose contributions I have attempted to synthesize, be it Louis Hjelmslev, Algirdas-Julien Greimas, Bernard Pottier or Eugenio Coseriu. Since I am part of a tradition, I hope that I have been capable of making my own contributions: a tradition also consists of ruptures.

Interpretive semantics is, in my view, independent of human will, at least mine: it is a line of research, not a school.[3] This should thus be considered an open body of theses, and not as a doctrine. On the other hand I have accumulated too many unpublished papers to be capable of assessing my actual contribution to the field. Anyway, here follow some principles of interpretive semantics which for the sake of brevity have been given a somewhat dogmatic shape:

- Meaning constitutes a level of objectivity which is irreducible to neither reference nor mental representations. It can be analyzed in terms of semantic features which are moments stabilized within a process of interpretation.

- The typology of signs depends on the typology of the interpretive processes of which they are the object.

---

[3] The notion of school is probably outdated and does not further inquiry in any way; I am by the way not member of any school, and it is just that I have not been mentioned in the work entitled *L'Ecole de Paris* (Greimas and Landowski, eds., Paris, Larousse, 1976).

- Meaning is made out of differences perceived and qualified within different types of praxis. It is a quality of texts, not of isolated signs (which lack any empirical existence).

- The meaning of a unity is determined by its context. The context is the whole text: micro-semantics depends thus on macro-semantics.

- The elementary textual units are not the words, but the *passages*. The expression of a passage is an excerpt, and its content is a fragment.

- At the semantic level, relevant features are organized so as to constitute *semantic forms*, such as the themes, which are detached from *semantic grounds*, among which primarily the isotopies. The semantic forms are moments stabilized within series of transformations, both within on and the same text and between several texts.

- If the morpheme is the elementary linguistic unit, the text is the minimal unit of analysis, for the global determines the local.

- Any text proceeds from a genre which determines, without constraining it, its genetic, mimetic and hermeneutic modes.

- Any genre is part of a discourse. By virtue of its genre, each text is connected to a discourse.

- Any text depends on a corpus and must be related to it in order to be correctly interpreted.

- The preferential corpus of a text is composed by belonging to the same genre. The generic and interpretive processes within the text are inseparable from the interpretive process in the structured inter-text constituted by the corpus.

- The validity of the interpretive problem exceeds the texts and can be extended to cover other cultural objects, such as images (amenable to being dealt with by the same methodologies: recollection of corpus, determination of genres, indexation in terms of features of expression).

- The typology and the analysis of cultural objects require an anthropological reflection. Contrary to the systems of animal communication, human languages allow three types of identification (notably in the domains of person, tense, space or mode): they distinguish a zone of coincidence (*identity* zone), a zone of adjacency (*proximal* zone) and a *distal* zone (the HE, the THEN, the OVER THERE, the UNREAL): in short, they make it possible to talk about that which is not there. The cultural objects warrant the mediation between the zones which allow the coupling of the individual and its semiotic environment: at the frontier between the identity zone and the proximal zone we find the *fetishes* (e.g. the cell phone); at the frontier between these two zones and the distal zone we find the *idols* (for ampler analysis cf. Rastier 2001a).

- Sketched by Aristotle in the *Peri hermeneias* and then elaborated in more detail throughout history up till Ogden and Richards, the *semiotic mediation* rests on a problematic connection between things, words, and concepts. The musings into which the semiotics of the sign has delved for millennia would improve a lot if they took into account the *symbolic mediation* between the identity zone, the proximal zone, and the distal zone: it would then be to understand the autonomy of the symbolic with respect to both things and concepts, and it would then be possible to define a field of objectivity proper without subsuming it under physical science (even in its folk version) or psychology (even in its cognitive version).

- Semiotics of cultural objects call for a reflection on the sciences of culture as a whole.

These suggestions are located at different levels of reflection.

At the gnoseological level, which is the one in which theory of knowledge is interested, the point consists in abandoning the claim to the effect that knowledge is a representation of being or human beings: it is a *praxis* or more exactly a reflexive and critical moment in a number of differentiated social praxes.

At the epistemological level, which is the one in which theory of science is interested, our task consists in characterizing and individualizing the cultural objects so as to make them permanently readable. We are here dealing with a progressive, but never-ending process: no scientific reading will ever exhaust a text; on the other hand these readings themselves can be called into question, they can be considered with respect to their conditions, and they can be hierarchized.

At the theoretical level proper, the point consists in abandoning both a too strong conception of theory, derived from claissical systematic philosophy, and the non-critical empiricism which today is predominant in what is called "normal science" (in Kuhn's sense) but which is in fact nothing but a non-critical routine: the theoretical apparatus cannot strive for any full systematicity and must know in advance how to warrant its own evolution, be it in terms of sophistication or in terms of simplification, as soon as the applications make this necessary. It must therefore mutually define the necessary descriptive concepts, but without any exaggerated axiomatic ambition. The acknowledgement of the complexity prevents us by the way from considering the sign systems as codes or the languages as systems: a *multiplicity* of systems are active in all semiotics. The interaction between the latter can be optimized, but they cannot for that matter be subsumed by a meta-system.

Finally, at the methodological level it must be possible to vary the methods according to the tasks; that is the prize to pay if the theory is to be applied on anything—hence my plea for an *applicable semantics*. These applications are of many different sorts, they apply both to Latin and medieval corpora and to contemporary corpora (literature as well as media). Also traductology is interested in these applications. Moreover, corpus semantics is called to renovate the domains of data retrieval and knowledge representation.

My intellectual project consists first and foremost in a redescription of linguistics based on the concept of text. This entails reestablishing the relation with new forms of philology and hermeneutics (cf. Rastier 2001b). Signs are generally considered as elementary units, and generally the word is taken in isolation and then analyzed with respect to its signification or polysemous character. However, texts and other complex semiotic performances are the genuine *fundamental data* and the real *empirical objects* of linguistics and semiotics. That is the reason why I have worked in the domain of corpus linguistics for the last fifteen years.

In the human sciences, data are what we give ourselves. Thus, any corpus is critically characterized by the fact that it depends on the point of view which preceded its constitution, and that it anticipates its own interpretation. Computational instruments are a necessary part of its objectivation, but they do not for that sake make the all as necessary digital philology and material hermeneutics less indispensable. As an illustration let me mention the thematic study of feelings in 350 French novels (1830-1970; cf. Rastier

1995); or the project *Morphogenres* which has given an experimental proof for the way in which global characteristics of discourse and genre determine local characteristics of morphosyntax: taking as our point of departure 2,600 texts, which had previously been codified in terms of their discourse type (say, law or literary texts) and their genre and then labeled by 251 different morphosyntactical tags, we were capable of proving that the average rate of tags varies in a sufficiently precise way so as to make it possible for an automatic blindfolded classification to match the discourse and genre classifications we had established while constituting the corpus. This justifies the conclusion to the effect that the morphosyntactical level (to which language is too often reduced) depends narrowly on global textual discourse- and genre-criteria, that is to say on *norms* still undescribed by grammars on the market (cf. Malrieu and Rastier 2001).

The European project *Princip.net* (2002-2004) has, along with the programs *Safer internet*, applied these results on the automatic detection of racist websites. By systematically comparing corpora from racist and antiracist websites, at different levels of textual analysis (lexicon, syntax, but also punctuation) and document analysis (typography, html tags) a thousand indices have been retrieved which make it possible to characterize sites online, in real time.

The stakes in the semiotic analysis are clear: when we succeed in correlating the local characteristics of expression (say, presence of capital letters) with global content criteria (being a racist or not) on the basis of certain rules (say: only racists write completely capitalized sentences), then we can improve the characterization of documents in a decisive way. At any rate we proceed from the global (characterization of discourses and genres) toward the local, according to the hermeneutic principle that the global determines the local.

Since meaning is made of established, interpreted and redefined differences, the problems that I am interested in concern diversity and history—not unity and origin, issues which in my eyes are metaphysical rather than scientific.

In the occidental tradition theories of signs and meaning have a logical and ontological foundation, starting with Locke and Peirce and up to our time. The intellectual framework of semiotics remains dominated by the opposition between Augustinian intentionalism (which Peirce endorsed) and Aristotelian referentialism (this neo-Thomism is still dominant in academic semiotics among writers like Eco, Courtés, Beuchot, Deely). Signs are too often considered as instruments of knowledge and cognitivism has simply upgraded this traditional claim, both in its Chomskyan or in its Californian version. The Aristotelian and Kantian categories are still listed in the inventories of cognitive universals, and people are still all too keen on (re)constructing the transcendental subject, now dubbed the cognitive subject, something we all are more or less.

In order to avoid isolating the signs and reifying meaning, I approach theories of signs and meaning from the outside with the aim of conditioning and sometimes refuting their legitimacy. This is done on the grounds of the following grossly formulated principles:

The characterization of signs depends on the interpretive processes: depending on the context the "same" sign can function as an index, a symbol etc. The study of interpretive praxes thus governs the study of signs.

The object of semiotics is not made out of signs, but of complex performances, such as an opera, rituals, etc. The complex precedes the simple, and since the oral or written texts are the empirical object of linguistics, already the delimitation of signs rests on non-trivial methodological operations. Since the characterization of texts and other semiotic performances is *differential*, it rests on the constitution and the critical analysis of a corpus.

Signs are not by nature the expression of reports of perceptual experiences. Semiotics, consisting of complex performances, constitutes the human environment: this environment is not an instrument, but the world in which we live and to which we have to adapt. The problem is no longer one of representation, but one of coupling—in Uexküll's sense.

Even though pragmatics privileges the *hic et nunc*, the human environment comprises a host of absent objects, or at least objects without any immediate perceptual tenor: they inhabit that which I have proposed to call the *distal zone*, to which all sciences as well as all religions intent to gain access. Since signs are not referential, they make it possible to create worlds: the one in which you are reading this book is just one among others.

Interactions in a given society are governed by the distal zone: we are here not simply talking of statistical norms but of laws. Thus, the question of communication should be substituted by the question of *transmission*: we establish and use our practical norms only relative to laws.

3. What is the proper role of a theory of signs and meaning in relation to other academic disciplines?

In the 19th century linguistics was seduced by models stemming from biology (cf. Schleicher's Darwinian theory); in the 20th century, notably in Chomsky, people have stressed the affiliation between the theory of grammar and the theory of formal language in order to include the former in the logical-formal sciences. Nowadays the failure of the formalization research programs have fueled the renaissance of the naturalization programs: people are looking for the language organ, without ever finding it, by the way, some scholars very seriously write small anthropological novels about the origin of language, others discover the "language genes," etc. These researches do not tell us anything, or hardly, about the natural languages themselves. The diversity of languages remains the founding problem of linguistics—in contradiction to what is the case in the other disciplines where language is addressed (philosophy, sociology, neuro-linguistics, etc.).

We have no data about and therefore no access to the origin of our languages, and we are better off considering them as collective creations that are reconstructed every day, for each of the uses we make of them is likely to modify them in some respect. They are made out of oral or written texts, cultural object produced within the frames of social praxes that are part of history. The same goes for all the other semiotic performances (images, films, music, etc.).

Semiotics of texts and other complex performances is therefore a genuine part of a *semiotic of cultures*. Now, a culture is understandable, i.e. characterizable in a critical manner, only within the framework of a corpus constituted by other cultures. This is why sciences of culture are necessarily historical and comparative. Semiotics of cultures remain by and large misunderstood because it is opposed both to cognitive universalism (which in its own way goes hand in hand with globalization) and the different nationalisms and communitarisms according to which cultures are monads, in the best case isolated such, in the worst antagonistic.

I leave open the question whether semiotics is one among many other sciences of culture—personally I do not consider it as a discipline, but a federative reflection which is relevant for all the other sciences of culture. Now, these sciences escape the canons of *Big Science*: this is due to their critical dimension, the difficulty they encounter in designing experiments with non-reproducible "results", their willingness to consider singular objects despite of the alleged fact that there can only be a science of general objects.

Therefore, they are being torn apart and redistributed among the different cognitive disciplines (hence the opulent programs dealing with the origin of language) and the disciplines of communication theory. In fact, this partitioning would by and large abandon the problem of culture to the industries of communication (from mass media in one end to the show business in the other): the issue of culture would then completely lose its critical dimension. This is the reason why it is so necessary for the sciences of culture to make clear their epistemological specificity: they are sciences of values and not of facts, of conditions and not of causes, of individuals and not of universals, of processes and not of beings, of occurrences and not of types; they are not founded on ontologies, but must elaborate a praxeology.

4. What do you consider the most important topic and/or contributions in the theory of meaning and signs?

There are a host of sources, and that is a good thing. In linguistics, I like recalling Humboldt, Steinthal, Bréal, Meillet, Dumézil; in anthropology Boas, Hocart, Lévi-Strauss, Geertz. Also Erwin Panofsky should be mentioned as regards iconology, Carlo Ginzburg in history, and so forth. Yet, the actuality of thought exceeds the limits of contemporary disciplines. Sources of inspiration, which may seem remote, have in fact kept all their actuality; this goes for Longinus' treatise *On the Sublime*, Augustin's *De doctrina Christiana*, in which you find an articulation of a theory of signs and a theory of text interpretation, Baltazar Gracián's *Agudeza y arte del ingenio*, a remarkable treatise on text semantics, Giambattista Vico's *Scienza Nuova*, Friedrich Schlegel's fragments, Schleiermacher's hermeneutics, etc.

The task of semiotics also consists in critically reading and describing the culture it is the upshot of. By multiplying our objects and intellectual traditions we make ourselves capable of turning the back to the speculative space of the universal theories of semiotics in order to construct a general semiotics of cultures, which is both historical and comparative. Since the creation of the International Association of Semiotic Studies at the end of the 1960's, Saussure and Peirce are traditionally seen as opposed figures, and people are therefore asked to choose between the two founding fathers. This *gigantomachia* is futile to the extent that their projects cannot be compared: Peirce is a first class philosopher, a genius metaphysician who claimed that man is a sign. Saussure, on the other hand, remains a linguist who refrains from any belief and even any ontology. Semiotics will be capable of becoming a discipline proper the day it accepts that everything is not a sign. Now, pan-semiotism has not ceased to grow, from zoo-semiotics to physical semiotics, semiophysics, DNA semiotics, etc.

As to me, I consider myself as part of the general Saussurean strand such as it has been represented by authors as different as Hjelmslev and Coseriu (both of whom I have edited in French). The import of this strand has been blurred by the ritual stigmatization of "structuralism," which is abusively reduced to a set of universalist theses, a sort of Jakobsonian binarism. By the way, a lot of different things are tossed together under the all too handy heading "structuralism", say, Czech functionalism, Danish glossematics, American distributionalism from the 1940's as well as the hyped conglomerate Lacan-Greimas-Barthes-Lévi-Strauss-Althusser-Foucault.

Saussureanism is nevertheless worth the detour. Since the discovery of Saussure's manuscript *De l'essence double du langage* in 1996, a vast international wave of edition and reevaluation of Saussure's work has made it possible once and for all to screen out the simplifications committed by the first editors of *Cours de linguistique générale*. Not only do we discover a thinker who comes to grips with complexity, but also this texts enables us to articulate the different aspects of Saussure's work while perspectivizing 20th century Saussureanism. This is why *neo-Saussureanism* (cf. www.institut-saussure.org) plays an important role in the renovation of linguistics.

5. What are the most important open problems in this field and what are the prospects for progress?

We are in need of an epistemological clarification, and I am convinced that the present book will further this. The field evoked in the question is not clearly delimited since all sorts of disciplines, scientific or not (such as philosophy) may pretend, and rightly so, to be concerned with signs and meaning. It is not enough to evoke transdisciplinarity, far from that, since contemporary semiotics, in some of its pity variants, marshals the constructivist ideas of cultural studies or the New Age reveries proper to the *Gaia* hypothesis which makes Nature to yet another avatar of the Great Goddess.

Neuroscience disposes today of new and powerful research resources, but neuro-linguistics and "neuro-semiotics" are still tributary to the outdated hypotheses of philosophy of language; they would gain from testing new hypotheses, for instance about the formation of representations while reading a book or watching a movie. The role of specialists of texts and other semiotic performances is then to come up with hypotheses and collaborate in the design of new experimental agendas. Several cognitive paradigms consider language as a report of perceptions, either connected to objects proper or to a phenomenological givenness. I'd rather say that language itself is an *object of perception*: this is evidently the case for the signifier, but it also holds true for the signified, and that is the reason why I have developed the notion and subject matter of *semantic perception*. A research program developed on the grounds of this topic seems promising.

The internet and the whole set of virtual worlds, including videogames and the assisted generation of interactive narratives, have taken on an increasing social signification. Now, semioticians have remained too passive with respect to this issue and have not sufficiently well addressed the issues connected with the digital documents—probably because of lacking technical competence. The Semantic Web, which has become a sort of international discipline (Web Science), is developed almost exclusively within the framework of the logical-positivistic semiotics proper to an outdated philosophy of language. This constitutes an obstacle for a Web semantics (and a Web semiotics): for instance, the ontologies on which it rests do absolutely not take into account criteria such as the genres of the documents, the trustworthiness and the authenticity of the sources, the cultural variability. When a web semantics is hooked up with a digital philology and a hermeneutics assisted by the instruments of corpus linguistics, it will become capable of dealing with these phenomena and thus lead us beyond the traditional problems concerning the representation of knowledge. As a consequence, data retrieval and processing are improved: data are indeed inseparable from their semiotic substrates.

17
Eleanor Rosch

Professor
Department of Psychology
University of California, Berkeley

Concepts–Think Again

From the time I started to develop what we call an intellect, around age eleven, I have also carried the intuition that the way mental forms structure the world and make pronouncements about it are not the whole story, perhaps not even a significant or deep part of it. My efforts to penetrate how things really are led first to literature, then to psychology with its scientific implementation, and finally to the insights of meditative and contemplative religious practices East and West. Within my professional milieu–psychology and cognitive science, particularly in their Anglo-American form–there is no field called theory of signs and meaning; however we do study concepts, categorization, language, and various issues concerning the relationship of the contents of minds to the external world. It is within that context that I have done work relevant to the topic of this book, and since that's what I know about, that's what I'll write about.

My work on such issues falls into three parts: 1) Early work on the nature of concepts and categorization 2) Later efforts to show how meditative and contemplative practices and texts (and daily life seen from such a point of view) transmit nonconceptual "wisdom" knowledge that may be more basic than the conceptual patterning that we take for granted, and 3) A new view of concepts and categorization from the broader perspective provided by such knowledge that I and my collaborators have been calling ecological.

Concepts and Categorization: The First Turning

Concepts are the central constructs in most modern theories of the mind and (arguably) in many theories of meaning. Concepts point, on the one hand, towards issues of categorization (how is it that we divide up, categorize, and label all the things in experience?) and, on the other hand, towards the relation between the mind that categorizes and its objects, usually seen as a relation between an inner and an outer world. Philosophy, psychology, computer science, and linguistics have all made contributions to conceptual theory and research. At the time when I began my work, a set of assumptions about concepts and categorization dominated all of these fields: this is what is now known as the classical view. The main impact of the first stage of my work was to identify this view and call the whole of it into question. Although, as a result, the classical view can no longer simply be assumed, at least in its overt and naïve forms, I believe its basic assumptions are, unregenerately, still the dominant mind-set of Western approaches to meaning. For this reason, I will describe it in some detail.

The classical view is the approach to concepts derived from the history of Western philosophy. When humans begin to look at their experience by means of reason, questions about the reliability of the senses and the bases for knowledge arise, as do more specific questions about how categories can have generality (called the problem of universals), how words can have meaning, and how concepts in the mind can relate to categories in the world. The Greeks, and most Western philosophers since, have agreed that experience of particulars as it comes moment by moment through the senses is unreliable; therefore, only stable, abstract, logical categories can function as objects of knowledge and objects of reference for the meaning of words. To fulfill these functions, conceptual categories had to be: a) exact, not vague (i.e. have clearly defined boundaries) and b) their members had to have attributes in common which were the necessary and sufficient conditions for membership in the category. It follows that: c) all members of the conceptual category were equally good with regard to membership; either they had the necessary common features or they didn't. Categories were thus seen as logical sets.

It is on the basis of conceptual categories as logical sets that categories could be the basis for logical inferences–as in the familiar "All men are mortal; Socrates is a man; Socrates is mortal." This is also the basis of the way words are defined by genus and differentia in our dictionaries. It was also the basis upon which concepts were turned into formal models in the fields that studied them and the processes of categorization and concept learning were studied as the attainment of such formal structures. For example, research on concept learning, led by the seminal work of Bruner, Goodnow, and Austin (1956), typically used artificial stimuli structured into micro worlds in which the prevailing beliefs about the nature of categories were already built in. In developmental psychology, the theories of Piaget and Vygotsky were combined with the concept-learning paradigm to study how children's ill-structured, often thematic, concepts developed into the logical adult mode.

In linguistics (perhaps the field most closely associated with theories of signs and meaning) most mainstream 20th century work in phonology, semantics, and syntax rested on the assumptions of the classical view. Phonemes were analyzed as sets of universal, abstract, binary features. Word meaning, the province of semantics, was analyzed by a componential analysis of features; for example, bachelor was rendered as the features +human, +male, +adult, +never married. A complex concept such as bald bachelor was considered the unproblematic intersection of the features of bachelor with those of bald. Synonymy, contradiction and other relational aspects of word meaning were accounted for in a similar fashion. Syntax was analyzed by formal systems such as Chomsky's transformational grammar that also relied on decomposition into features. (See any history of modern linguistics, such as Taylor 2003, for summaries.) A logical componential understanding of language was adopted with enthusiasm by computer science because meaning could be divorced from world knowledge and readily represented by the substitutable strings of symbols on which computers work.

This view of categories, concepts, and meaning seemed to me to violate everything from common sense observation to learning theory in psychology to the penetrating understanding of meaning in later Wittgenstein. Consider the color red: is red hair as good an example of your idea or image of red as a red fire engine? Is a dentist's chair as good an example of chair as a dining-room chair? Are you immediately sure how to classify and name every color and object you see? From the inception of psychology as a discipline separate from philosophy, psychology has investigated types of learning and behavior that show graded effects. For example, Pavlov's dogs produced decreasing amounts of saliva as tones grew farther from the tone originally combined with meat powder. This is called stimulus generalization. Note how different it is from the classical view of conceptual categories.

My challenges to the classical view began with cross-cultural work on color categories (Rosch, 1973) and soon extended to a variety of other types of categories, included those that could be argued to not have a perceptual basis or cross-cultural universality. In a programmatic series of empirical studies of the mental representation, learning, retrieval and real world uses of these categories (summarized in Rosch 1978, 1999, in press b), a wide variety of conceptual categories were shown to have gradients of membership; that is, subjects can easily, rapidly, and meaningfully rate how well a particular item fits their idea or image of its category. This is true for perceptual, semantic, social, biological, and formal concepts. (Note that these are not probability judgments but judgments of degree of membership.) In contrast, subjects cannot list criterial attributes for most categories (Rosch and Mervis, 1975). More importantly, the psychological import of gradients of membership were demonstrated by their effects in a series of experiments on virtually every major method of study and measurement used in psychological research: learning, association, speed of processing, expectation, inference, probability judgments, and judgments of similarity. Boundaries of most naturally occurring categories are anything but precise and whether or not particular items are members of a category can be the subject of much academic, societal, legal, and personal dispute.

To summarize and account for all this, I suggested a general model in which categories formed around perceptually, imaginally, emotionally, and/or conceptually salient stimuli, then, by stimulus generalization, spread to other similar stimuli–without necessarily any analyzable criterial attributes, formalizable definitions, or definite boundaries. There is graded, rather than uniform, membership in such categories. I called the salient centers of such categories prototypes, their structure graded structure, and proposed that once learned it is the prototype that mentally represents the category for most purposes; that is, that when people perform most psychological tasks in relation to concepts and categories they do so by referring present experience back to full bodied, multifaceted representations containing imagery, emotions, habits, and world knowledge not to the formal, stripped down, necessary-and-sufficient-for-membership attributes that are the hallmark of the classical view.

Any time a concept or category is used, it is in a concrete situation; thus we may ask how it is that the world of complex concrete concept-producing situations becomes segmented and tagged in the way that it does? Why are chairs a different category from tables or sofas? Why does chair seem more like this object's real name than piece of furniture, material object, or desk chair? Why does the category kangaroos weighing between 1.3 and 2.9 pounds seem neither basic, coherent, nor likely? In the classical view, categories could just is well be arbitrary sets of attributes and, indeed, were just that in traditional laboratory concept learning tasks. In a another programmatic set of experiments (Rosch, Mervis, Gray, Johnson, and Boyes-Braem, 1976), I proposed that under natural conditions there is a great deal of relational structure between perceptions, actions, and life activities, and that categories form so as to maximally map that structure. For taxonomies of common objects (studied from within this culture), I called this level the basic level, showed how it was the default level at which categories were interpreted, and offered evidence that this level had perceptual, linguistic, and developmental priority. Since named objects and events can be considered "props" in socio-cultural as well as biological life activities, research into basic levels of conceptualization and their variation across cultures potentially provides an entrance into study of some of the basic forms of human functioning.

What has been the effect of this body of work? On the one hand it has been at times credited with overturning the classical view and helping to make the nature and origin of concepts and categories a nexus of new research and thought (see Laurence & Margolis, 1999, and Rosch, in press b, for overviews of the field today). However, while prototypes and other effects that I studied are highly robust, much replicated, and each of the new theories seems to feel the need to address these findings in some way even if it be to misrepresent or strongly disagree with them, it is not clear how deeply the implications have actually penetrated. The strongest objections to the work seem to be that prototypes cannot be represented in a formal model that accounts for contradiction, synonymy, and all the other claimed necessities for a theory of meaning (for example, Osherson & Smith, 1981), precisely the sort of model that the work was disputing. On the other side, support is often in the form of a demonstration that such effects can be produced by some other kind of model, as for example in the subsymbolic mechanistic neuron-like processes of connectionist computer models (Rogers & McClelland, 2004). Much concepts research simply uses the idea of prototypes or of a privileged level of abstraction in order to study a specific domain without general theoretical concerns. I believe it is time to situate the field of concepts and categorization (along with our assumptions about what constitutes a proper explanation in science) in a broader context of understanding. The next two sections will explore this.

II. Contributions from Meditative and Contemplative Traditions

By the time I finished the first round of research on concepts and categories, I was haunted by the sense that this was becoming a field of technical disputes, hardly touching what seemed most meaningful and basic to people in terms of their lives. For the past 30 years, beginning with Buddhism, I have increasingly turned to studying the meditative and contemplative aspects of religions— what William James speaks of as "that which is seen as most primal and enveloping and deeply true" (James, 1902, p. 34). I believe that some of what we classify as religious experience can be directly relevant to science, particularly to psychology (Rosch 2002, 2007a,b, Rosch & Fallah 2007, Varela, Thompson & Rosch, 1991). Psychology and cognitive science generally take religions to be no more than cognitive beliefs about personified deities whose purpose it is to provide illusory comfort or to explain things that science can explain better. But I have found that as people pursue inner meditative or contemplative paths, their vision of religious objects changes radically as also, ideally, does their relationship to their own minds, hearts, and environments (Rosch, in press a). In a less explicit and organized way, the arts can have a similar effect (Rosch, 2004).

Here is the psychological portrait that has emerged for me (Rosch 2002, 2007 b, in press a): the human mind consists of different levels (or different modes of functioning or ways of knowing) of increasing depth. On the surface is the mind of ordinary concepts, emotions, desires, fears, even boredom–the mind with which everyone is familiar and from which psychologists and cognitive scientists take all their ideas and assumptions. Below that are levels of mind more in contact with various kinds of basic wisdom and better able to see and act from it.

This point may be clarified, hopefully, by a computer analogy. Imagine the ordinary surface mode of knowing as a particular computer program running on a more basic operating system. In daily life–and in psychology and cognitive science–researchers mistake the limited surface program for the whole system. The research community keeps trying to study how the system works, but all it can see is the functioning of the program in which it, as well as the people it is studying, are confined. On the other hand, various aspects of society such as religions and the arts specialize in communications that, at their best, can penetrate through the surface level of minds to touch and evoke intuitions and wisdom from the deeper levels.

Of course different traditions speak of the potentials of the human and the paths to realize those in different ways. Their focus is on the nature, meaning, and proper conduct of human existence (Rosch 2002, 2004, 2007a, b, in press a) and not primarily on concepts, categorization, language, signs, nor any of the other aspects of our topic here. However, the expanded vision provided by these traditions may allow us to see such issues in a new light. The account below begins with forms of experience most emphasized by Buddhism, but I believe it to be also consonant with contemplative vision more generally and, perhaps most importantly for present purposes, with the common-sense rationality of science–if one but keep an open mind.

III. Concepts Again–Not What You Think

Theories of categorization and concepts tend to begin from a vision of a lone human mind stationed in a perennially unknown world trying to master its environment by continuously classifying everything it encounters. The mental concepts produced by these classifications are assumed to derive their meaning through reference to the objects in the world. The only parts of the picture not assumed and thus made the subject of research are the rules determining the classifications. But is this actually the correct picture of the way language and thought work? The way time and causality work? As you enter your kitchen in the morning, do you stand gawking anew at each object trying to figure out what it is and what you can do with it? Actually, we move about in a locally known, not an unknown, world in which mind and environment are already linked by a vast interdependent causality, not a one-billiard-ball-at-a-time causality.

To begin to understand this, let's look first at the time dimension. What we have is the present. The actual functioning of the mind is only right now. A memory of the past is something happening now. Likewise, a fear, hope, or plan about the future is something happening now. Similarly the environment, whether one takes it as an independent external world or the phenomenological experienced world, is only happening right now. The mind and world mutually occur right now. A concept in use occurs only in a particular situation right now. I emphasize time because some realization of the presentness of experience seems to be necessary in order to appreciate causal interdependence and/or the particularity of actual concept usage. Throughout the universe, the great interdependent web of what is happening is occurring right now.

The content of right now, however, is the result of causal histories. Those causal histories are vast, complex, and interrelated. (For a model of the creativeness of such causality using the formalisms of quantum mechanics see Gabora, Rosch & Aerts, 2008.) As one stands in one's kitchen in the morning, both one's mind and the objects around one are the inheritors of mutually interlocking causal histories. Oneself and the objects have already been categorized and conceptualized (and largely turned into habits) not only by oneself individually but by the language, culture, and the whole of interconnected human history. Concepts themselves never exist individually but only within a web of other concepts. Moment by moment one is born (Heidegger uses the term thrown) into an inherited and known, not a primitive and perpetually unknown, world.

As stated, concepts never occur in the abstract but only in use in concrete situations–even if that situation is no more than a philosophical example. And because it is people who use concepts in those situations, if we want to know what concepts and categories are and how they work, we need to ask what people are doing with their concepts. People are acting with intentions and purposes; at any moment they are trying to achieve something. Another way to say this is that people are purposively participating in life games, the meaningful activities of life. Concepts, categories, and the rest of conceptualization are participating parts of these life games. There is nothing else for them to be. Yes, there are life games in which referring to objects plays a role but the reference always has some purpose; it occurs not in isolation, but as part of the game (see for example Wittgenstein's famous discussion of "slab" in the *Philosophical Investigations*, 1953).

Each life game has a motive (what the player is trying to do), and it has a loose set of rules for how it is to be played (parameters that instantiate what kind of a game it is). There are all kinds of life games at various levels of abstraction: survival, relating to people, marriage, playing social roles, predicting the physical world, playing an instrument, solving a math problem, re-enacting childhood traumas, raking leaves, removing a splinter, obtaining pleasure, following an ideal, teasing a friend, going to sleep, and so on. Structurally, life games are hierarchically nested; for example, doing an assignment in class may be nested within passing the class, which is nested within getting an education, which is nested within preparing for a career, etc. Life games are also horizontally interpenetrating; e.g. one is usually playing multiple life games by means of the same activity. For example, one can be exercising for both pleasure and health while perhaps simultaneously enacting an unconscious theme from childhood.

How are concepts learned? The core effort of a child is to find how to participate in life games from the earliest scenarios of getting what (s)he needs from mother (think of the highly influential pictures of Harlow's infant monkeys clinging to their cloth mother facsimile) to the most sophisticated later intellectual endeavors. Questions about how the social and physical world work, whether they are enacted by a prelinguistic infant or researched by an adult scientist, are always asked from a participant's point of view and thus from within the life games in which that participant is immersed. And concepts are developed as participating parts of those life games.

This view has implications for many endeavors. For example, educators already recognize that the concepts taught in schools need to be made "relevant" so that students will learn, but efforts to do so are far from a general success. What relevance means is relevance to the life games in which students are most invested, so a life game analysis might prove a key aid for curriculum development. Likewise, in cross-cultural contact, we need to realize that learning new concepts from another culture means also learning the life games in which they are embedded; without that the contact will remain shallow at best and potentially rife with misunderstandings. Translation of texts raise similar concerns; it may often be best to leave key terms in their original language to signal that the reader needs to enter a different mind set or life game view to understand their meaning.

In light of this view we can also see how the current conflicting academic theories of concepts and categorization each touches on an aspect of the process and may not be as contradictory as they first appear. The view of concepts as theories (Medin, 1998) gains credence from the part of the web of interdependence that consists of conceptually shared world knowledge. The Putnam-Kripke-Fodor use of history in accounting for concepts acknowledges an aspect of causal inheritance. Prototypes deal with the form in which concepts occur and highlight concrete wholistic mental representations. The classical view describes those life games in which people are explicitly seeking to define meanings and essences in terms of necessary and sufficient criterial attributes, something taught and honored in our culture. Connectionism (Rogers & McClelland, 2004) reminds us of a subsymbolic neuronal substrate. Various combination models attempt to bring other theories together. And the ecological approach (which this paper endeavors to clarify and extend) seeks to provide an umbrella understanding in terms of the ways concepts participate in real-world uses.

In summary: the primary unit of meaning is not cognition or language per se but the real-world uses of concepts and categories within the contexts I am calling life games. Cognition rests on the intentions of the person and those in turn emerge from his desires, fears, and past experiences, all of which are the result of the workings of the vast interdependent world (and whatever else one may think guides human life) beyond our view. Our surface conceptual mind can have little grasp of any of this as long as we remain fixated on local causality or constrained by our theories of what a proper scientific model of concepts, categorization, and meaning should look like.

Where Next?

We need to emerge from the current feuding academic theories of concepts, categorization, and the origins of meaning to study these activities in their living context. To break out we need an expansion of perspective. Children begin at a local level of seeking one-on-one causal relations (Gopnik & Meltzoff, 1997) in their quest for mastery of how things work. But here we are as adults still doing that—even when we are scientists, or government officials (the term blowback is used when a myopically local causal manipulation goes wrong), or parents, romantic partners, pet owners... all of it. I honestly think that the study of concepts, categories, signs, and meaning needs just what the rest of the world needs, that the individuals engaged in that study also engage in some form of wisdom practices (and perhaps personal emotion work, see Barron, 2005) so that they can begin to emerge from the cage of the surface conceptual mind and tune in to the broader context of relations that make research and the rest of human life meaningful in the first place. Einstein said that problems can never be solved with the same mind that created them. Those who study concepts might think on that.

18
Lucia Santaella

Professor

São Paulo Catholic University

The omnirelevance of the theory of signs and meaning

1. Working on semiotics below the equator

I did my postgraduate studies in Linguistics and Literary Theory at São Paulo Catholic University in the 1970's. The French intellectual influence on Brazilian academic culture had always been pervasive, but in those times of French structuralism and poststructuralism, this influence was even more intense. São Paulo Catholic University was the first in Brazil to include structuralism in the Humanity programs. Hence, my research at that time was impregnated by the work of Michel Foucault, Louis Althusser, Roland Barthes, Claude Lévi-Strauss, Jacques Derrida, and Jacques Lacan. The main books of these writers were translated and published very early in Brazil by two avant-garde publishing houses, Perspectiva and Cultrix, quite in tune with the most recent European trends in the humanities.

It is curious to note that works of seminal structuralists, such as Ferdinand de Saussure and Louis Hjelmslev, were divulged, translated, and read at the same time and in parallel with their French poststructuralist critics. This is why the difference between structuralism and poststructuralism was never very clear-cut in Brazil. As both arrived simultaneously, the difference or even rupture between the two trends remained somewhat opaque. After all, both structuralism and poststructuralism were being studied in a thread of continuity and the growth of complexity proper of the development of ideas. Nor is it surprising that the great impact which the work of Derrida, under the name of deconstruction, produced in the North-American academic environment was never very well understood in the Brazilian context.

As far as the Brazilian intellectual life is concerned, the above tableau is all part of what Nestor Garcia Canclini, the important Mexican sociologist, has diagnosed as the cultural hybridity characteristic of Latin American countries which has always acquired a peculiar intensity in Brazil. In his award-winning book, *Hybrid Cultures*, Canclini (1989) analyses Latin American cultures as mixed and temporarily multidimensional. The adjective "hybrid" includes notions such as cross-breeding, *mestizo* culture, mixed ethnic groups, miscegenation, syncretism, and religious fusions with indigenous symbols from African and American cultures, and it refers to many other kinds of intercultural mixture, dense intercultural contact, and exchange at the crossroads of highly diverse historical temporalities.

The Latin American culture, despite its affiliation to the Western World and with its predominant languages certainly stemming from the Indo-European root, presents certain peculiarities which distinguish it from the other cultures of the West. Latin American culture evinces certain condiments–sometimes even eccentric or even weird ones –making it mix things up: social strata, diverse temporalities, or high and low cultures. The melting pot of ethnic groups and the phantoms of alterity must have reached a boiling point in Latin America which is much higher than the one allowed by the recipes of order, strict hierarchy, homogenized gestures, and linearity of reasoning.

The emphasis I am giving to these features may give an idea of the cultural frame in which I developed my academic and intellectual career. Despite its interdisciplinary character, it has never lost its center of interest in semiotics. Living in Brazil as well as in any other Latin American country encourages such centralization. Almost twenty years ago, in an article entitled "Brazil: a culture in tune with semiotics" written for T. A. Sebeok and J. Umiker-Sebeok's *Semiotic Web* of 1990, I argued that culture in Brazil is a semiotic culture in which nonverbal signs are a large-scale phenomenon extending not only throughout daily life but also into popular festivals, informal celebrations, and formal ceremonies, not only in formal, informal, and spontaneous processes of teaching and learning but also in the activities of scientific research. Brazilian culture is fundamentally an oral, visual, tactile, and corporeal culture. This is why folklorists, anthropologists, and ethnomusicologists from other countries have displayed so much interest in the exuberance of the Brazilian nonverbal manifestations, which is more than the attraction exerted by any exoticism on foreigners. In the whole country, irrespective of the degree of development or social class, apparent or concealed, there is a copious stream of nonverbal culture, especially in music and dance.

Under these circumstances, it is not by chance that, every semester for the last thirty-two years without interruption, I have been giving graduate courses on semiotics. From all over Brazil, these students converge in São Paulo Catholic University, attracted by the possibility of studying semiotics in the only graduate program in Semiotics in the country. As a member of a postgraduate program which originated in Literary Theory (1970) and was later extended to Communication Studies and Semiotics (1978), I was twice fortunate to belong to this university. On the one hand, literary theory was the first area to bring semiotics to Brazil, on the other, this program offered me the privilege of becoming a student of two of the eminent founders of the concrete poetry movement, Haroldo de Campos and Décio Pignatari.

The semiotic orientation of concrete poetry is well known. Concrete poetry has faced the task of rethinking the poetic code as well as a broad spectrum of questions concerning the techniques and problems of composition, structure, form, dynamic movement, isomorphism which this rethinking involves. The starting point was the statement that a poem exists in a graphic space, a plastic field which sets in motion the use of typefaces in various sizes and shapes as well as the positioning of printed lines as essential elements of composition and the generation of meaning. A new dynamic syntax was the result. Operating by juxtaposition, superimposition, interposition, dismemberment, or derivation of the design of the signs and shapes, this syntax could no longer be considered from a merely grammaticolinguistic point of view but had to include multiple relationships between materials and significations on the page. It is on this basis that concrete poetry creates the intersemiotic potential of which poetry can be the bearer. It was not by chance that the work of these poets led to a crisis in the traditional methods of reading and criticism until then considered exclusively literary.

Under the influence of the concrete poets, who brought their poetic creativity also to their academic activity, I came to see literature in close connection with the visual arts, music, film, and other sign systems in a web of relations which included the semiotics of poetic translation and the translation between systems of signs which Roman Jakobson had called intersemiotic translation. These connections became ubiquitous when the program enlarged its orientation from literary theory to "Communication and Semiotics" with an emphasis on the interrelations between music, visual arts, literature, and the mass media. It was at that time, five years after my PhD, that I was incorporated as a professor in the same program of which I had been a student. Attracted by semiotics, my students came from diverse backgrounds: literature, arts, geology, journalism, film studies, even mathematics and medicine. They intended to rethink their own field of research in light of semiotics. This was a challenge that I could face due to the audacity proper of youth and to the fact that by that time I had already been submerged for some years in my research on Charles S. Peirce's philosophy and semiotics in which I could find fertile means to face interdisciplinarity.

Although I was to become a Peirce scholar, it was not in Peirce's writings that I began my studies of semiotics during my graduate studies but in Saussure's, Hjelmslev's, Barthes's, and Greimas's parallel with the study of the works of the Russian Formalists, the Prague School, and the Bakhtinian Circles. I also had the privilege of being a student of the outstanding Brazilian specialist in Russian studies, Boris Schnaiderman who was a professor of the University of São Paulo, but occasionally also a visiting professor of my own university. Besides being poets and academics, Haroldo de Campos and Décio Pignatari (who completed 80 years in 2007) were also authors of theoretical works. Both also served as advisors to the excellent publishing houses Perspectiva and Cultrix. De Campos and Pignatari did not only introduce Peirce's semiotics to Brazil, but they also organized the translation of books of such well-known Peircean semioticians of their time as Max Bense and Umberto Eco.

The first time I heard about Peirce was from Décio Pignatari in a class in which he briefly introduced Peirce's famous triad of the icon, the index, and the symbol. That classification intrigued me, and looking for more information about it, I could find in Eco's *Struttura Assente* the expansion of this triad into the three trichotomies of qualisign/icon/rheme, sinsign/index/dicent, and legisign/symbol/argument. Eco's brief but talented presentation fascinated me, and I immediately recognized that those classifications of signs opened a promising path for fertile analysis and understanding of the most diverse systems of signs besides the verbal ones. Peirce's classification of signs became highly influential in the Brazilian context. As poets, Haroldo de Campos and Décio Pignatari were interested in the consequences that could be derived from the theory of iconicity for the study of poetry and the arts. The insights gained from this new perspective as well as the typically Brazilian antilogocentrism make it easy to understand why the category of firstness and its possible applications has always been privileged by semioticians in this country.

In those years, the importation of books to Brazil was extremely difficult and expensive. Thus, I had to wait until a friend went to the States to bring to me the eagerly awaited volumes of the *Collected Papers*. At this point, in 1972, I began my exploration of Peirce's writings which has continued until today. From phenomenology and semiotics, which took me years to penetrate, I gradually began to scrutinize Peirce's entire philosophical architecture. In the history of philosophy, most of the philosophers that I read, and they were not few, were always read in parallel with and as a means to better understand Peirce.

In the long course of the development of my perusal of Peirce's work–a perusal which confirmed Peirce's notion that our ideas evolve by creative love–there was a remarkable fact that was decisive for my richer understanding of Peirce in particular and semiotics in general, my participation, both in 1983 and in 1985, in the memorable International Summer Institutes for Semiotic and Structural Studies organized by Thomas Sebeok in Bloomington, Indiana, at that time the most outstanding semiotic center in the whole world. In 1993, I had the opportunity of attending courses given by Umberto Eco, John Deely, Joseph Ransdell, and Michael A. K. Halliday, in 1985, by Gerard Deledalle, Thomas Sebeok himself, and Erika Fischer-Lichte. It was also during both Institutes that I met, and became friend with, Dines Johansen who, by the way, generously gave to me a copy of hundreds of pages containing his notes from and on Peirce's manuscripts, which he had taken during his year as a visiting scholar at Indiana University. Besides the Institute, I also paid several visits to the Peirce Edition Project where I met Max Fisch and profited from his generosity of opening his precious archives for my consultation.

I can say that these two stages in Indiana worked as a great divide in my academic life, particularly in my research on Peirce. Ransdell's course was superb, and since then his writings have illuminated my reading of Peirce's work. In my judgment, Ransdell is indeed one of the most lucid and brilliant interpreters of the intricacies of Peirce's philosophy and semiotics. With his thorough exegesis of Peirce's writings, Ransdell produces a personal interpretation without loosing the due loyalty to Peirce's ideas.

Furthermore, Ransdell brings Peirce's concepts to the face of the contemporary debates of ideas, highlighting Peirce's philosophy and semiotics and contribution to them at the same time. I certainly owe a lot to many of Peirce's interpreters but, since 1983, my understanding of semiotics has been profoundly in debt to Ransdell's writings.

2. Thirty-seven years of semiotic endeavor

With the exception of psychoanalysis and my constant reading of Freud and Lacan, I gradually began to leave behind the poststructuralist and other trends of semiotics in the back of my mind to dedicate myself more and more to the study of Peirce's writings. This project meant several research residences at Indiana University, from 1987 to 1994. In fact, for decades Peirce's semiotics has been at the foundation of my work as a scholar and author. However, as my students are not philosophers but come from diverse areas of communication studies and the arts, semiotic concepts had to be put to the test of being applied. Facing the necessity of understanding the specific sign systems with which the students work to guarantee the dialogue between semiotics and communication studies, I was led to pursue in depth studies in films, advertising, and in the visual arts. Fortunately, my background in music made things easier in this field. Since communication is embedded in culture making the two inseparable, theoretical and applied cultural studies with the explicit or implicit support of semiotics has always been a strong facet of my work.

Being the author of twenty-nine books and nearly three hundred articles and the editor of another eleven, I think I am authorized to say that I am a prolific writer. My books can be clearly divided into two groups, those dedicated to the work of C. S. Peirce and those dedicated to topics of culture, more recently cyberculture. From a semiotic point of view, I have been discussing the current reconstitutions of social, cultural, and artistic lives and their impact on the psyche and the body of human beings.

Peirce has been the topic of eight of my books and one more in progress. Without premeditation, but as a result of pure instinct–in the sense that Peirce gives to this word, that is, a capacity to guess–these books have followed the hierarchical organization of Peirce's architecture of philosophical disciplines. My first booklet, *O que é semiótica?* (*What is semiotics?*), addressed to beginners, is mainly dedicated to semiotic phenomenology. Since 1983, the title has sold more than a hundred and thirty thousand copies in Brazil. Under the title of *A assinatura das coisas* (*The signature of things*), looking for the roots of the semiotics of literature, I gave a general account of Peirce's classification of the sciences, the role of his philosophical architecture in this system, and of the place of literature in the whole. The next book, on the *General Theory of Signs*, was dedicated to Peirce's first branch of semiotics. The headings of its chapters are able to give a good idea of its contents: the sign, the object, the interpretant, and the sign revisited. Next came another booklet, at present being enlarged, about Peirce's theory of perception (*A percepção: Uma teoria semiótica*), followed by one which addresses Peirce's aesthetics as one of the normative science (*Estética de Platão a Peirce*). The sequel was a book dedicated to the second and third branches of semiotics, the three kinds of reasoning (abduction, induction, deduction), and methodeutics (*O método anticartesiano de C. S. Peirce*). The book in progress touches metaphysical questions in an approach towards the theory of a pervasive semiosphere based on Peirce's concepts of tychism and synechism. Pressed by the students' interest in applied semiotics, I wrote a book specifically turned to facilitate the work of students whose aim is to find the paths for the application of Peirce's semiotic concepts to concrete processes of signs (*Semiótica aplicada*).

Although many of my articles are published in English and other languages, all of my books, with the exception of the Spanish title *Imagen: Comunicación, semiótica y medios*, written with Winfried Nöth, are in Portuguese, which has greatly diminished their potential of reaching an international readership. Among my books on Peirce, the most relevant and certainly the most ambitious is probably *Matrizes da linguagem e pensamento: Sonora, visual, verbal* (*Matrices of language and thought: Acoustic, visual, and verbal*) which brought me the most important book prize of Brazil, *Jabuti*, in 2002. According to Winfried Nöth, who wrote the preface to the book, its central thesis confronts us with a paradox. "On the one hand, sign systems are manifested in metabolic processes of permanent mutation and the media universe produces a multiform hybridization of codes, on the other hand, the semiotic study of this diversity reveals that there are only three semiotic matrices from which, through processes of combinations and mixtures, the multiplicity of different sign forms are generated".

It is not difficult to recognize that the thesis of the three matrices is founded on Peirce's three categories of firstness, secondness, and thirdness. In Nöth's judgment, the innovative hypothesis is that there is a basic correspondence between Peirce's categories, human perception, and sign systems: sound belongs to the matrix of firstness, the one of the icon; vision to the matrix of secondness and the index, whereas verbal language falls into the domain of thirdness and of the symbol. Due to manifold mixtures of the three categories, each of the three matrices is triadically subdivided into nine modalities, their further combination and mixture resulting in twenty-seven modalities for each matrix in a total of eighty-one modalities of sign systems. The classification can be applied to a variety of sign processes from music to film, from poetry to the visual arts.

From 1978 until today, I have been the principal adviser of no less than 168 MA and PhD dissertations, all of them related to semiotics in some way or other. Since 1995, I have been the director of the Center of Peirce Studies at São Paulo Catholic University, which congregates students with an interest in developing in depth research in Peirce's writings. Numerous international congresses, colloquia, and symposia on semiotics have been organized by me since 1985, in which many semioticians of international renown have participated.

In sum, since the early 1970's until today, my intellectual endeavor has unceasingly been devoted to the development and consolidation of semiotic studies in Brazil. Although I have certainly not been alone in this enterprise, it has been a task which has always been in the center of my scholarly interests.

3. The interdisciplinary scope of semiotics

Since the nineteen-sixties, there has been an enormous expansion of the semiotic field: from textual structures to communication in general, from human verbal to nonverbal communication, and from human to animal communication. Under the name of zoosemiotics, the latter was one of Thomas A. Sebeok's major contributions to the semiotic field. According to Sebeok, semiosis begins with the origins of life. Hence, semiotics and biology have the same object of study, although their perspectives of study differ. With the new interdiscipline of biosemiotics, semiotic processes in microorganisms and cells, including those that take place within the human body, began to be investigated. In sum: as the semiotic investigations proceeded, they allowed an increasingly broad recognition of a variety of sign processes: microsemiosis, endosemiosis, mycosemiosis, phytosemiosis, and more recently ecosemiosis. Besides all these domains of the organic, with the development of computers and digital culture, the domain of nonliving systems from machines and computers to artificial intelligence and artificial life constituted a new challenge for semiotic research.

Fundamental questions discussed during this phase of expansion are: Is semiotics a scientific field, a discipline, or an interdisciplinary method? Is it is a theory, a method, a metatheoretical perspective, or is it an art? The difficulty of arriving at an immediate answer is evidence of a pluralist field of inquiry in which differences seem to be the rule, and therefore it is necessary and better to distinguish between theoretical, formal, and applied, empirical, experimental, or descriptive semiotics, between general and special, regional and global, critical and comparative semiotics. The semiotic fact that any science and any discipline involves sign processes places semiotics in the position of a metadiscipline which is by nature multidisciplinary. Hence, semiotics is necessarily in dialogue with interdisciplinary fields of inquiry such as hermeneutics, gestalt theory, information theory, system theory. Furthermore, there is also an explicit and implicit semiotics, in the latter of which researchers deal with signs without being aware or admitting doing so.

Faced with this diversity, I have come to the conclusion that there are two types of semiotic theories, namely general and special semiotics. Semiotics of culture, semiotics of space, visual semiotics, or narrative semiotics are special types of semiotics in the sense in which Peirce defined the idioscopic sciences, that is, sciences that have an empirical territory of investigation. General or formal, on the other hand, are the characteristics of the semiotics developed by Peirce. This does not involve the claim of any superiority for Peirce's semiotics, but it does involve the necessity of a distinction between the nature and the scope of a special and a general semiotics.

Although I have written a book of applied semiotics, in which Peirce's theory of signs has been applied to the study of diverse sign processes, I am convinced that application does not exhaust the real scope of Peirce's semiotics. For years and at several occasions, I have defended the idea that following Peirce's vision means to explore his work and thought as a general map towards inquiry in general. I am aware that this sounds like an echo of Apel's claim that Peirce's pragmaticism should be taken as the outline of and the program for a future logic of science. However, it is true that I had begun to defend a similar idea several years before learning about Apel's thesis.

This is not to say that scholars in film, television, music, art, or internet studies may not profit from the powerful theory of signs which Peirce's semiotics offers as a tool of investigation to back up their studies of signification. Nevertheless, it can not be forgotten that Peirce's semiotics is a philosophical discipline, or better, the third of the normative sciences and as such the most theoretical of the theoretical sciences, which means that it is a formal and abstract science disconnected from the practical concerns that affect applied semiotics. Hence, the philosophical and cognitive scopes of Peirce's semiotic concepts should not be underestimated. It is the abstraction of his concepts in their interrelations that allow them to work as a logical diagram, as a conceptual map for the more specialized theories of the idioscopic sciences, as he called them. Indeed, it is the uncommon level of generality of Peirce's concepts which turns possible their broad range of applications to the most diverse fields of knowledge.

Peirce's endeavor was to create elementary and systematic conceptions in order to turn philosophy itself into a science applying in philosophy, with all necessary modifications, the methods of observation, hypothesis, and experiment of the natural sciences. Hence, he created a system *of* and *for* scientific thought as a guideline for the development of an authentically scientific understanding of any special philosophical field.

Peirce's classifications, which are not classifications *sensu stricto*, have to be interpreted in the framework of the logic of vagueness and the doctrine of continuity. Thus, they provide the necessary grounds for dealing with the complex problems of ontology, epistemology, philosophy of mind, philosophy of science, and all other subdivisions of philosophical thought to which Peirce intended to lay a common semiotic ground and to contribute a new perspective according to which semiosis is synonymous with intelligence, continuity, learning, growth, and life. Peirce's semiotic foundation of the sciences was based on a method whose aim was the development of a highly abstract conception of mind derived from the study of an evolutionary tendency towards truth which he postulated to exist in the depths of the human soul.

4. The relevance of the theories of signs and meaning

Of my semiotic leitmotifs, the most pervasive one has probably been the idea that signs are undergoing an uninterrupted expansion at an ever increasing speed, a major evidence of this growth being the emergence of the new technologies of communication. The exponential progression of this growth has been the cause of much intellectual concern on the part of social scientists. From a semiotic point of view, it is most certainly evidence of the expansion of the semiosphere in which signs are destined to ever increasing proliferation.

In the nineteenth century, Charles Baudelaire interpreted the city as a forest of symbols, but today we know that the whole planet and its galactic environment, our homes and our own bodies are dense forests of the most diverse kinds of signs, images, signals, and symbols. The global semiotic diversity is expanding in its vastness and profundity, and this expansion demands from us an interaction not reduced to the level of mere intuition. Instead, permanent advances towards a more critical and reflexive dialogue with signs are required. The most apparent relevance of the theory of signs and meaning is to give us the ability to read and interact with signs with analytical penetration. Considering that the proliferation of signs is not limited to certain fields of knowledge but appears everywhere and that the production of meaning demands understanding, we can conclude that the relevance of the theory of signs is ubiquitous.

Even in physics, a field which until recently was dominated by the laws of mechanical causation, with the advances of science and technology, physicists are beginning to recognize that we are living in a world in which matter speaks. In the organic world, the study of the fantastic codifying machinery of the cell has given plenty of evidence that biology is a semiotic science. After all, the components of the organic cell are able to recognize, memorize, copy, replicate, multiply, differentiate, prescribe instruction, direct, guide, regulate, control, store, transfer, and transmit information, and they can respond, communicate, obey rules, correct errors, edit, incorporate new information, and finally mutate. Since the 1970's, the study of such processes has been the aim of the new biosemiotic research paradigm of a number of outstanding scholars who have given evidence that semiotic concepts are more pertinent to the understanding of the secrets of the living world than any concept imported from the information sciences.

In the biological world beyond the human realm, Peirce's phenomenology, semiotics, and philosophy have shown to be increasingly relevant. At the root of this relevance is Peirce's notion of final causality, which allows biology to go beyond the bare limits of physicalism and explore a new conception of teleology free from determinism and metaphysical burdens.

A further important aspect of Peirce's relevance to contemporary thought, which I have been focusing on for years, is its interdisciplinarity. Since the 1950's, together with the emergence of new paradigms in the sciences, scientists have been proclaiming the necessity of interdisciplinarity. In this context, I have become convinced that Peirce's classification of the sciences, updated and founded on his architectonic philosophy, can function as a cartography for the implementation of guiding principles toward interdisciplinarity. Semiotics questions raised in this respect are: How can interdisciplinarity be approached without some kind of guide and signalization? How can the frontiers imposed by the extreme specialization of the sciences be transposed? How can the fragmentation of knowledge be overcome?

Some years ago, at the occasion of his being awarded an important prize of the *National Endowment for the Humanities*, the late Walker Percy emphatically proposed that Peirce's monumental scientific and philosophical work may function as an antidote against the separations of the sciences. In Peirce's work, Percy affirmed, one can find the most sophisticated and complex paths to reflect on and to accomplish the tasks of interdisciplinarity. In the same line of argument, I may add that the transdisciplinary cartography of the sciences designed by Peirce is founded on a philosophy of science and a philosophy of nature which enables us to face the challenges posed by contemporary techno-scientific advances.

Without following the easier and more common roads suggested by pseudo-scientific mysticisms, without having to abandon the modern conquests of specialization, Peirce's architecture of the sciences provides us with keys for the comprehension of the subtle webs of interrelation between the different sciences. Although a comprehensive classification of the sciences in their present state of the art seems hardly possible any more, given the impressive development and the many new subdivisions and ramifications of the sciences during the last century, Peirce's classification allows us to visualize the intricate web of the sciences with the many interdependencies among them. To Peirce, knowledge substantially embraces everything that we think or say, and this is why so many orders of the universe of science are possible. The most useful modes of classification of the sciences are those which consider the logical interdependencies between their levels of specialization. Indeed, the most fundamental aspect of such classification is its being supported by a philosophy able to provide the sciences with ontological and epistemological principles founded on a broad logic conceived of as a semiotics founded itself on phenomenology.

5. Open problems and paths to the future

It is difficult to speak about the problems which have remained open in our field of knowledge without imposing the perspective given by the state of the art of our own research. Aware of this fact, I will not try and go beyond my personal point of view but will, on the contrary, fully assume it. My most recent concern, addressed in my presidential lecture for the Charles S. Peirce Society in December 2007, is turned to what I decided to call "pervasive semiosis". A few years ago, I stated the following five steps leading the main ideas which have been guided this work in progress:

1. The radical antidualism and evolutionism implied in Peirce's synechistic ideas, have to be taken to their ultimate consequences. According to these ideas, there are no strict separations or divisions between the classes and categories of study but only differences of degree between nature and culture, between the organic and the inorganic, the psychical and the physical.

2. Peirce's disturbing semiotic credo that "all this universe is perfused with signs if it is not composed exclusively of signs" (CP 5.448, n.1) can only be properly understood in the light of his synechism.

3. Peirce's even more disturbing statement that "matter is effete mind, inveterate habits becoming physical laws" (CP 6.24), can only be properly understood in light of his broad concept of mind and in the context of his theory of final causation.

4. Final causation can only be properly understood from the perspective of semiosis. It is in Peirce's classification of signs in the range from quasi-signs to genuine signs that we find the basis for the analysis of the different degrees of semiosis from the inorganic to the organic, from the physical to the psychical, from protosemiosis to the most developed forms of semiosis, namely, in the self-control that human reason can exercise over thought and conduct.

5. Metaphysics and semiotics will appear even more deeply connected when we consider that Peirce's emphasis on continuity was vital to his evolutionary logic and pragmatism. His methodeutics, the liveliest branch of semiotics, highlights the scientific method as the prototype of final causation. The laws of nature have been discovered by abductive inference, revealing an affinity between the human mind and the design of nature. Hence, the formal laws of thought are not simply laws of our mind but laws of the intelligibility of things.

These five steps have been my working hypotheses for the proposal of an all-encompassing concept of a semiosphere and the omnipresence of semiosis in the universe; its elaboration will certainly still take many years of my intellectual life.

19
John Searle

Slusser Professor of Philosophy
Department of Philosophy
University of California, Berkeley

---

1. Why were you initially drawn to the theory of signs and meaning?

I am somewhat hesitant to the word "signs" because most of the things I deal with in my work in the philosophy of language are not literally signs, but words, sentences, speech acts, and texts of various kinds. The stop sign on the road outside my window is literally a sign. The words that I am now writing on this page are not literally signs; they are words. However, if we interpret the question to ask "How was I initially drawn to questions in the philosophy of language and to some extent in linguistics?" then here is the answer: when I first seriously began the study of philosophy in Oxford in the early 1950s, the dominant strand in Oxford philosophy, and by far the most exciting area of research going on in philosophy in the world at the time, was the philosophy of language. Many people felt that all, or at any rate many, of the traditional philosophical problems could be solved by paying close attention to language, and even those of us who did not believe that the analysis of language would provide the solution to all of our philosophical worries, were fascinated by questions about language. The central question was, "How do words relate to the world? How do we get from sounds to reality?" And the answer, of course, is that we get from sound to reality because the sounds have meanings, and speakers utter the sounds with intentions that convey meanings. But that opens the next question: "What is meaning?" So the two most fascinating questions to me were really the same question in different formulations: What is the relationship between words and the world? What is the nature of meaning?

There were two strands to the approach to the language in the heyday of so-called "ordinary language philosophy". One was based on the supposition that all (or perhaps many or at least some) philosophical questions could be solved by paying close attention to the use of words. For example, many people thought that the correct way to answer skepticism was to show that traditional skeptical arguments rested on a systematic misuse of words like "know", "evidence", "certain", "reason", etc. This was the view of philosophy according to which philosophical problems arise when we fail to understand the actual functioning of words. And we solve the philosophical problems by bringing a word back to its real-life use and away from its abstract philosophical misinterpretation. The leading theorist on this conception was, of course, Wittgenstein. And Austin, though he was not at all influenced by Wittgenstein, held a version of this view. The second strand was to me more interesting and that was the idea that language was an object of philosophical study in its own right. The main purpose of investigating language was not just to solve traditional problems by examining the use of words. Rather, the aim was to get a general, systematic account of speech and language. And in this field, my work was concerned with speech acts. I had no objection to studying language for the purpose of solving traditional problems, but that was not my primary objective. My first book *Speech Acts* stated an overall position and then in subsequent works, notably in *Expression and Meaning*, I went into more detail on such topics as metaphor, fiction, indirect speech acts, etc. In my book *Intentionality*, I tried to show how linguistic meaning and speech acts in general were based on more biologically fundamental forms of intentionality of the mind. And in my book *The Construction of Social Reality*, I tried to show how language enables us to create an institutional reality of money, property, government, marriage, etc.

2. What do you consider your contribution to the field?

I have written a fairly large number of books and articles about the philosophy of language, and I will not attempt to summarize them all here. Much of my work was concerned with the theory of speech acts. How is it possible, and how does it work in detail, that when I make these sounds through my mouth or these marks on paper, I can make a statement or ask a question or make a promise or give an order, request, apology, thanks, etc.? I think the fundamental unit of meaning in human communication is the speech act of the type that Austin baptized as "illocutionary acts." The parts of my work in the philosophy of language that I feel best about have to do with the general theory of speech acts as stated in two books of mine, *Speech Acts* and *Expression and Meaning*, and within the general theory, the accounts of meaning and its relation to intentionality that I give especially in my book *Intentionality*, and the attempt to use all of that, both to give a taxonomy of speech acts as I give in my article "A Taxonomy of Illocutionary Acts" and also to relate the theory of speech acts to the philosophy of mind in general.

I said I would not summarize my various claims, but I will list half a dozen of my results that had proved influential, at least in the sense that they have provoked discussion–sometimes agreement, sometimes disagreement:

1. *Speech Acts*. My first serious effort in the philosophy of language was the analysis of speech acts and that culminated in *Speech Acts: An Essay in the Philosophy of Language* (1969). This was one of the first systematic attempts to get a general theory of speech acts. One way to see the book is as an attempt to combine Austin's theory of speech acts with Grice's theory of meaning and put them together in a systematic fashion. It is important for me to emphasize how much my work owes to the work of my teachers Austin, Grice, and Strawson, and I think especially to Austin.

2. *Intentionality*. In my book *Intentionality: An Essay in the Philosophy of Mind* (1983), I tried to show how the philosophy of language is grounded in the philosophy of mind. Fundamental linguistic notions such as meaning and speech acts are derived from and dependent on the more fundamental forms of intentionality of the mind. Meaning, as applied to words and sentences, is an extension of the more fundamental intentionality of beliefs, desires and other mental states.

3. *"Ought" from "Is"*. Once you understand the commitments that are built into the structure of speech acts, then you can see that the traditional doctrine that one cannot derive an "ought" from an "is", that no set of descriptive statements can ever entail an evaluative statement, is false. Of course you can derive evaluative statements from descriptive

statements because the whole notion of a descriptive statement is already an evaluative notion. The notions in which the traditional doctrines were stated, notions like "entailment", "validity", "meaning," "statement," and "truth" already contain evaluative components. The first place where I published this was in an article "How to Derive 'Ought' from 'Is'", *Philosophical Review*, 1964. So this is one area where my work in the philosophy of language actually did have an application to traditional problems.

4. *Taxonomy of Speech Acts.* One much discussed work was my attempt to get a systematic theoretically motivated taxonomy of speech acts. My analysis of meaning attempts to show that there are really only five different possible types of speech acts and all of the others can be seen as variations and permutations on those five. These five are Assertives, where we try to tell people how things are (for example, statements), Directives where we try to get them to do things (for example, orders and commands), Commissives where we commit ourselves to courses of action (for example, promises), Expressives where we express our feelings and attitudes (for example, apologizing and thanking), and Declarations where we bring about changes in the world through our utterances (for example, when we declare war or adjourn a meeting by saying "War is declared" or "The meeting is adjourned").

5. *Social Ontology.* I regard my work on social ontology as essentially an extension of my work in the philosophy of language. Basically, we create an institutional reality of money, property, government, marriage, universities, cocktail parties, etc. by using words in certain ways and I have written a book trying to explain that, *The Construction of Social Reality* (1995), and I am working now on another book in which I extend the analysis. The basic idea is that human social-institutional reality is created by a certain type of linguistic representation. These representations I call "status function Declarations", and I will say more about them later in this interview. But right now, I want to emphasize that when create money, private property, or a government, we are creating a set of power relations and these power relations work because we use language to create a set of facts which give people desire-independent reasons for acting; that

is, reasons which are independent of their immediate inclinations.

6. *Systematic Theories.* Perhaps the most influential feature of this work is one that is so to speak invisible. By attempting to get an account of language which was systematic and theoretical, I went against the grain of Wittgensteinian ordinary language philosophy. Wittgenstein tried to teach us that we could not have theories in philosophy and especially we could not have theories about language. We could only "assemble reminders for a purpose", but language is so various and so unsystematic and so complex that it would be impossible to have a general theory of language, meaning or speech acts. I tried to show by example that that view is mistaken. The best way to refute this antitheoretical conception is to actually create a general theory or set of general theories and that is what I have tried to do.

I have worked on a whole lot of other topics concerning language and meaning, and I would not want to give the impression that these half dozen that I mention are the only ones I am interested in. For reasons of space, I confine my discussion to these few. I have also written on reference, metaphor, indirect speech acts, fiction, predication and a whole lot of other subjects in the philosophy of language.

3. What is the proper role of a theory of signs and meaning in relation to other academic disciplines?

Remembering that I am interpreting "signs and meaning" to mean the study of language, or the philosophy of language. I think that the study of meaning, in my sense, is absolutely crucial for a number of academic disciplines besides just philosophy. The one that interests me most, and the one I have been working on for the past few years, is the role of language in the constitution of social and institutional reality. Most of the world exists independently of our representation of it. Molecules, mountains and tectonic plates exist regardless of how we think of them or describe them, and they would continue to exist, even if we had never invented any of these words that I just used to name them. But when it comes to money, property, government and marriage, all of these exist only in so far as they are represented as existing, and their representation is linguistic representation. I regard this is an absolutely fascinating field of investigation, and I have written one book about it already, *The Construction of Social Reality*, and I am working on a second book, developing the ideas further.

I think the social sciences have had inadequate theoretical foundations. Human societies differ importantly from the forms of society that exist among other species, even other primate species. What is the difference? One could begin to state the difference by saying that humans have a language in a way that other species do not. Other species have signaling systems, some of them quite complex. But with human language, we have the remarkable capacity to create what I call "status functions." These are functions that an object or a person can perform only because the object or person is recognized as having a certain status and with that status, a function that can only be performed in virtue of that collective recognition. Examples are pretty much everywhere. The President of the United States, a ten dollar bill, and the University of California, Berkeley are all examples of status functions. Status functions can only exist in so far as they are represented as existing. I will say more about this in answer to a later question.

4. What do you consider the most important topics and/or contributions in the theory of meaning and signs?

There are so many topics and important contributions, that I really cannot list all of them. Let me just pick a few highlights.

Frege. The entire subject was invented by Gottlob Frege in the late nineteenth and early part of the twentieth century. Most of what happened after Frege are responses to Frege's philosophy of language.

Russell's "On Denoting". A decisive event in the history of philosophy occurred a little over a hundred years ago when Bertrand Russell published his classic article "On Denoting". This article, though generally misunderstood at the time of its publication, was immensely influential in philosophy for a number of reasons. First of all, it showed how to use the methods of logical and linguistic analysis to solve philosophical problems. And a second feature was that it actually used the logic that had been invented by Gottlob Frege, what later was called the predicate calculus or first order logic, and this inspired a large number of important philosophers to use logical methods of this kind in solving philosophical problems. And third, it was done without the epistemological obsession that had characterized the history of philosophy, and it was not in any sense a phenomenological analysis. Russell did not ask himself what it felt like to utter the sentence "The King of France is bald," nor did he ask himself how he knew that the King of France did not exist. He just stated the truth conditions. That is, his philosophical method was neither phenomenological nor epistemological. It was analytic.

The Tractatus. A subsequent important development was Wittgenstein's *Tractatus Logico-Philosophicus*. It is a very complex work and it was immensely influential; however its influence has waned. One hears very little about it now, and I won't attempt to discuss it here.

Logical Positivism. An important subsequent influence was really crucial in the history of philosophy and the history of intellectual life generally, and that was the movement known as "Logical Positivism". The logical positivists thought that most of traditional philosophy was simply meaningless. I don't think anyone today accepts the positivist doctrine that traditional metaphysics is meaningless but the positivists did help to create a type of analytic philosophy: The positivists thought that all meaningful utterances were either analytic or empirically verifiable, that is, they were either true or false by definition or they were true or false as a matter of empirical fact. All else was meaningless. This thesis was called "The Verification Principle." It did not survive very long, but it did lead to a certain conception of philosophy which survived for a long time and is in some sense still influential and that is as follows:

Conceptual Analysis. The aim of philosophy is to state the truths. And what sorts of truths can the philosopher state? Well, the philosopher does not do lab-research, so he does not attempt to state empirical truths. But now, because of Hume's famous proof that it is impossible to derive an "ought" from an "is", it is impossible that there can be any true statements in ethics. The function of ethical statements is not to state truths, but rather to express our feelings and attitudes to try to encourage people in certain sorts of behavior and so on. So the traditional task of the philosopher of giving a large picture of reality would be excluded because these would be synthetic propositions and would have to be verifiable like any other scientific proposition. And another traditional task of the philosopher, to tell people how they ought to live, is also removed, because statements about how one ought to live cannot be true or false, and it is the aim of the philosopher, as in any other systematic discipline, to state the truth. What is left then is that philosophy analyzes language and particularly analyzes the conceptual relations between language, experience and the world. So the topic of ethics, for example, was transformed into the study of ethical language or ethical discourse. On this view then, which was dominant in the middle decades of the twentieth century, the aim of the philosopher is conceptual analysis.

I have attacked various aspects of this conception of philosophy, one of which I mention above, the supposed dichotomy between fact and value, between descriptive statements and evaluative statements, but a second aspect I have also criticized and that is the conception that philosophy can only do conceptual analysis, that the philosopher can only state analytic truths which are the results of his analysis of the various concepts to be found in language. What actually happens when you are really working on a serious problem is that you don't have much use for these sharp distinctions between the analytic and the empirical, the conceptual and the substantive. For example, a few paragraphs back I said that all human institutional reality is partly constituted by language. Now, is that statement analytic or empirical? It is a bit of both. That is, it is an essential characteristic of institutions like money and private property that they can only exist if they have a linguistic component, if they are represented as what they are, and that makes the proposition look analytic, but then of course it is a contingent fact that we have these institutions at all and that they function the way they do. Philosophers continue correctly to be obsessed by conceptual worries and these are in a broad sense linguistic investigations. But it is a mistake in proceeding with these investigations to make too sharp a distinction between the linguistic and the non-linguistic, between the conceptual and the substantive. And similarly it is a mistake to make a sharp distinction between philosophy and the sciences. I find my work on the philosophy of mind, for example, to be constantly using results from the neurosciences and contributing to the neuroscience discussion. With the decline of the acceptance of these two distinctions, between analytic and synthetic, and between descriptive and evaluative utterances, philosophy has become much messier but much more interesting.

Later Wittgenstein. Wittgenstein's later work, culminating in his *Philosophical Investigations* (1953) had a profound influence on philosophy. Wittgenstein thought that it was a mistake to get general theories of language and he thought that philosophy should be, in a sense, a "therapeutic" discipline in which one tries to remove philosophical puzzles by analyzing the ordinary use of words: what Wittgenstein called "language games."

Linguistic Pragmatics. Part of the heyday of conceptual analysis, and in a sense part of the same movement, was the growth of the study of the use of language by philosophers such as Austin, Grice and myself. I think that in the philosophy of language, this is the most useful line to pursue. This branch of the study of language is sometimes called "pragmatics."

5. What are the most important open problems in this field and what are the prospects for progress?

I think a lot of the current research in philosophy of language suffers from a kind of scholasticism whereby the authors go round and round the same sets of questions about reference, semantics and truth. There is a great deal of technical expertise combined with philosophical superficiality. However, I don't wish to condemn the scholastic element out of hand, as some important results might still come from this. To me, though, the two most interesting areas of investigation are the following.

First, it seems to me we need a much more naturalistic conception of language than has been characteristic of our tradition. It may seem a strange accusation to say that we have been insufficiently naturalistic because, of course, philosophers such as Quine and Davidson thought of themselves as very much empirical. What I mean by naturalistic is we must show how language is based on prelinguistic, biologically fundamental forms of intentionality. I began that work in my book *Intentionality*, and I am continuing it in a recent article called "What Is Language?"

Second, I am continuing to try to investigate the linguistic basis of all human social ontology. In some abstract sense, everyone would agree that language is the fundamental social institution. You can imagine a society that has language but does not have money, property, government or marriage, but you cannot even imagine a society that has money, property, government and marriage but does not have language. I think everyone would agree to that. The problem is to say exactly how and exactly why is language constitutive of society. The right way to approach this, and the way that I have been approaching it, is this: we ought to be looking for the fundamental principles on which human social ontology is based. I believe that there is in fact a single unifying principle that underlies all of human social and institutional reality. As I mentioned earlier, there is a distinctive and fundamental human social phenomenon and that I call a "status function." A status function is a function that a person or object can perform only in virtue of the fact that there is collective acceptance of the person or object as having a certain status and with that status, a function that can be performed because of that status. I earlier gave some examples: Being a twenty dollar bill, President of the United States, a licensed driver, or a University professor are all examples of status functions.

Status functions are important in human life because they create a species of power. They create a kind of powers that I call "deontic powers," those involving rights, duties, obligations, authorizations, requirements, permissions, etc.

All status functions are created by the same logical linguistic maneuver. The maneuver has the logical form of a Declaration of the sort that I described in my 1974 taxonomy, even though the actual speech acts are not always in the surface form of Declarations. It is an interesting enterprise to try to work out the details of this conception of human social ontology, but I am quite confident that I am on the right track, and I continue to work on these questions.

20
T.L. Short

Private Scholar

---

1. Why were you initially drawn to the theory of signs and meaning?

I am not now nor have I ever been interested in the theory of signs, as that is usually understood. I will not confess even to being a fellow traveler of the semiotics movement. My interest has been in the philosophical issues framed by the success of modern science. I would divide those issues in twain. Firstly, modern science has seemed to entail a mechanistic world-view in which human reality–consciousness, freedom, moral responsibility, aesthetic delight, the pathos of yearning–has no place. Secondly, modern science has seemed to pull the rug out even from under itself, implying that objective knowledge and objective inquiry are impossible. None of this is utterly new: cynicism, skepticism, and the like were debated also in ancient Athens. But it is the success of modern science–the fact that its major theories cannot be dismissed, even though flawed or problematic–that has given old questions new urgency. I turned to the philosophy of C.S. Peirce because Peirce, it seemed and still seems to me, had gone further than anyone else, including any of our contemporaries, in grasping the spirit of modern science and in affirming its promise, while at the same time maintaining its consistency with (in my terms, not Peirce's) human dignity and the ideal of objectivity. I wanted to find out how he did it. This led me, eventually, to his theory of signs, or semeiotic (a spelling he sometimes used, which I have adopted to distinguish this theory from the semiotics movement), as part of his philosophy. I mean 'part'. Contrary to many of Peirce's recent devotees, I do not hold that his philosophy is 'semiotical' from top to bottom. He himself, in his architectonic of the sciences, made semeiotic to be but one of the philosophical sciences, dependent on phaneroscopy (phenomenology), aesthetics, and ethics, and depended on by metaphysics.

My own interest in that theory, likewise, has been limited to its philosophical use.

As this answer may seem to many to be deeply wrong-headed, if not indeed offensive, I shall add some explanations, both as to the limits of Peirce's semeiotic and as to why I view it as important, limited as it is. Let us begin by considering one reason why it may be supposed to apply broadly, as a comprehensive theory of... everything! Semeiotic is divided into three parts: grammar, or sign taxonomy, the logic of inference, and rhetoric (or 'methodeutic'). (In some places, Peirce used 'logic' in this encompassing sense, calling the second branch 'critic'.) Clearly, like logic narrowly construed, semeiotic is an organon. It applies to every study and hence to everything we can study, and hence to everything. Because it covers all forms of representation, it applies to everything representable, and hence to everything. Therefore, it is easily mistaken to be a comprehensive theory of everything. But that is a non sequitur. It is like saying that, because biologists should be logical in their inquiries, biology is logic–a most illogical inference.

In order to explain why I became interested in Peirce's semeiotic, I must first mention its two most striking features (that distinguish it, for example, from Saussure's semiology). One of these is that rhetoric, or the theory of the interpretant, is the key to Peirce's semeiotic. An interpretant of a sign is an actual or potential effect of it *qua* sign; it is how it is or may be interpreted as signifying this or that. Nothing is a sign apart from the ways in which it may justifiably be interpreted. This is utterly characteristic of Peirce's thought, which sees each thing in terms of its relations to other things, its place in the whole, its potential uses, and, hence, with reference to the future. As Max Fisch once said, the fundamental idea in Peirce's theory of signs is not that of sign but is that of semeiosis, or sign-interpretation. But use and justification are purposeful, and therefore semeiosis cannot be explained by mechanical cause and effect alone. The explanation of semeiosis is teleological and belongs to metaphysics and the special sciences; therefore, it is posterior to semeiotic, at least as far as the architectonic ordering of the sciences is concerned.

The second striking feature Peirce's semeiotic is its breadth (I refer to the mature semeiotic alone, not to its precursors in his early thought). Objects signified may be of any ontological category, including qualities, types, laws, fictions, possibilities, and impossibilities. Signs may also be of any category, though those not actual signify only through being instantiated by or embodied in or signified by signs that are actual (for example, examples are signs, and Pegasus is an example of a mythical creature). Signs–samples, examples, diagrams, symptoms, evidences, gestures, words, thoughts, arguments–may be natural or conventional; they may be formed with a purpose to signify or independently of any purpose. Interpretants may be other signs, including thoughts, or they may be habits, actions, or feelings and emotions. Interpreters need not be human and even when human they need not always be conscious of what they are doing. The purposes interpretation serves may be intrinsically semeiotical, that is, satisfied only by signs, as in the arts and sciences, or they may go beyond semeiosis, in effects called practical. All signs are related to their objects by signifying them, i.e., by being so interpretable on some ground; but the grounds of interpretation are various. Grounds may be rules of interpretation, conventional or instinctive, or existential connectedness, such as something's being a cause or an effect, or mere embodiment, as a color sample exhibits its own quality. Semeiosis thus encompasses everything from the actions of the lower animals to science, moral suasion, music, prayer, and mystical experience.

When I was in graduate school, my interest, which I had thought was mostly in logic, turned out to be mostly in the philosophy of mind. Led by the neural-identity theory of mind, then new, which presented itself as an empirical hypothesis, I reflected on how identifications in physical science (e.g., of heat with molecular motion) are made and confirmed, and I concluded that the neural-identity theory could not be established in that way. Those reflections led me into the philosophy of science, which had just become the most exciting area of philosophy, due to the ideas of Karl Popper and to the attack, by Paul Feyerabend, Thomas Kuhn, and others, on the reigning orthodoxy of logical empiricism. Peirce's anticipation of Popper's view of scientific inquiry as conjectural and self-corrective, i.e., as approaching truth on stepping-stones of error, was generally known. But it was not well-known that he had also anticipated the view of Feyerabend et al. that observation, as it embodies general ideas and presupposes general beliefs, is subject to revision as our theories change. It follows that the test of theory against observation is not so straight-forward an affair as had been assumed. It also follows that the meanings of words cannot be established, as empiricists had assumed, by association with types of sensory experience. Meaning does not precede belief and, thus, changes with changes in our theories. All of this was part of Peirce's philosophy. However, remarkably, he did not conclude that truth is relative and that inquiry is subjective. Unlike Feyerabend, who gleefully embraced subjectivism, and Kuhn, who never succeeded in wholly evading relativism, though he agonized over it, Peirce retained the Popperian view that science is self-corrective. It is in that sense objective, though Peirce did not use the word 'objective' in that connection. How did Peirce manage this? It was on that topic that I wrote my dissertation.

I did not cover in that dissertation another respect in which Peirce had anticipated the attack on logical empiricism, namely, the arguments of Kuhn and Stephen Toulmin that revolutions in scientific theory entail changes in ideals of explanation and standards of theory-evaluation. Here, too, the specter of subjectivism shimmers before us, on the moonlit road we are traveling. For, ideals and standards are values, and it has been a persistent theme of modern philosophy that values, as they seem to have no home in reality as portrayed by physics, must be subjective. Once again, the question arises: how did Peirce manage to evade subjectivism and relativism? Or did he simply not see the implications of his own ideas?

Another item omitted from my dissertation was Peirce's theory of signs. At the time, I did not know much about it. Such acquaintance with it as I had, was from George V. Gentry, one of G.H. Mead's students. Gentry emphasized the interpretant, the identification of ultimate logical interpretants with habit-changes, and the dependence of significance thereon–a key teaching that I have retained and elaborated. Although my dissertation advisor was I.C. Lieb, who had written on Peirce's taxonomy of signs and was the first editor of Peirce's letters to Lady Welby, I do not recall ever discussing Peirce's semeiotic with him. Nor did he discuss that theory in the course I had with him, where it would have fit in very well (nor was Peirce mentioned in the course I had with Charles Hartshorne). But when I contemplated turning my dissertation into a book, I thought it should be completed by using Peirce's sign-theory to explain the connection between idea and sensation in perception. How does sensation occasion judgment? How is the particular brought under the general? What is the nexus of experience and theory? The first thing I found is that there was vast confusion about Peirce's semeiotic, and thus began my long detour through the jungles of sign theory, attempting to trace Peirce's semeiotic Nile to its source.

One consequence of the breadth of Peirce's semeiotic is that, by encompassing such a diversity of kinds of sign within one structure, it can account for the connection of thought to mind-independent reality. Signs are not exclusively conceptual and, thus, in their combined uses, they allow thought to break out of its own circle. The crux, here, is that the replica of a symbol is an index and, thus, it can be existentially connected to its object while being general in meaning; that is what happens in perception. To understand this, however, you must first know much about Peirce's conceptions of indices and symbols, legisigns and their replication, and so on–in short, his entire complex though unfinished theory of signs. You must also know his phaneroscopic categories, which semeiotic presupposes. In this way, the argument of my dissertation may be completed, though I have not yet written on perception in the detail I should like to.

A second consequence of the breadth of Peirce's sign-theory is that the fine arts and moral suasion, military commands and moral imperatives, and much else that makes up human experience and human life are encompassed in a semeiotic structure that entails the possibility of objectivity, i.e., corrigibility. Significance is always relative to interpretative purpose, and interpretation, as it has a purpose, is subject to correction. Therefore, even those interpretants that are actions or feelings are subject to correction, as are, then, the signs they interpret. Objectivity, therefore, is not unique to science. As interpretants may be feelings and actions, objectivity extends to our judgments of aesthetic and moral value, to works of art and to feelings of remorse. Indeed, if scientific inquiry presupposes cognitive values–ones not fixed by definition but that are subject to revision–then its own objectivity depends on the objectivity of those values. Again, I should like to develop this use of Peirce's semeiotic in more detail; so far, I have only issued hints.

A third consequence of semeiotic breadth is that it locates human mentality in a continuum with the lower animals and thus with the rest of nature. Animals respond without deliberation but nonetheless purposefully to stimuli, by their actions interpreting scents and sounds as signs of prey or predator. They, too, can make mistakes. Peirce's semeiotic therefore makes significance to be broader than human thought and thus it explains the distinctive features of thought as a special case, especially complicated, of processes found also outside of thought. In particular, significance, whatever the ontological type of the interpretant and no matter the primitiveness of the interpreter, has the characteristic Franz Brentano named 'intentionality' and which he mistakenly supposed to be unique (or nearly so) to the human mind. Intentionality consists in something's 'having an object', where that object may fail to exist or obtain. But wherever there is interpretation, there is the possibility of error; hence, signification is of that which may in fact not exist or obtain. Any explanation of semeiosis therefore explains intentionality. In my view (see below), there is such an explanation; it is naturalistic; and it does not always presuppose consciousness. In this way, the study of Peirce's semeiotic led me back to the philosophy of mind, which, in the meantime, by pleasant coincidence, has supplanted the philosophy of science as the liveliest area of contemporary philosophy.

2. What do you consider your contribution to the field?

As far as the interpretation of Peirce's theory of signs is concerned, which is my only contribution to the 'field' indicated, it has been focused on making sense out of his various and fragmentary remarks about the interpretant. It was necessary, first of all, to emphasize the identity of significance with a potential interpretant, not with actual interpretants–a potentiality that is grounded in one or another relation of sign to object or of signs of that type to objects of a corresponding type. For otherwise significance would be arbitrarily imposed and therefore useless. The kind of semiotic idealism, or endless and arbitrary interpretation of sign by sign, that Derrida read into Peirce's theory, is fundamentally opposed to that philosopher's deepest aims. Derrida's reading, however, may seem to be justified by Peirce's writings of 1868-9. Thus it is important to show, as I have tried to do, that Peirce later corrected certain key features of his early theory.

Secondly, it was necessary to recognize the various divisions that Peirce made of interpretants, as that is essential (a) to establish the breadth of his semeiotic, (b) to account for his taxonomy of signs, and (c) to explain how semiotic idealism is avoided, viz., by there being interpretants that are not signs.

Finally, the end-directedness of interpretation had to be explained on a naturalistic basis. Otherwise, Peirce's semeiotic would reproduce the same dualism of mind and nature that he had explicitly and forcefully opposed from the very beginning of his career to its very end. This last, which I would say is my major contribution, required taking a bare hint in one of Peirce's posthumously published manuscripts c.1907 (it was Gentry who first drew attention to the passage) and interpreting that hint in terms of his late and brief discussion of final causation c.1902. The latter discussion, in turn, demanded extensive explication and defense. But that, of course, belongs to metaphysics and not to semeiotic. Those who suppose that Peirce's idea of final causation is itself 'semiotical' get the matter precisely backwards. Everything that was on the point of becoming illuminated, they have cast back into darkness. I deeply regret that some of them have cited my own work, as if agreeing with it.

A word, then, about final causation. Remarkably, Peirce found in some of the best-established departments of modern science explanations that are not mechanistic. They are usually assumed to be mechanistic, because they introduce none but mechanistic assumptions. However, what they explain are anisotropic phenomena, i.e., those involving tendencies irreversible or nearly so, whereas mechanistic laws are isotropic. These explanations are statistical, but not in the sense of subsuming the phenomena explained under probabilistic laws. Instead, they explain a tendency by the type of outcome that defines it. This is done in one way in explanations of the thermodynamic Second Law, in another way by Darwinian natural selection. In the latter, a type is explanatory by its having been selected-for. Thus we say that organic features exist for the sake of those types of outcome for which they were selected; we say, e.g., that the purpose of eyes is to see (even when defect prevents them from fulfilling their purpose). Avoiding the perhaps misleading connotation of the word 'purpose', we may identify the type selected-for as a final cause. A final cause is independent of there being an agent that does the selecting; natural selection is agentless. (Notice, also, that natural selection itself has no final cause or purpose or end; it was not selected, ergo, it was not selected for any type of outcome.) This idea of final causation is diametrically opposed, in one or two respects, to Aristotle's idea, but is like his in identifying a final cause, or *telos* or purpose, as a general type rather than as a particular event, body, or force. As the general has no location and can exert no force, final causation is not at all like mechanical causation; as types of possible outcome must nonetheless be cited to explain the anisotropic aspect of anisotropic processes (which in other aspects are mechanical), final causes are real.

Much that has a purpose, such as a heart's beating, is mechanical: its having a purpose is due to the anisotropic process in which it was selected for the type of result it normally and mechanically has. Animal behavior, however, is guided by a type of outcome for which the individual selects: the individual varies its behavior in the absence of outcomes of a given type and reduces variation in their presence. Thus the individual corrects its behavior, which often is mistaken. And thus animal behavior may be described not only as having a purpose but as being purposeful, whether or not the purpose is consciously entertained. All such behavior involves sign-interpretation, as nothing done purposefully is done arbitrarily (even when choice is made by tossing a coin, there is a basis: that we do not know which alternative, if either, is better). Animal action always takes something to be a sign of that which would make its action appropriate to its purpose. This is where semeiosis begins, nowhere earlier. And as mistakes are possible, that which is signified may fail to obtain: thus, intentionality.

Earlier, I mentioned the distinction between signs that occur without a purpose to signify and those (legisigns) that exist to be used (=replicated) to signify. That occurs already in animal communication, but humans are able to devise new legisigns. And thus we are able to represent, and hence to adopt, new purposes, not subordinate to biological goals. Among these are intrinsically semeiotical purposes, as in science and art. Some of Peirce's remarks on final causation indicate how the adoption of new purposes may escape arbitrariness. Human freedom is a semeiotic and teleological phenomenon.

All of this is drawn from Peirce's brief references to statistical explanation and final causation, but it is my own formulation, introducing distinctions he did not make; and elsewhere I have made arguments in its support that he did not make. The upshot is a double-aspect theory of mind and matter that goes all the way down, or almost all the way down. (It would go all the way down if Peirce's speculative cosmology could be completed.) The human mind is a semeiotic phenomenon *a fortiori* teleological *a fortiori* anisotropic, explained not wholly by mechanical causes but crucially by types of possible outcome. The semeiotic extends down through the animal kingdom, the teleological down through all biological phenomena, and the anisotropic down at least as far as clouds of molecules. The details are mechanistic, but the shape things take can only be explained statistically, by the types of outcome toward which some processes tend. And the statistical cannot be dismissed as mere averages, as merely our way of looking at reality. The steam engine would be impossible but for the irreversible flow of heat, a fact purely statistical; so also for all other engines. What, then, could be more consequential than statistical phenomena, including the teleological organization of all living things, the semeiotic orientation of all animal behavior, and the intellectual and moral life of human beings? Peirce used the word 'mind' and its cognates to denote the aspect of reality that cannot be explained mechanistically, but he did not thereby mean to attribute personal agency and consciousness to unthinking nature. He meant only to emphasize that our mental and moral nature is a development of the irreducibly non-mechanistic aspect of reality. That is what his 'objective idealism', often cited, less often understood, amounts to.

3. What is the proper role of a theory of signs and meaning in relation to other academic disciplines?

As I have never studied semiotics, I am incompetent to answer this question. As far as Peirce's semeiotic is concerned, I mentioned above that it is but one department of his philosophy, albeit an organon; it is definitely not 'a philosophy', much less a theory of everything. To be sure, the breadth of the theory is essential to it: it makes each thing, real or unreal, to be one or more signs. But it does not follow that everything is to be explained by this theory, as it were, 'semeiotically'. Except for legisigns and their replicas, nothing is explained by its being a sign. Except for interpreters and the interpretants they form, nothing is explained by semeiosis.

In the spirit of modern science, there is nothing to prevent inquirers in other specialties from adopting the techniques and/or conclusions of Peirce's semeiotic, if they find them to be useful. But the exercise is justified only if it produces new insights, new discoveries. I would suggest that the same criterion should be applied to other sign-theories. Merely to cast a web of semiotic jargon over every topic imaginable, without revealing anything new—a deplorable act of semiotic imperialism—is pointless.

As to the specific question of hermeneutic interpretation versus scientific explanation, the line I have taken requires that their distinction, and several like distinctions, be rigorously maintained. The upshot, however, is to show that hermeneutics, historical explanation, and explaining a person's conduct by his reasons (so-called rational explanation) are continuous with forms of teleological explanation, and, more broadly, statistical explanation, that are well-entrenched in natural science. All of these presuppose various forms of mechanistic explanation but are not reducible to them. Nor would mechanistic explanations by themselves account for the order, or reality, of our world. Again, this is the double-aspect theory that Peirce named 'objective idealism'.

4. What do you consider the most important topics and/or contributions in the theory of meaning and signs?

Again, I plead ignorance of the field. Within the philosophy of language specifically, many would say, and I agree, that the idea of rigid designation, developed by Saul Kripke and others, has been the most notable achievement of the past fifty or so years. But then I have to go and spoil the party by arguing that that achievement was anticipated by Peirce, in some ways in a much superior form, in his concepts of indexical signification, hypostatic abstraction, and the 'growth of symbols' (see Ch.10 of my recent book).

5. What are the most important open problems in this field and what are the prospects for progress?

Again, I am incompetent to say. But the new development named 'biosemiotics', as it has adopted Peirce's sign theory, poses a problem to me. For it takes that theory down to a level at which in my view it does not go and cannot go. Now, other sign theories, or fragments of Peirce's, might be useful or not (I would not know) in understanding biological processes, much as the concept of 'information' has been helpful, if only in a heuristic way, in thermodynamics and in genetics. The key question, however, is whether such talk–*or equivalent talk*–is inescapable if we are to understand these phenomena. What we cannot avoid saying in order to explain the facts, no matter how bizarre it may seem to us, must be accepted; and what we can avoid saying in explanation, no matter how pleasing it is to us, we should avoid saying. But what counts as equivalent talk? The answer is what I take to be Peirce's deepest insight (it is not part of his sign-theory): equivalence in this case consists in citation of irreducible relations of the same order (=number of relata).

21
Barry Smith

SUNY Distinguished Professor of Philosophy, University at Buffalo

Research Director of the Institute for Formal Ontology and Medical Information Science, Saarbrücken

---

1. Why were you initially drawn to the theory of signs and meaning?

My dissertation, completed in 1976, is entitled: *The Ontology of Reference. Studies in Logic and Formal Ontology*. It is a study of theories of meaning and reference in Frege, Husserl, and Michael Dummett. I had earlier attended many classes given by Dummett, during my time (1970-73) as an undergraduate in Oxford. I had been tremendously impressed by Dummett's passion for philosophy; but also dissatisfied with the sorts of answers to philosophical questions which he (channeling Frege) was proposing. I thus became interested in exploring alternatives to Frege-inspired approaches to philosophy, which seemed to me to rest on an oversimplified repertoire of ontological categories.[1] I very quickly became convinced that Husserl, and especially the sort of ontological thinking set forth by Husserl in the *Logical Investigations*, provided the key to what I was looking for. *The Ontology of Reference* embodies my early attempts to solidify this conviction, using Dummett and Frege as foils.[2]

I spent the next 20 years or so exploring the thought of Husserl, of his teacher Brentano, and of his great students Roman Ingarden and Adolf Reinach, with almost exclusive attention to themes in ontology (including the ontology of works of art, and of speech acts). I collaborated throughout this period with Kevin Mulligan

---

[1] Barry Smith, "Against Fantology", in Johann C. Marek and Maria E. Reicher (eds.), *Experience and Analysis*, Vienna: HPT&ÖBV, 2005, 153–170.

[2] It was never published, but you can find it, along with my papers on Husserl, here: http://ontology.buffalo.edu/smith/articles/husserl.html.

and Peter Simons, with whom I still share many views on the nature of philosophy and on its current state.[3]

2. What do you consider your contribution to the field?

I have in the last 20 years been working primarily on applying ontology in a variety of extraphilosophical areas, above all biomedicine. In 2002, drawing on Husserl's coinage of the term 'formal ontology' and on a generous award by the Alexander von Humboldt Foundation, I established in Germany the Institute for Formal Ontology and Medical Information Science (cf. http://ifomis.org/.) I have during this time been in the peculiar position of witnessing how, what had initially seemed a private concern of Mulligan, Simons and myself, namely applied ontology – roughly: the application to real-world problems of ontological tools and theories deriving from philosophy – has burgeoned into a veritable industry, in which philosophical work overlaps with computer science, database engineering, and scientific research. Representatives of all of these disciplines are attempting to solve the problem of how, in an era of information-based science, it might be possible to make different sorts of scientific information work well together even though it is collected at different times and places by different researchers using different vocabularies.

There are theoretical (logical, computational, linguistic, and also philosophical) problems to be addressed here; but also, and perhaps most importantly, there are non-trivial socio-cultural problems of coordination, in the addressing of which I have also become heavily involved.[4] In addressing these multiple sets of problems, each disciplinary community has, it seems, contributed its own set of idiosyncrasies, often resting on what, from a philosophicological point of view, seem to be obvious confusions. I believe that my main contribution is (1) to have persuaded at least some of those working in the field that some of the repeating elements in these confusions can be addressed using standard philosophical theories and methods; and (2) to have demonstrated that resolving these confusions may bring positive practical benefits.[5]

---

[3] See Kevin Mulligan, Peter Simons and Barry Smith, "What's Wrong with Contemporary Philosophy?", *Topoi*, 25 (1-2), 2006, 63-67.

[4] Cf. http://obofoundry.org/; http://bioontology.org/.

[5] Barry Smith, Michael Ashburner, Cornelius Rosse, Jonathan Bard,

Some of the most influential ways people go wrong – for example in the use of circular definitions – are addressed already in beginning courses in logic. Another significant contribution, therefore, has been a series of attempts on my part to convey to working biologists some of the lessons of basic logic. The paper on the logic of relations[6] which grew out of this work has been downloaded some 25,000 times, and it has been cited in over 200 other papers published in biology and biomedical informatics journals in the last 2 years. The Gene Ontology, thus far the world's most successful ontology, has been especially influenced by these efforts, in ways which its developers see as bringing genuine benefits to its users.

3. What is the proper role of a theory of signs and meaning in relation to other academic disciplines?

One important contribution which those working on meanings and signs might make for the future is to clarify the thinking of those – a multidisciplinary community predestined to play an increasingly influential role in our lives – who are engaged in what is variously called 'information modeling', 'conceptual representation', 'knowledge modeling' and so forth.

Here what we might call the UM axiom (for 'Use-Mention Confusion') is especially important:

> UM: Terms (and other units of representation, for example in computers) should be distinguished strictly from the objects they represent in reality.[7]

All those involved in addressing the increasingly urgent need for theoretically well-founded methods and resources to manage the

---

William Bug, Werner Ceusters, Louis J. Goldberg, Karen Eilbeck, Amelia Ireland, Christopher J Mungall, The OBI Consortium, Neocles Leontis, Philippe Rocca-Serra, Alan Ruttenberg, Susanna-Assunta Sansone, Richard H Scheuermann, Nigam Shah, Patricia L. Whetzel, Suzanna Lewis, "The OBO Foundry: Coordinated Evolution of Ontologies to Support Biomedical Data Integration", *Nature Biotechnology*, 25 (11), November 2007, 1251-1255.

[6] Barry Smith, Werner Ceusters, Bert Klagges, Jacob Köhler, Anand Kumar, Jane Lomax, Chris Mungall, Fabian Neuhaus, Alan Rector and Cornelius Rosse, "Relations in Biomedical Ontologies", *Genome Biology* (2005), 6 (5), R46.

[7] Barry Smith, Waclaw Kusnierczyk, Daniel Schober, Werner Ceusters, "Towards a Reference Terminology for Ontology Research and Development in the Biomedical Domain", O. Bodenreider, ed., *Proceedings of KR-MED*, 2006, 57-66. Also available online at: http://ceur-ws.org/Vol-222

burgeoning wealth of information brought by the use of computers in science should be thoroughly apprised of this axiom at least several times a day. They should be reminded, for example, that an entity in reality is not identical to a website describing this entity, and that neither are identical to the website's URL.

4. and 5. What do you consider the most important topics and/or contributions in the theory of meaning and signs? What are the most important open problems in this field and what are the prospects for progress?

As someone trained as a philosopher ontologist, I was at first completely at sea in my attempts to understand the odd statements made by many of those developing or using ontology-like artifacts in the information technology field. I have become especially involved in trying to understand how ontologies are being used in healthcare information technology, for example in fostering a more coherent treatment of patient data in electronic health records.[8],[9] The more I looked into the way such data are treated at the moment, the more I was confronted with the confusions in the handling of signs, meanings and objects referred to already above.[10]

Notorious examples of such confusions are to be found in the relevant ISO (International Organization for Standardization) standards in health informatics, where the ideas of a certain Eugen Wüster, a Viennese semiotician/philosopher/terminologist/businessman/Esperanto advocate and professor of woodworking machinery, have been extraordinarily influential.[11] From Wüster's

---

[8] The same confusions are present elsewhere; for example in the oil and gas industry. See Barry Smith, "Against Idiosyncrasy in Ontology Development", in B. Bennett and C. Fellbaum (Eds.), *Formal Ontology in Information Systems* (FOIS 2006), Amsterdam: IOS Press, 2006, 15-26.

[9] I became intrigued also by questions pertaining to the nature of records more generally, for example in the sphere of economics and commerce. See Barry Smith, "Searle and De Soto: The New Ontology of the Social World", Barry Smith, David Mark and Isaac Ehrlich, *The Mystery of Capital and the Construction of Social Reality*, Chicago: Open Court, 2008, 35-51.

[10] Barry Smith, "Beyond Concepts, or: Ontology as Reality Representation", Achille Varzi and Laure Vieu (eds.), *Formal Ontology and Information Systems. Proceedings of the Third International Conference (FOIS 2004)*, Amsterdam: IOS Press, 2004, 73–84.

[11] Barry Smith, Werner Ceusters and Rita Temmerman, "Wüsteria", *Medical Informatics Europe* (MIE 2005), Geneva, Stud Health Technol Inform. 2005;116:647–652.

point of view, through the sensations with which we are bombarded in the initial stages of our life, we begin to acquire what he calls "concepts" – entities existing in the heads of people. Before we can assign a term to such a concept, Wüster says, we must first "delineate" the concept by listing 'the totality of "characteristics" which form the concept's content or intension.' Sometimes, Wüster suggests that such characteristics are themselves just further concepts (so that, like other concepts, they would exist in the heads of people). At other times he suggests that they are properties of objects existing in the world. But when faced with the problem of defining clearly whether given characteristics are concepts in the head or properties of objects in the world, one standard response of Wüster and his epigones is to assert, in effect, that there is no difference between the two. This is in keeping with a general failure to discriminate clearly between objects and concepts that runs through terminology work as a result of the influence of Wüster's thinking (counterparts of which I find also in some other types of semiotic thinking, in some work in cognitive linguistics, and in so-called 'conceptual modeling').

The influence of this failure is illustrated most clearly, and perhaps most tragically, in the work of HL7 (for "Health Level 7"), a large and influential body, comprising representatives of different parts of the health care information technology industry in some 66 countries. HL7's pride and joy is its 'Reference Information Model' (or RIM), an artifact which has, strangely, been elevated to the status of an ISO standard. Central to the RIM is the concept 'Act', which is defined as meaning:

A record of something that is being done, has been done, can be done, or is intended or requested to be done.

An Act, then, is (in normal English) something like: the record of an act. The term 'Act', for the RIM, embraces: assessments of health conditions (such as problems and diagnoses), healthcare goals, and observations. An observation is defined, in its turn, as:

An Act of recognizing and noting information about the subject, and whose immediate and primary outcome (post-condition) is new data about a subject.

Unfortunately, the HL7 documentation conveys a deep-rooted uncertainty as to whether an Act should most properly be conceived as a record of something that is being done, etc., or as the act of doing that is recorded. Both views are represented prominently in different places in the relevant manuals, and efforts which have been made in various circles to resolve the resulting contradiction have thus far led nowhere. The HL7 organization, one might think, would by now, after more than 10 years of RIM development, have resolved this contradiction through some official diktat as to which of these two evidently conflicting interpretations is correct. Incredibly, however, they resolve the issue with the following declaration (English and punctuation as in the original):

> Act as statements or speech-acts are the only representation of real world facts or processes in the HL7 RIM. The truth about the real world is constructed through a combination (and arbitration) of such attributed statements only, and there is no class in the RIM whose objects represent "objective state of affairs" or "real processes" independent from attributed statements. As such, there is no distinction between an activity and its documentation.[12]

The solution to the logical contradiction between 'An Act is a record' and 'An Act is an action in the world' is, thus, to deny that these two statements are in logical conflict – because an activity and the record of an activity are one and the same.[13]

In the specific field of biomedical informatics, and biomedical ontologies, there are on the other hand some signs of progress. Some ontology developers, for example, are beginning to learn that when they use a word like 'kidney' in an ontology, then this word should not be interpreted as referring to some representation in a computer, or to some concept in someone's head, but rather to an entity on the side of reality. This leads to another central axiom for ontology developers, which we might call TC, or: the axiom of terminological coherence:

> TC: For any expression 'E' in an ontology, 'E' means E.

I am sometimes asked what might be the pragmatic consequences of ontology developers getting the mentioned axioms right or wrong. The answer to this challenge can most easily be illustrated, again, by the case of HL7. First, the consequences of multiple, cascading violations of UM and TC are that the documentation guiding successive cohorts of users of HL7 artifacts is (as the HL7 organization has recently been forced to admit[14]) often

---

[12] ANSI/HL7 V3 RIM, R1-2003: RIM Version V 02-11. Membership Normative Ballot Last Published: 11/22/2005 8:05 PM. Section 3.1.1, emphasis added.

[13] Barry Smith and Werner Ceusters, "HL7 RIM: An Incoherent Standard" (MIE 2006), *Studies in Health Technology and Informatics*, vol. 124, 133–138.

[14] http://hl7-watch.blogspot.com/2007/09/piece-of-good-news-has-been-posted-on.html.

painfully unintelligible. HL7 initiates themselves have thereby become involved in interminable disputes, documented in HL7's own public email fora. Another is that multi-million-dollar projects fail,[15] leading, I believe, to the entrenchment of what thereby begins to appear to be a well-justified pessimism as to the very viability of information technology in the domain of healthcare.

It must be admitted that the goals of HL7, and of multiple similar projects in a variety of domains, are exceedingly ambitious, and that the problems which need to be addressed are far from trivial. If computers are to work well together, then they must as far as possible adopt common ontologies to describe the entities in common application areas. At the same time, however, in areas like science and medicine, the terms and definitions used must be marked by sufficient flexibility to accommodate the changes that result from new discoveries. We still do not know how to establish a methodology to determine the appropriate response in the face of such problems. To the extent that philosophical issues are involved in addressing them, however, this means that philosophy itself is subject to new kinds of empirical and practical constraints and influences.

---

[15]Examples of all of the mentioned phenomena are documented at http://hl7-watch.blogspot.com/.

22

Göran Sonesson

Full Professor
Department of Semiotics
University of Lund, Sweden

Like many other young people, I thought I was going to be a fiction writer. While I was waiting for the big fit of inspiration, I took up the study of literature. But literature did not seem to have anything new to tell me. On the contrary, linguistics opened up entirely new vistas on such a common sense object as language. What fascinated me was the later much maligned structuralist linguistics, from phonology to grammar. On the contrary, I was very unhappy with the reigning Chomskyan paradigm: it seemed to me to be about some figment of Noam Chomsky's imagination, not about language. Pragmatics was not enough. It treated all kinds of meaning except for language as some kind of auxiliary means for conveying linguistic meaning. Only semiotics seemed adequate for treating all meaning on a par. This impression was very much reinforced, when I travelled repeatedly to Paris to visit my sister who lived there and discovered, in the Parisian bookshops, semiotic books by many of the authors I knew from linguistics, such as Roman Jakobson, Emile Benveniste, Luis Prieto, A. J. Greimas, etc.

Thus I became an unwilling Greimasean. The Parisean seminar of A. J. Greimas was more or less the only place where you could go to prepare a doctorate in semiotics at the time. But I did not like the *a priori* character of the theory, nor, in particular, the postulate that all meaning was born equal. I though semiotics was about the *differences* between semiotic resources as well as about their common ground. My basic formation having been in linguistics, I was very much disturbed by linguistic terms being used in quite different senses. It did not only seem confusing: it created obstacles to the important task of finding real differences and similarities between semiotic domains.

I spent almost ten years in Paris and later in Mexico City, working in Paris within the Greimas group with the semiotics of gesture, and in Mexico as an ethnolinguist involved with Mayan languages. Apart from what this taught me about gesture and Mayan language, respectively, I think it gave me a very pronounced feeling for the differences between human cultures, which served me well in my later work on cultural semiotics–and in general strengthened my interest in semiotic *differences*. It was an appeal from the Swedish Research Council in the Humanities that brought me back to Sweden in order to introduce semiotics (belatedly) to the Swedish academic public. I have since then remained in Sweden in different functions.

My main contribution to the study of meaning so far has no doubt involved pictorial and, more generally, visual semiotics. This came about in a curious way. To understand language, you must account for the whole situation of communication, which, apart from the verbal elements, is mainly a visual phenomenon. I got interested in the psychology of perception and cognition but also in Husserlean phenomenology. My first teaching at Lund University, in the late seventies, well before this became a fashionable blend in semiotics and cognitive science alike, was about semiotics *and* phenomenology. This focus brought me from language to gesture and from there to pictures. Thus I came to occupy myself with the similarities and differences between language and visually conveyed meaning instead of their interaction in the situation of communication.

Within the semiotics of pictures, my contribution has been at least twofold. Although a lot of scholars have expressed their misgivings about the conventionalist theories of pictures formulated by Umberto Eco (1968; 1976) and Nelson Goodman (1968), notably, and although the true Peirceans have never given up their belief in the existence of icons, I think I am the only one to have given, in *Pictorial concepts* (Sonesson 1989) a complete account of the arguments, of both a theoretical and empirical nature, for the untenability of these theories. I took the empirical arguments from the psychology of perception and cognition, and this emphasis on empirical study has followed me ever since. The theoretical arguments were my own: they consisted in a refutation of the best arguments against the possibility of iconic signs, those formulated by Goodman, and actually much clearly before him, by a little known thinker, Arthur Bierman (1963). The most important ones are the *argument of regression*, according to which there are similarities between all things in the world, and so this cannot be the foundation of a sign relation, and the *argument of symmetry*, according to which similarity is symmetric, which the sign relation is not. I showed that iconicity must either be applied to something which was for other reasons known to be a sign, or else it must be a property of things which are universally prominent in the human Lifeworld, giving rise to *secondary* and *primary iconic signs*, respectively (Sonesson 1993; 1998; 2001). As against the symmetry argument, I claimed, on the basis of experiments by the psychologists Eleanor Rosch and Amos Tversky, that similarity, as understood in the common sense world, is really asymmetric. One twin, the one I knew beforehand, is more similar than the other–which is an awkward, but therefore also, I believe, effective way of saying that a comparison always is made from the point of view of one of the elements involved, the one which is more well-known or otherwise more prominent.

In the second place, I have tried to bring together, and bring to bear on each other, the theoretical models for picture analyses proposed by, mainly French, semioticians and the empirical work accomplished within the psychology of picture perception, creating finally what Gombrich called "the linguistics of the visual image" (Sonesson 1988; 1989; 1998). The most important contributions in the first domain are no doubt those of Jean-Marie Floch (1984) and Felix Thurlemann (1990). But it was necessary to liberate their models from the *a priori* character given them by the Greimasean paradigm to see that other variants were possible. The true pioneer of the latter domain was really the psychologist James Gibson (1982), who, contrary to most other perceptual psychologists, always insisted on the difference between the perception of pictures and direct perception. Building on Gibson and his followers, as well as on phenomenology, it was also easy to show why the structuralist tenets concerning the picture sign were completely mistaken (Sonesson 1989; 1995). It is true that, already at the time, these ideas (such as the double articulation of pictures) were out of fashion–but I have always believed it was important to understand *why* they deserved to be out of fashion.

A relatively more recent contribution of mine involves the semiotics of culture, which I have understood as a study of the models a culture constructs about its relations to other cultures. This conception has permitted me to develop the analytical tools of the Tartu school (Lotman et al. 1975) in the direction of the analysis of intersubjectivity, in terms of *Ego*, the one whose point of view defines the model, *Alter*, the one with whom he or she is on speaking terms, and *Alius*, the one who is only talked about. Thus understood, semiotics of culture has turned out to be a potent tool for the study of history, such as the conquest of America, as well as an aid to the understanding of modernity, globalization, and worldwide migration, as I have tried to show in a number of articles (Sonesson 2000a; 2004). Indeed, a quite separate line of work, the study of "performance", in the art historical sense, which first inspired me to analyse theatre, play, ritual, and many similar phenomena–the *spectacular* function (Sonesson 2000b), turned out to be fundamental for the understanding of urban space, as manifested in the boulevard, the coffee house, and other public places (Sonesson 2003), and then for the understanding of semiosis generally. This branch of study is important to me also, because as an "old left wing intellectual", I tend to believe that the fact that we live in a (particular) society has important consequences for all semiotic resources.

Semiotics, like so much else, is first of all an intellectual tradition, a series of questions and the answers to them that have provoked new questions through the centuries. But it is our task to try to make something more out of it–something that can serve to bring the human and social sciences together, offering a bridge to parts of the natural sciences erected on the conditions of the former. Contrary to what Saussure said, the place of this discipline is certainly not determined beforehand. Elsewhere I have discussed this issue (most completely in Sonesson 2006a), rejecting the idea that semiotics is a method, a model, and even a branch of the philosophy of language. I think it is–or should be–a science. Some sciences are defined by the particular part of reality that they describe, like Art history or French studies, others by the particular perspective they take on all or some part of reality, such as sociology and psychology. Semiotics, in my view, is of the latter kind: it is defined by its interest in how something comes to carry meaning. However, I also believe there is a limit to the domain to which such a research interest may be applied. Perhaps it is too broad to say, following Sebeok, that meaning is coextensive with life. I would rather say that it requires some degree of consciousness.

For a long time now, a lot of semioticians have argued that the sign is not the fundamental unit of semiotic analysis. There is a paradox to this, of course, since semiotics literally means the science of signs. However, I am quite willing to redefine semiotics as the science of meaning (Sonesson 2006b). Not because I accept the kinds of arguments against the existence of the sign propounded by, notably, Eco and Greimas. The notion of sign is, I think, quite adequate, not only for characterising linguistic meaning (even though it might be a rather superficial phenomenon of language, as Ferdinand de Saussure maintained), but also for defining at least pictures and some kinds of gesture. But there is much more to meaning than signs. The notion of sign is not at all useful for analysing the meaning with which perception is imbued. It does not account for the way symptoms serve to signify some particular kind of illness: for once all possible symptoms are known, the illness is also known (and the patient is normally dead). Indeed, this is how ordinary perception works: when we know all items of the expression, we know the content. This is why it is better not to talk about expression and content in these cases. The picture sign and the verbal sign, on the contrary, consist of two units that are clearly *differentiated* from each other, using a term first proposed by Jean Piaget (1945; 1970; cf. Sonesson 1992; 2006b). One of the units, the expression, is *directly accessible* but it is *not in focus*, whereas the other one, the content, can only be reached over the expression, and yet it is *the focus* of our interest. This characterisation builds on some passages from Edmund Husserl (1913; 1939; cf. Sonesson 1992; 2006b). At first, I was interested in establishing this difference between language and pictures, on one hand, and perception on the other, for systematic reasons–to understand how semiotic resources may differ. Nowadays, however, I think it is more important from the point of view of evolution and development. In the different phases of evolution (which may have parallels in child development) described by Merlin Donald (1991), we have to pinpoint the emergence of the sign function–somewhere in the mimetic phase, well before language and picture, but not, perhaps, before tool use. Not only does it appear that sign use is something of which most, if not all, animals, apart from human beings (and perhaps some other higher primates) are incapable, but the child goes through a number of phases in learning to grasp the nature of the picture sign, as well as the verbal sign. Indeed, in the on-going EU project SEDSU in which I am involved, together with primatologists and psychologists, we have failed to find clear indication of sign use in the precise sense given to the term here (See http://www.sedsu.org/).

There is an immense number of contributions to semiotics that I admire very much. Of course, Charles Sanders Peirce (1998) is among the two or three most important thinkers in our domain, but he is also very obscure, and I am not interested in forming part of the Talmud crowd. I don't care very much to know "what Peirce really said". There is such an enormous amount of ideas in Peirce's work. One must read Peirce to get ideas, and there is really no way of knowing if these are really the ideas intended by Peirce. Thus, Peirce's notion of sign is probably not at all the sign that I have characterised above, at least not in the case of many of his numerous definitions. The issue is not, as it is often stated, that Peirce, contrary to Saussure, was interested in all kinds of signs, not just verbal ones. As Peirce noted late in life, the term "sign" was really too narrow for what he intended. Instead he suggested the terms "mediation", "branching", "semiosis". I think what Peirce is describing really comes much closer to the situation of communication or, even better, the situation in which a signification is conveyed (from somebody or something) to someone. In this sense, it would also apply to perception. It is a pity, however, that Peirce never took care to separate this very general notion from the more precise and limited concept of sign (Cf. Sonesson 2006b).

The fundamental work of the Prague school is today sadly neglected, as is that of Louis Hjelmslev and Luis Prieto. I am fascinated by the former, because it permits a serious analysis of society as a socio-cultural lifeworld, in which some things are taken for granted, already because it is a human lifeworld, and other things only seem obvious and uncontested because they are embodied in the norms and canons of this particular society (cf. Mukarovsky 1974; 1978). The social dimension added by the Prague school to the situation of communication stands in stark contrast to the abstract notion of semiosis propounded by Peirce. It is a pity that, even today, scholars who want to add a social dimension to their semiotic work, like for instance Gunther Kress and Theo von Leeuwen, rely on the fuzzy ideas of Roland Barthes, instead of building on the much more useful and precise notions of the Prague school (to which could be added the partially similar work of the Bakhtin circle). The interest of the work of Hjelmslev (1943) and Prieto (1975), on the other hand, lies in their formalism. They allow us to discover the system character, which, for instance, separates verbal language from most other semiotic resources. I was very much helped by their ideas when I tried to show how different pictures were from language, and I found their notions helpful also recently (in Sonesson 2006b), when criticising some ideas of Deacon's (1997) about the semiotic specificity of language.

Few people within semiotics have set the standards of rigour and creativity as high as Groupe μ (1977; 1992). Jean-Marie Klinkenberg once said to me that, if I only hade been a Belgian, I could have been a member of the group. I really take that as a very big compliment. If I had ever been able to form part of a school, that would certainly have been the Liège group. Sometimes I do regret not being a Belgian. It is a remarkable fact that both the two traditions that have renewed rhetoric in our time, Chaîm Perelman and Groupe μ, have their origin in Belgium, in Brussels and Liege, respectively. But, not being a Belgian, I have built on their work and tried to extend it in different dimensions. Most notably, I have treated the norms as being something basically social, as in the Prague school model. But, of course, this supplement depends on the earlier distinction between norms as *normalcy*, the things taken for granted in the Lifeworld, and as *normativity*, that which is required in a particular society. My second contribution has consisted in showing that the rupture of norms with which Groupe μ is concerned really involves relations of contiguity and of parts and wholes in the Lifeworld, and that transgressions of norms may also pertain to other dimensions, among which must be counted more or less similarity than expected, more or less levels of signs than expected, as well as the unexpected combinations of channels of circulations, social function, and kind of construction (See Sonesson 1996; 2004).

To me, however, Eco has been exceptionally important, not only because he has formulated many of the essential questions of semiotics, but also because he tends to come up with answers that I find inadequate. So thanks to Eco I am in business. Indeed, I have found faults with Eco, both when he argued that pictures were conventional and made up of features, and when, more recently, he has argued that most of them, and notably television images, are like mirrors, and that mirrors are no signs, but examples of what I would have called direct perception. In my early work on iconicity (Sonesson 1989; 2001), I opposed his idea, formulated during the first period of his iconicity critique, in *La struttura assente* (Eco 1968), that pictures were conventional and made up of features, thus having double articulation, just like language, being constructed from something similar to phonemes and something similar to words, and that, as a consequence, the cinema has a triple articulation. I also argued against Eco's conception in *Theory of semiotics* (Eco 1976 - what I have called his second period in Sonesson 2001), according to which pictures were conventional but not made up of features, that, on the contrary, they were basically motivated by similarity, but still made up of a kind of features (in accordance with the tenets of the psychology of picture perception). As against Eco's (1997) third conception of iconicity, I think the mirror can be shown to be a sign by the same token as the Peircean weather-cock: more exactly, a given *mirror image* is a sign, just as a particular constellation of the weather-cock in space and time is. But although the mirror is more picture-like than Eco would admit, the television image is not at all like the mirror: it is very much amenable to manipulation, even when, as happens today very rarely, it is based on direct transmission, which is the ideal case considered by Eco (cf. Sonesson 2003).

Finally, I cannot see the point of Eco's claim that special branches of semiotics, like the study of gesture, are sciences, but general semiotics is some kind of philosophy, in fact a part of the philosophy of language. My basic complaint is not that it should be the other way around, because general semiotics must have a more general subject matter than whatever is concerned with language, but that if general semiotics is a philosophical school, it would have no continuity with the study of specific semiotic resources– and this would be a very inconvenient relationship. If, as Eco suggests, general semiotics should define what a sign is, then the special disciplines would only be valid for those who accept this philosophical conception. I am not saying, of course, that science can do without philosophy: but, rather than being a scientific conception, semiotics, like any other science, can by conducted from many different philosophical points of view (Cf. Sonesson 2006b).

But the real cultural heroes of my brand of semiotics are some thinkers who would hardly call themselves semioticians: Husserl, who used the term only once, in an earlier article on the "logic of the sign", to refer to his own writings, Piaget, who only late in life talked about the semiotic function, Ernst Cassirer, who used the term sparingly, Lev Vygotsky, James Gibson, Aron Gurwitsch, and Karl Bühler, who never used the term, and so on. I must insist immediately that I admire Husserl, and his one true follower as well as best critique (notably involving the function of the ego), Gurwitsch, not as builders of a philosophical system, but as scholars dedicated to the painstaking, ever repeated scrutiny of meaningful phenomena. Before the word was invented, and at least before I heard the term, I have been "naturalizing" phenomenology. It is really interesting to compare the detailed research manuscripts found in Husserl's *Nachlass*, where he tries, over and over again, to arrive at an adequate analysis of some apparently simple, mundane phenomenon (in the everyday, as well as the technical, sense), with Peirce's *Collected Papers*, which never stops rehearsing the abstract definition of semiosis. I think Husserl's advantage consists in staying closer to the facts. The facts of consciousness, of course. As for Gibson, he did not only initiate the psychology of picture perception, but his theory of perception is really an early instance of naturalizing phenomenology. Curiously, he often uses the same examples as Husserl. Although Gibson never refers to Husserl in his published works, it has been said by at least one of his students that he often referred to him in his classes. If Gibson did not read Husserl, they were certainly kindred spirits. Or perhaps the concordance of their work shows that phenomenology is not as subjective (in the sense of common sense) after all.

Cassirer and Bühler are interesting for their ability to combine general, "philosophical" reflection with empirical information. The same observation applies, in practice, to the work of Gurwitsch, although he officially insists very much on the difference between phenomenological psychology (which is a way of describing the mind) and phenomenological philosophy (which is about the world, how it can appear to us, but since the world only appears through the mind, the structures found in both cases are identical). As I said before, this is how I see the spirit of semiotics: combining what is traditionally known as philosophical reflection with empirical work. For the same reason, I am not very happy with Eco's suggestion that general semiotics is a kind of philosophy. Rather, philosophy that is worthwhile is a kind of semiotics.

I very much admire the work of both Piaget and Vygotsky, although they are often presented as (and, to some extent, really are) diametrically opposed. As is well known, they could not agree which came first, the chicken or the egg–or, as we also say, the individual or society. Basically, however, I think there was some kind of misunderstanding between them. They did not mean the same thing by the term "society". The society from which the Vygotskyan individual starts out is society in terms of the common cultural values, the norms that are taken for granted by all members of the crowd. This is a society which is imposed on us–and, which, in Simmel's phrase, which Cassirer (1942) takes over to turn it against him, is not only "a tragedy of culture", not only structural violence acted out on the individual, but a common ground to stand on, in order to grow and learn. The Piagetean society is were the individual ends up after a long journey: it is society in the sense of interaction, of dialogue, modelled, now doubt, less on the marketplace, as in Mikhail Bakhtin, or on the political sphere, as in Jürgen Habermas, but rather on scientific discussion, closer, in the respect, to the scientific community according to Peirce. It has long been said that the stages of Piaget's theory are stages in the emergence of the little scientist. As a corollary, however, the Piagetean society is the scientist's discussion club (Cf. Sonesson 2003).

In terms of topics, I think the plurality, and difference, of meaning or semiotic resources is the most important one contributed by semiotics (though this insight is not shared by all who call themselves semioticians). This can be understood in several ways: there are many kinds of semiotic resources, and the choice of one over the others changes the message that they convey; and there are other kinds of meaning than signs. I have already discussed signs as opposed to other meanings above. Let me add a few words about the diversity of semiotic resources.

We know the idea that language determines thinking from Wilhelm von Humboldt and, with a different emphasis, from Edward Sapir and Benjamin Lee Whorf. Piaget, on the other hand, thought that (the stages of) thinking determine(s) language. His disciple Hans Furth even believed he had shown that since mute children went through the same stages of development as other children, language could not be important. But he forgot that even mute children's thinking might be mediated by other semiotic resources. Vygotsky seems to open up for a wider interplay of thinking and different kinds of semiosis, even though, in practice, he hardly considers other examples than language. There is nothing wrong with finding semiotic universals, but I think too little has been done trying to define the difference between semiotic resources. Goodman, with his "ways of world-making", has been more explicit about the different ways of representing (thinking about) the world. But, in the end, Goodman's stipulation of a nominalist metaphysics renders impossible any descriptive approach. The deepest thinker in this domain, in spite of all his shortcomings, remains Gotthold Ephraim Lessing. Udo Bayer and David Wellbury did a great job trying to rework Lessing's observations into a more modern semiotic terminology, that of Peirce and of Hjelmslev, respectively. I have myself tried to go on from there, using observations from cognitive psychology on the "dual coding" of memory, to criticise some of their contentions (cf. Sonesson

2007). However embryonary the state of this work, it is certainly much more worthwhile than the arbitrary declarations of Kress & van Leuuwen about the difference between language and pictures. They have done a great harm to semiotics, because their work, instead of more serious contributions to pictorial semiotics, has proved acceptable to linguists.

There is of course any number of open problems remaining within semiotics–as there always will. The most important task at present may well be to integrate the contributions of semiotics and cognitive science. Semiotics, it will be remembered, like most sciences in the course of time, has separated out from the magma of philosophy. The case of cognitive science is very different. It represents the amalgamation of fully-fledged sciences like biology, neurology, computer science, philosophy, linguistics and cognitive psychology. This latter-day marriage of the arts, however, received its benediction from the computer. The possibility of simulating theories on the computer may have been useful at times. But the most important thing cognitive science accomplished was the rapprochement of theory and empirical facts. Semiotics should have done that long before. A few semioticians, like Martin Krampen, René Lindekens, Paul Bouissac, and myself have long argued for the use of psychological, biological and other kinds of data in semiotics. Since cognitive science has already realised this, it is rather the integration with cognitive science that must now take place. I do think we have something to contribute. The notion of representation in cognitive science, like the notion of sign in semiotics, is at present too general and vague to accomplish any theoretical work. It does not help denying the existence of representations, as George Lakoff, Mark Johnson and their followers do. We need to understand the *different* ways of representing the world. And before we can do that we need to define "representation" (and/ or "sign").

Another meeting with biology has taken place within semiotics proper. Biology-minded thinkers have opposed their own biosemiotics to what they call anthroposemiotics, which turns out to be a vast waste-basked containing all other kinds of semiotics. In the strict sense, however, anthroposemiotics must be a part of biosemiotics, because the way human beings convey signification cannot be completely independent of their being part of the animate world. So, again, we need to take a comparative approach: in what way are human beings like other animals, and how are they different? In order to answer these questions, and to help integrate anthroposemiotics within biosemiotics, the latter first needs to be informed by anthroposemiotics, or rather, by classical approaches to semiosis. Biosemiotics needs to limit its semiotic imperialism. All life is not semiotic–only life which is aware of being life. Meaning is an intentional concept.

One issue which is important and which has some prospects of being elucidated in the near future is that of the evolution and development of semiotic resources, how the capacity for using gesture, pictures, and of course language grows in time, in the history of the individual and the species–and perhaps even in historical time. Adding this diachronic dimension helps justifying the classificatory approach that has always been a feature of semiotic theory. It also affords semiotics the possibility of saying something that no other academic discipline has even been able to say: to show us how, in a number of stages through evolution and development, life has become consciousness of life. Life signified.

23
John F. Sowa

Private Scholar

---

1. Why were you initially drawn to the theory of signs and meaning?

I had been interested in science and language since I was a child. The science came from my father, who had studied chemical engineering and gave clear scientific answers to all my questions. The interest in language came from my maternal grandmother, who spoke only Polish at home. At MIT and Harvard, I majored in mathematics, but I also studied languages and philosophy. I spent 30 years working on research and development projects at IBM, and by focusing on artificial intelligence and computational linguistics, I was able to combine all my interests while still doing work that was useful to the company.

In my studies of philosophy, I knew of Peirce only as a friend of William James. At Harvard, I took some courses in logic, but I never heard anything about Peirce from the philosophers there, despite the fact that his manuscripts were buried in the Harvard library. In 1978, I finally came across an article about Peirce's existential graphs by Martin Gardner in the mathematical games section of the *Scientific American*. I immediately noticed a similarity between Peirce's existential graphs and my earlier article on conceptual graphs (Sowa 1976). In my first book (Sowa 1984), I redefined the logical foundations for conceptual graphs in terms of existential graphs. From that initial attraction to Peirce's logic, I have been continuing my studies of his semeiotic and its relationship to all branches of cognitive science.

2. What do you consider your contribution to the field?

In my work in artificial intelligence, I have been trying to relate the enormous power and flexibility of language to the mathematical precision required for science. But research in philosophy, linguistics, and AI has been polarized between the "scruffies" and the "neats". Those terms were coined by Roger Schank, who proudly called himself a scruffy because of his often *ad hoc* computational methods for addressing the complexities of ordinary language. He denounced the logic-based methods of the neats, such as Richard Montague, as irrelevant for linguistics and AI. Although I admired the precision of logicians such as Carnap, Quine, and Montague, I realized that the cognitive mechanisms must be flexible and that absolute precision is a highly unusual special case. My solution was to develop conceptual graphs as a notation for logic with a continuous range of precision. At one extreme, CGs are as formal as Montague's logic, but they can be used in approximations that are as scruffy as Schank's. The key innovation is not in the CG notation itself, but in the methods for relating CGs to background knowledge.

Before I began to study Peirce's writings, the two philosophers who had the strongest influence on me were Whitehead and Wittgenstein. Like Peirce, both of them had a strong background in logic, mathematics, and science, but they appreciated the full complexity of language. Another influence was Pike's *Unified Theory of Human Behavior*, which addressed the distinction between the *etic* (continuous) and *emic* (discrete) aspects of all modes of language and behavior. Those influences led me to develop methods for relating the rigid notations of mathematical logic to the flexible, but vague aspects of natural languages. In my first book (Sowa 1984), I devoted Chapter 2 to a survey of cognitive psychology that emphasized the issues of perceiving and interacting with a continuous world and talking about it in terms of discrete words. The concluding paragraph of Section 2.3 captures the essential point:

> Advocates of AI, who concentrate on the discrete aspects, are optimistic about the prospects for simulating intelligence on a digital computer. Critics who concentrate on the continuous forms maintain that simulation of intelligence by digital means is impossible.
>
> Since the human brain uses both kinds of processes, a complete simulation may require some combination of digital and analog means.

The final chapter of that book, "Limits of Conceptualization," surveyed "the continuous aspects of the world that cannot be adequately expressed in discrete concepts and conceptual relations."

More recently, I used the term *knowledge soup* (Sowa 2000, 2005) to describe the complexity of what people have in their heads. Whitehead (1937) aptly characterized the problem:

> Human knowledge is a process of approximation. In the focus of experience, there is comparative clarity. But the discrimination of this clarity leads into the penumbral background. There are always questions left over. The problem is to discriminate exactly what we know vaguely.

The poet Robert Frost (1963) suggested a solution:

> I've often said that every poem solves something for me in life. I go so far as to say that every poem is a momentary stay against the confusion of the world.... We rise out of disorder into order. And the poems I make are little bits of order.

Logic and poetry are complementary disciplines that use analogy to find relevant knowledge and assemble it in a tightly structured proof or poem. All methods of formal reasoning — deduction, induction, and abduction — are disciplined special cases of analogy (Sowa & Majumdar 2003). But as Peirce observed, discipline is "purely inhibitory. It originates nothing" (CP 5.194). Yet discipline is necessary to prune away irrelevant or misguided excess. To support high-speed reasoning, both formal and analogical, Majumdar invented algorithms for mapping discrete conceptual graphs to and from continuous geometric fields. Two aspects of those algorithms are critical for meeting the challenge of knowledge soup: First, their speed enables them to simulate an associative memory that can store and retrieve arbitrary volumes of background knowledge. Second, with varying constraints on the mapping, the reasoning can be as vague or precise as appropriate for any given application. The tight constraints of generalization and specialization support the disciplined methods of deduction, induction, and abduction. Looser constraints can be used for analogies at any degree of vagueness. By tightening the constraints in incremental steps, a reasoning engine can systematically tailor a vague guess to a precise solution.

3. What is the proper role of a theory of signs and meaning in relation to other academic disciplines?

Peirce convinced me that a theory of signs is the proper foundation for cognitive science, which includes philosophy, psychology, linguistics, anthropology, neuroscience, and artificial intelligence. Some people have suggested that neuroscience might someday provide a suitable foundation for the other branches, and others have suggested that AI would. But both of those views are misguided. Neuroscience and AI have strongly influenced other branches, including each other. Yet both of them have been guided by the branches that study the external effects of cognition: psychology, linguistics, and anthropology. Since the same topics can be studied from different points of view, cognitive science, by its nature, must be interdisciplinary.

Language affects and is affected by every aspect of cognition. Only one topic is more pervasive than language: signs in general. Every cell of every organism is a semiotic system, which receives signs from the environment, including other cells, and interprets them by generating more signs, both to control its own inner workings and to communicate with other cells of the same organism or different organisms. The brain is a large colony of neural cells, which receives, generates, and transmits signs to the cells of the complete organism, which is an even larger colony. Every publication in neuroscience describes brains and neurons as systems that receive signs, process signs, and generate signs. Every attempt to understand those signs relates them to other signs from the environment, to signs generated by the organism, and to theories of those signs in other branches of cognitive science. The meaning of the neural signs can only be determined by situating neuroscience within a more complete theory that encompasses every aspect of cognitive science.

Philosophy is considered the foundation for all other subjects, but philosophy itself has many branches, some of which are more fundamental than others. Aristotle called metaphysics *first philosophy* because it studies the nature of being itself. Yet the first six books of the Aristotelian corpus, the *organon* or instrument for carrying out any philosophical or scientific study, present Aristotle's theory of signs. Metaphysics is a prerequisite for science, but an understanding of signs is a prerequisite for studying anything, including metaphysics.

In short, neuroscience is one component of the larger field of cognitive science, whose ultimate foundation is the theory of signs. Like neuroscience, artificial intelligence relates cognitive signs to lower-level signs, which happen to be the data structures and operations of computer systems. In another galaxy, living things might have a totally different biology and neurophysiology, but all their life processes must be governed by signs. For all forms of life, evidence for the meaning of the internal signs comes from external signs of an organism interacting with its environment. For human life, psychology, linguistics, and anthropology study the external signs. Understanding the relationships between levels can clarify many issues, but it cannot "reduce" the external to the internal.

4. What do you consider the most important topics and/or contributions in the theory of meaning and signs?

The single most important contribution was Peirce's integration of the theories by the Greeks and Scholastics with modern logic, science, and philosophy. Aristotle laid the foundation in his treatise *On Interpretation*. His opening paragraph relates language to internal affections (*pathêmata*), whose existence is not in doubt, but whose nature is unknown:

> First we must determine what are noun (onoma) and verb (rhêma); and after that, what are negation (apophasis), assertion (kataphasis), proposition (apophansis), and sentence (logos). Those in speech (phonê) are symbols (symbola) of affections (pathêmata) in the psyche, and those written (graphomena) are symbols of those in speech. As letters (grammata), so are speech sounds not the same for everyone. But they are signs (sêmeia) primarily of the affections in the psyche, which are the same for everyone, and so are the objects (pragmata) of which they are likenesses (homoiômata). On these matters we speak in the treatise on the psyche, for it is a different subject. (16a1)

In this short passage, Aristotle introduced ideas that have been adopted, ignored, revised, rejected, and dissected over the centuries. By using two different words for sign, he recognized two distinct ways of signifying: *sêmeion* for a natural sign and *symbolon* for a conventional sign. With the word *sêmeion*, which was used for omens and for symptoms of a disease, Aristotle implied that the verbal sign is primarily a natural sign of the mental affection or concept and secondarily a symbol of the object it refers to.

In the last sentence of that paragraph, Aristotle noted that the study of the psyche is a distinct, but related topic. That point is key to Aristotle's success in avoiding the dangers of psychologism. Any system that interprets signs is affected by those signs and must therefore have some internal affections. Aristotle called such systems psyches, and he assumed that the affection must have some likeness (*homoiôma*) to the external object. That assumption would be just as true of the "psyche" of a robot that relates linguistic signs to images of the environment.

The triad of *sêmeion*, *pathêma*, and *pragma* forms a *meaning triangle*, which Ogden and Richards (1923) drew explicitly. Although they didn't draw triangles, the Scholastics were far ahead of Ogden and Richards. Their Latin terms for the triad were *signum*, *significatio*, and *suppositio*. They originally followed Aristotle in saying that the signification was an affection (*passio animae*), but they also called it a mental concept (*conceptus mentis*). They extended Aristotle's point that written signs are symbols of the spoken to a more general theory about signs of signs. They adopted the term *prima intentio* for a triad whose supposition is a real or imaginary physical object, and *secunda intentio* for a triad whose supposition is another sign. At the same time, they began to think of concepts less as likenesses (*similtudines*) than as language-independent signs of things (*signa rerum*). With this shift, all nodes of the meaning triangle became signs or even signs of signs. In logic, they combined Aristotle's syllogisms with a propositional logic that included a version of De Morgan's laws. An important achievement was Ockham's *Summa Logicae*, which included a model-theoretic semantics for Latin. Ockham wasn't as formal as Tarski, but he went beyond Tarski by stating truth conditions for temporal, modal, and causal propositions. He also went beyond Russell by accommodating suppositions of fictional things, such as a chimera, or intended things that did not yet exist.

Peirce had studied the Greek and Scholastic theories in depth and boasted of having the largest collection of medieval manuscripts on logic in the Boston area. He combined their innovations with the categories of Firstness, Secondness, and Thirdness, which he had discovered by analyzing the relationships implicit in Kant's table of twelve categories. Unlike Aristotle, whose categories are the most general types of entities, Peirce used his triad in a metalevel procedure for generating new triads by subdividing signs of any kind. Instead of two interlocking triangles for first and second intentions, Peirce could apply his method to any node of any triangle to spawn another triangle. Peirce also introduced new ideas that went beyond the Scholastic theories. Among them is the principle of continuity, which led him to the conclusion that the precision of logic is the goal of analysis, not the starting point:

> Get rid, thoughtful Reader, of the Okhamistic prejudice of political partisanship that in thought, in being, and in development the indefinite is due to a degeneration from a primal state of perfect definiteness. The truth is rather on the side of the Scholastic realists that the unsettled is the primal state, and that definiteness and determinateness, the two poles of settledness, are, in the large, approximations, developmentally, epistemologically, and metaphysically. (CP 6.348)

According to Peirce, the meaning of a symbol grows during the stages of learning and use, both in science and in everyday life. He recognized that a formal logic, in which every symbol has a single precise meaning, is valuable for recording the results of analysis. But he also realized that such a language, by itself, cannot support novelty and creativity. It would be unusable for learning, planning, discovery, negotiation, and persuasion.

5. What are the most important open problems in this field and what are the prospects for progress?

The most important problem is to correct the "grave errors" (*schwere Irrtümer*) that Wittgenstein (1953) recognized in the framework he had adopted from his mentors, Frege and Russell. One of the worst was the view that logic is superior to natural languages and should replace them for scientific purposes. Frege (1879), for example, hoped "to break the domination of the word over the human spirit by laying bare the misconceptions that through the use of language often almost unavoidably arise concerning the relations between concepts." Russell shared Frege's negative view of natural language, and both of them inspired Carnap, the Vienna Circle, and most of analytic philosophy. Some philosophers who had read Wittgenstein's later work and commented on it favorably continued to preach the same grave errors. Dummett (1981: 316), for example, still claimed that vagueness was "an unmitigated defect of natural language." Dummett (1993:170) also said that Austin's work on speech acts "was harmful and pushed people in the wrong direction." During a dialog, however, the language games can change, and the symbols can grow in continuous and unpredictable ways. In a written text, the author plays language games with the reader and may develop those games during the exposition. Even a textbook on mathematics shifts games from explanations and applications to conjectures, proofs, counterexamples, and exercises. In a narrative, the characters play language games with each other. Contrary to Chomsky, language competence is the ability to recognize, invent, and play those games.

Unlike Frege and Russell, Peirce had a high regard for language, and instead of trying to reform it, he did his best to understand it. A crucial experience came in the late 19th century, when he was employed as an associate editor of the *Century Dictionary*. During that period, he wrote, revised, or edited over 16,000 definitions — more than any other editor of that dictionary and much more than most philosophers of language accomplish in a lifetime. The combined influence of logic and lexicography is evident in a letter he wrote to the general editor, B. E. Smith:

> The task of classifying all the words of language, or what's the same thing, all the ideas that seek expression, is the most stupendous of logical tasks. Anybody but the most accomplished logician must break down in it utterly; and even for the strongest man, it is the severest possible tax on the logical equipment and faculty.

As logicians, Peirce, Whitehead, and Wittgenstein were as good or better than Frege, Russell, and Carnap. The former, however, embraced vagueness as the starting point for analysis, but the latter tried to build a fortress that would exclude any possibility of vagueness. Unfortunately, their fortress is a fragile glass house that collapses at the first contradiction. Some logicians tried to develop formal logics of fuzziness and ambiguity, but what they built is a metalevel glass house to protect the object- level glass. Some pioneers in formal semantics, such as Kamp (2001) and Partee (2005), admitted that logic alone is not sufficient to solve the problems, but they had no alternative to offer. Peirce never rejected logic, but he had a more encompassing system:

- A detailed ontology of signs as the basis for analyzing all aspects of cognition.

- Linguistic and logical signs as special cases of the more general theory of signs.

- Context dependencies, marked by indexes and indexicals, as the mechanism for relating language to the world.

- Versions of Austin's speech acts, Grice's conversational implicatures, and Davidson's event semantics.

- Continuity and its corollary that symbols grow out of vague beginnings.

- Induction, abduction, and analogy as prerequisites for discovering the axioms used in deduction.

- The fundamental principle of pragmatism: "Consider what effects, that might conceivably have practical bearings, we conceive the object of our conception to have. Then, our conception of these effects is the whole of our conception of the object." (CP 5.402)

Whitehead and Wittgenstein accepted most of these principles in one form or another, but every one of them was ignored, deliberately rejected, or considered a defect by Frege and his followers. Wittgenstein's language games, for example, are compatible with Peirce's principle of pragmatism, context dependencies, the idea that symbols grow, and the minor role of deduction in language understanding and use. The willingness to accept vagueness is an implicit recognition of continuity, but Peirce emphasized it explicitly. A promising approach by Thom and Wildgen (1982, 1994) derives the discrete structures of language and logic from continuous fields. The elegant crystals of logic are like diamonds that form in a continuous flow of magma.

As an application of his categories, Peirce recognized that the language arts of grammar, logic, and rhetoric are a clear example of his principles applied to linguistic signs. He generalized all three fields to more general approaches that included natural languages as well as the formalisms of mathematics and symbolic logic. To avoid the connotations of the traditional fields, Morris renamed the three terms of that triad as *syntax*, *semantics*, and *pragmatics*. During the 20th century, natural language syntax was studied in depth, but the fields of semantics and pragmatics were fragmented in competing approaches to a confused mass of techniques applied to a wide range of language-related phenomena. Although Peirce himself is no longer available, his method can still be used to find order in that chaos.

Semantics, loosely speaking, is the study of meaning, but the meaning triangle has three sides, and different studies typically emphasize one side or another: the link from words to the concepts they express; the link from words and sentences to objects and truth values; or the link from concepts to percepts of objects and actions upon them. Instead of integrating all three sides in a single subject with different aspects, linguists usually narrow their focus to competing, one-sided approaches named *lexical semantics*, *formal semantics*, and *cognitive semantics*:

1. *Lexical semantics* addresses the link between words and concepts. It follows Saussure's definition of language (*langue*) as "the whole set of linguistic habits, which allow an individual to understand and be understood" (1916). Lexicographers analyze a corpus of contextual citations and catalog the linguistic habits in lexicons, thesauri, and terminologies.

2. *Formal semantics* bypasses the concept node of the triangle and relates words and sentences directly to objects and configurations of objects. An alternate name, derived from the formalism, is *model-theoretic semantics*. Although some linguists developed versions of formal semantics, most of the proponents come from philosophy and computer science. Yet despite 40 years of sustained research, none of the computer implementations can translate one page from an ordinary textbook to any version of logic.

3. *Cognitive semantics* relates language-independent concepts to perception and action in a social context. Linguists who specialize in cognitive semantics often collaborate in interdisciplinary studies with psychologists and anthropologists. Among them are Lakoff (1987), Langacker (1999), Talmy (2000), and Wierzbicka (1996).

Pragmatics or rhetoric analyzes the language games. Like semantics, pragmatics can be studied from different perspectives: the structure of a text or discourse; the intentions of the author or speakers; or the social function of a game in the culture. Unlike the single semantic triad, the intentions of two or more participants in a social setting can entangle the pragmatic triad with multiple triads and subtriads. The plots of literary and historical narratives illustrate the complexity that can develop from a clash of perspectives and motivations. Much more research is needed to analyze all these relationships, but a Peircean approach provides the vocabulary and framework.

24

Frederik Stjernfelt

Professor
Center for Semiotics
University of Aarhus

1. Why were you initially drawn to the theory of signs and meaning?

What attracted me to semiotics, and more broadly, the study of signs and meaning, was, I think, several different vectors. One was as a student of Nordic literature: the interest in the interpretation of texts – and the interest in which theories might support and explain the interpretation of texts. This interest led me to semiotics taken as the study of text structures and interpretation. Before choosing literature as my field of study at the universities, however, I had been studying philosophy at the University of Copenhagen and had been close to stumbling into that University's mathematics-physics department. So another force which made me gravitate towards semiotics was more general: that of the interest in philosophy of science. Here, semiotics seemed to promise not only insights into the structure of texts – but also in the relation to reality of these texts, the basic scientific issue of the description and understanding of reality. And, finally, semiotics seemed to make possible the combination of the two: the study of text and other human and social entities – but with formal, scientific means.

These general forces seemed somewhat alien, however, in the environment of the late 70's Danish humanist academia where the more scientific aspirations of parts of the 68 movement seemed to whither away under the pressure of Marxism. Here, however, a small Copenhagen Semiotic Circle involving persons such as Per Aage Brandt and the late Harly Sonne acted as an oasis where issues semiotic were discussed in a free-floating way, liberated from the moralist and political straitjackets of the period. Here, I discovered one of the main scientific attractions of the semiotic program: it is basically anti-relativist due to the fact that the objective existence of signs, their contents, and their referents rejected all sorts of fashionable reductionisms: that of psychologism, reducing the content of signs and intentions to psychological states; that of historicism, reducing the same contents to contingent and ever-changing surface material on the process of history, and that of sociologism, reducing contents to be ineffable social constructions or mere instruments for power –let alone deconstruction and vitalism, reducing contents to the "play of differences" or to the dynamics of life itself. All these -isms failed to respect the difference between *Genesis* and *Geltung* and aimed at reducing the alleged validity of any claim to its process of origin, inevitably leading into relativism and, consequently, skepticism. Any claim, even the most evident ones, of course has a process of origin and may, for all these genealogical approaches to see, be dissolved into concealed motivations in this origin. Semiotics thus seemed to form an oasis in this climate of general humanist suspicion. Not that semiotics was never inspired by such genealogies – quite on the contrary, Danish semiotics around 1980 often looked to Foucault, Baudrillard, Derrida, and other Nietzschean figures, interpreting them in a strongly relativist way, thus creating an internal tension with the more formalist, realist, and scientific aims of semiotics. In the mid-80s, I wrote a book on semiotics and catastrophe theory, that is, on Rene Thom and Jean Petitot, as a response to a prize contest at the University of Aarhus. To me, this experience decisively took me to the rationalist, realist side of semiotics, and some of Rene Thom's slogans still stand out as guidelines for a realist semiotics: The task is to make a theory of language which makes the construction of knowledge about the world a corollary of the theory. This idea should not be taken in a Sapir-Whorf-like interpretation; rather, Thom's idea was that the validity of science must be based on the overall epistemological validity of ordinary language. On this basis, I tend to conceive of semiotics as a necessarily interdisciplinary endeavor, uniting insights from ontology, linguistics, logic, epicstemology, mathematics – and, in turn, psychology, sociology, anthropology, comparative literature, the neurosciences. My personal trajectory through semiotics led me to the involvement not only with Thom and Petitot, but a long series of figures mentioned below under section 4.

2. What do you consider your contribution to the field?

I have been interested in different branches of semiotics: mid-20 C Danish structuralism; catastophe theoretical semiotics; semiotics of pictures; narratology; interpretation; semiotics and the history of philosophy; biosemiotics; the relation between semiotics and phenomenology; semiotics and cognitive linguistics, semiotics of religion and sport, etc. My main contribution, however, is probably focused around the notion of diagrams.

In the mid-90's, I chose as the subject of my postdoctoral dissertation iconicity and diagrams based on the idea that diagrammatical reasoning forms the overlooked core of the mature Peirce's semiotics – tucked away in an obscure corner of the 4-volume edition of Peirce's mathematical writings. I did not want to become a Peirce addict, trying to find the answer to every possibe issue in some enigmatic parcel of Peirce's unpublished grocery bills, but rather to pick out and actualize a specific bundle of interrelated issues in the mature Peirce: continuity, semiotic realism, iconicity, abstraction, diagrammatical reasoning. At the same time, I saw these treasures as being closely connected to early European phenomenology, especially in the early Husserl where the concepts of formal and regional ontologies, the doctrine of parts and wholes, and categorial intuition played a theoretical role analogous to the Peircean cluster of concepts just mentioned. The result of this work became the book *Diagrammatology. An Investigation on the Borderlines of Phenomenology, Ontology, and Semiotics* (2007) which I consider as my major contribution to semiotics. In addition to the first half, containing the material on the issues indicated, it contains a second half pertaining to diagrammatical reasoning in biology, pictorial arts, and literature. Thus, the book also collects my contribution to the so-called Copenhagen School of Biosemiotics, an informal network appearing around 1990 with the biochemist Jesper Hoffmeyer and the biologist Claus Emmeche as central figures. I became part of that network and have enjoyed the collaboration with these great persons and have served as a sort of semiophilosophical sparring partner of the group. In this context, I have insisted on semiotic realism and the importance of Ernst Cassirer's doctrine of Symbolic Forms and his overlooked philosophy of biology. The chapters devoted to visual art and literature in the *Diagrammatology* book draw the connection to the phenomenologies of these fields and thus graft Husserl and Ingarden onto the basically Peircean conception of diagrams.

On a more general level, it is my vain hope that my work in

the field has contributed to the shaping of a semiotics in the spirit of the Enlightenment: an anti-skepticist, realist theory of signs and meaning which has no obscure, anti-scientific agendas and does not preclude political standards like liberalism, democracy, the rule of law, human rights, and I am increasingly interested in articulating a political philosophy on this basis, having published two books on the 90s Balkan Wars and one on multiculturalism and freedom of expression. Thus, I tend to think it is a duty for scientists to support free speech: the most liberal exchange of signs compatible with democracy.

A polemical aspect of my temperament has often led me to attack reductionisms like the -isms listed above – most often in Danish papers and books. My hope that these attacks have been influential remains, however, not enormous.

3. What is the proper role of a theory of signs and meaning in relation to other academic disciplines?

One of the results of the iconic or phenomenological turn of semiotics during the recent decades is that its close affiliation with the Linguistic Turn is weakening. Thus, linguistics ceases to be the model science of semiotics, even if language as an object, of course, remains a core issue of semiotics. Language appears as the most central of many cognitive and communicative tools of man, and semiotics – as indicated by the predicate "cognitive" in cognitive semiotics – must base itself on the study all such tools. This implies the empirical connection of semiotics to all aspects of cognitive science (from sociology over psychology to neuroscience) – and the conceptual connection of semiotics to epistemology, philosophy of science, and ontology. Peirce famously attempted to define a science by the community of researchers pursuing it. Measured by this criterion, it seems like it is no coincidence that among the practicing semioticians I know of, you will find both mathematicians, physicists, biologists, anthropologists, neuroscientists, philosophers, psychologists, linguists, literary scholars, logicians, philosophers, and many more. The more precise role of the semiotic project in academia is, of course, dependent on the future development of semiotics and the university as a whole.

Institutionally, it is probably not too pessimist to say semiotics is, for the time being, in a sort of crisis. Semiotics was institutionalized during the 60's with the foundation of the IAAS and the establishment of the periodical *Semiotica,* and many of the founding uncles of this era have left us or are in the process of retiring. In many cases, this implies that semiotic chairs, programs, and departments are dwindling, if not disappearing. The cognitive revolution in (parts of) semiotics seem, however, to work against this destiny, at least in some cases, including Bologna, Sao Paolo, Helsinki, Tartu, Paris, Kassel, Cleveland, Aarhus, and elsewhere. This points to the fact that it is only in the ongoing interaction with other disciplines that semiotics finds its place as the non-skepticist mediator between formal and material, humanist and scientific, strands of academia.

4. What do you consider the most important topics and/or contributions in the theory of meaning and signs?

Such contributions are so diverse and vast in numbers that they are easiest indicated by way of name dropping. In addition to Greimas, Thom, and Petitot, the heroes of my first book, my trajectory through semiotics has brought me in contact with figures like Aristotle, John Duns Scotus, Spinoza, Leibniz, Locke, Bayle, Voltaire, Kant, Humboldt, Bolzano, Frege, Peirce, Brentano, Stumpf, Reinach, Husserl, Meinong, Hilbert, Saussure, Ingarden, Lesniewski, Uexküll, Russell, Wittgenstein, Carnap, Cassirer, Arnheim, H.H. Price, Mukarovsky ,Jakobson, Brøndal, Hjelmslev, Tesnière, Merleau-Ponty, Lévi-Strauss, Barthes, Genette, Thomas Sebeok, Umberto Eco, Jaakko Hintikka, Roderick Chisholm, Wallace Chafe, George Lakoff, - as well as a series of figures contributing to this volume.

5. What are the most important open problems in this field and what are the prospects for progress?

The broadness of the domain of semiotics connects it to a large number of unsolved problems. Here, I pick out five.

1. I guess Peirce is right in seeing that chief among these is the ontological and mathematical notion of the continuum. Continuum comprises discontinuity, but not vice versa, claims Peirce, which is why continuity is more basic than the discontinuous singularities contained within it. Semantics, in turn, seems to be impossible without some notion of intensional meaning, and Peirce's argument claims that such

meaning is impossible to grasp without an ontological concept of continutiy – intensional meaning referring to a continuum of possible referents. Thus, continuity is connected both to semiotic realism, to the reality of powers or propensities, to iconicity (the existence of continuous signs like many images and diagrams), and to diagrammatical reasoning (such reasoning being based on the continuous deformation of a diagram). Semiotics thus must seek to integrate and contribute to the mathematical and ontological investigation of the continuum.

2. The central role played by diagrams in epistemology and semiotics points to an important task: the elaboration of a taxonomy of diagram types. This may sound easier than it is, because diagrams may make use of all formalisms of mathematics which is why the issue of diagram types is closely connected to – if not outright identical with – the basic issue of philosophy of mathematics: which basic mathematical objects are there and how is our mode of access to them? This problem is, of course, connected to the basic semiotic and epistemological issue of the connection between the formal and mathematical formalisms of semiotics and the empirical structures they are taken to describe. Furthermore, this issue also commits semiotics to its often overlooked connection to logic and epistemology: how do which signs facilitate reasoning and the ongoing growth of knowledge?

3. The biosemiotic insight that the use of sign vocabulary in biology is not mere surface verbiage but refers to real semiotic phenomena, even in the simplest biological processes, points to a central task of biosemiotics: the construction of a biosemiotic "ladder" indicating which sign types occur on which levels of biological evolution, forming a nested series of thresholds. Two basic methods to this end may be outlined a priori: a compositional one, taking higher biological sign types to be composed out of interrelated sets of simpler such signs; and a "physiological" one, taking arguments as the simplest full semiotic process to be rudimentarily present even in the simplest biological cases, and taking more complicated sign types to stem from specializations and compartmentalizations within specific segments of metabolism (much like organs form such functional specializations in organisms). Maybe this investigation needs a difficult integra-

tion of both approaches. The construction of such a ladder, moreover, will presumably shed new light upon many of the basic concepts of semiotics which will now be endowed with a biological ancestral tree of simpler such forms. The construction of such a ladder of thresholds is important in order to avoid naive anthropomorphism: the semiotic concepts used in biosemiotics must be scrutinized so to avoid the export of unwarranted assumptions from the human world onto other species.

4. A special case of 3), of course, is the semiotic "missing link" issue: what is the semiotic competence which human beings possess and higher animals do not? Earlier proposals like tool use, sign use, consciousness, metacognition etc. are being discarded in the ongoing research into animal cognition which never ceases to surprise in its charting of intricate animal competences. The missing link issue has resurfaced during the recent years' research into the origin of language (itself a crucial scientific issue uniting human biology, archeology, and comparative linguistics), and a growing number of different proposals are already around. The specificity of human semiotic competence is due to an autonomous syntax module of the brain (Chomsky), symbol use (Terrence Deacon), to double scope blending (Fauconnier/Turner), to joint attention (Michael Tomasello), to the coupling of the four capacities of 1) recursive information recombination, 2) application of same rules to different situations, 3) creation and understanding of symbolic representations, and 4) detaching modes of thought from perceptual inputs (Marc Hauser) – and several more. The intricate nature of this task stems from the fact that it involves both empirical and conceptual problems; the former of course because evidence from the missing link period is in itself sparse; the latter because it is not evident how the different proposals interrelate: maybe some of them will appear, on closer scrutiny, to be corollaries of some of the others or even identical to them, or some of them may turn out to be mutually dependent. The fact that this is not clear forms a central part of the very problem, and any full solution must establish the role of all concurrent claims in relation to the explanation given. Personally, I tend to think the Peircean notion of "hypostatic abstraction" should play some role in a satisfactory answer: it is the ability to shape new objects of thought by hypostatization

(thus making the object of "redness" out of the colour quality "red"). Such hypostatization allows for human beings to ask new questions about such ideal objects ("What is "redness"? What does it amount to? How is it produced? etc.). The establishment of such explicit, ideal objects moreover facilitate the possibility of changing such objects in a trial-and-error process and thus facilitate the control our very use of such abstractions in thought and language. Hypostatization would thus be what makes it possibe for human beings to *make explicit* a long series of semiotic processes which are taking place implicity in higher animals – and, by the same token, to actively and speedily monitor, control, and critique our own sign use and reasoning.

5. The issue of how human language relates to human cognition, perception and action capacities in general has appeared as a central issue after the weakening of the Linguistic Turn in philosophy, semiotics, and elsewhere. This question has, of course, come to the forefront thanks to the cognitive semantics and linguistics movement during the recent decades, as well as through ongoing semiotic research in the neurosciences. Here, many newer and older ideas are being recombined: embodiment, gestalt structures, blending, the localist hypothesis, neo-Whorfianism..Semiotically speaking, I tend to think that a conceptual revolution is needed where diagrams cease to be seen as mere illustrations to more basic linguistic or mental articulations – so that language is rather seen as a highly sophisticated and hetereogeneous tool made possible, inter alia, by diagrammatical reasoning. Thus, both syntax and cognitive semantics of concepts and metaphor in general seem to involve diagrammatical structure and its manipulation, and it is a crucial task to articulate an integration of a semiotic understandig of language with the understanding of other central semiotic devices.

25

Leonard Talmy

Professor Emeritus of Linguistics

University at Buffalo, State University of New York

---

1. Why were you initially drawn to the theory of signs and meaning?

I have always been interested in how the mind works. Although I began college in mathematics, the fascination of cognition overtook me. I think I might have concentrated on any branch of psychology that addressed cognitive structure if one had existed at the time or on cultural anthropology as easily as on linguistics. But a combination of factors did lead me to focusing on language. Still, I've always seen language as one system of mental functioning through which the mind could be studied more generally. So I'm glad that in more recent years, while keeping language as the base of my expertise, I've been progressively examining its relations to other cognitive systems, with the aim of our advancing in understanding cognition in general.

2. What do you consider your contribution to the field?

3. What is the proper role of a theory of signs and meaning in relation to other academic disciplines?

4. What do you consider the most important topics and/or contributions in the theory of meaning and signs?

My interest in how the mind works has especially attended to what is now often called higher levels of cognition. As I see it, such cognition includes major "substantive" cognitive systems like perception (in its various modalities), motor organization, affect, thought (including inferencing, planning, and imagining), culture (I proposed a cognitive culture system in Talmy 2000, Vol. 2, ch.

7), and language. Applying to these in turn are such major "operational" cognitive systems as memory, perspective, and attention and consciousness. Further, these can all function with respect to different organized "domains"–also implemented as systems in cognition–such as spatial structure, temporal structure, and causal structure. Critical to understanding how all these systems work is determining their principles of organization–that is, their structure and patterns of operating. Some further major issues that concern these cognitive systems are: how genuinely separate (modular) they are as against grading into each other; how extensively they function with distinct principles of organization vs. with common ones; how they interact and do or do not integrate; and the extent to which they or related forms of them exist in other animals. In my work, I have referred to this perspective as the overlapping systems model of cognitive organization.

I have been asked why I think that the analysis of conceptual structure in language is central to the study of language and cognition. In my view, understanding how the mind works entails understanding the principles of organization that characterize it overall and that characterize its various systems. And understanding the organizing principles of any single cognitive system is not only valuable in its own right, but can also serve as an entree to further understanding those of other systems or of the whole, whether by generalizing the similarities or by contrasting the differences. This certainly holds for language. More specifically, language consists of components with relatively distinct principles of organization, perhaps even distinct principles for different subcomponents within phonology, morphosyntax, and semantics. Each of these sets of organizational principles–besides their necessity in understanding language as a cognitive system– needs to be compared for similarities and differences against the principles found in other cognitive systems and in cognition overall so that we can map out how cognition is organized.

Semantics–that is, how conceptual content is organized in language–may well have several different subcomponents each with its own set of principles. One such subcomponent that I've already written much on is the semantics of the closed-class system. This system consists of those classes of forms that have relatively few members and have difficulty adding more. Closed-class forms can not only be morphemes, but also word order patterns, lexical categories, grammatical relations or, importantly, grammatical complexes such as case frames and constructions. While the closed-class system is largely the same as what is generally meant by "grammar", my work has focused on its meaning–that is, on its representation of conceptual material–hence, it has focused on the semantics of grammar. The principles of organization for the closed-class system and its conceptual representations include the following features.

There may well be an approximately closed, universally available inventory of concepts that can ever be expressed by closed-class forms. This inventory consists not only of the basic concepts, but also of the immediate conceptual categories that these concepts belong to, and of the large-scale schematic systems that these conceptual categories in turn belong to. The closed-class forms in anyone language express a selection of the concepts and categories from the universally available inventory–no language expresses them all–though possibly all the schematic systems have at least some closed-class expression in every language. Any individual closed-class form could represent a single basic concept, but more often it represents a schema consisting of a selection of basic concepts in a particular arrangement (as described most fully in Talmy 2006). The crucial finding is that there is a difference in the functions performed by the open-class system and the closed-class system of a language. In the conceptual complex expressed by any portion of discourse, the open-class system determines most of the conceptual content, while the closed-class system determines most of the conceptual structure. As a whole, the universally available inventory–its basic concepts, conceptual categories, and schematic systems–constitutes a pervasive and important–perhaps the most fundamental–conceptual structuring system of language. And the selection from this inventory present in any single language plays the same role for that language.

It is valuable to have this understanding about language in its own right–that it has a system dedicated to representing structure, in particular, a system of formal structure for representing conceptual structure. Even more striking, though, is the possibility that this organizational feature might be unique among cognitive systems. To use the colloquial expression, language hands you structure on a silver platter. It has an explicit structured formal system readily distinguished by its peculiar properties that represents conceptual structure as distinguished from conceptual content. For a contrast, consider visual perception. Much of the work of perception psychologists seems to consist of tracing out what they often implicitly take to be structural about vision. Yet there may be no overtly distinct subsystem in perception dedicated to establishing visual structure as distinguished from visual content. Put another way, no readily identifiable system responsible for a "grammar of vision" seems to mark itself out. As one consequence, there is no definitive way to conclude that any particular visual feature is a feature of structure or of content, nor that such a distinction can be made. For example, which of these two, if either, is color, as with the colors present in a scene? Further, there seems to be no definitive way to settle on some point along the visual processing stream, from the retina through the visual cortex and beyond, as being responsible for the main system of structuring in the perception of a visual scene or activity (whatever such structure might be thought to be). Accordingly, insofar as comparisons can be made across different cognitive systems, since language has an explicit indicator of its structural properties, it may offer the best entree to a cross-systems study of cognitive organization.

My analysis of how grammatically specified concepts group into conceptual categories and how these, in turn, group into schematic systems has been laid out systematically in the very first chapter of my two volumes (Talmy 2000), which sets the tone and much of the organization of those volumes. But a sense of the analysis at the schematic-system level can be given here.

Three of the schematic systems that I propose might be considered together as the "architectonic" systems. The first of these schematic systems I call that of "configurational structure". This system comprehends all the respects in which closed-class schemas represent structure for space or time or other conceptual domains often in virtually geometric patterns. It thus includes much that is within the schemas represented by spatial prepositions, by temporal conjunctions, and by aspect and tense markers. It also includes the uniplex or multiplex instantiation of a type of object at various points of space–what is often represented by number markers on nominals–parallel to similar distinctions for events in time already understood as part of aspect. Two instances of configurational schemas can be seen in a sentence like *Poles stood across the road*. The spatial schema represented by the English preposition *across* includes–to select only some of its elements and portray them broadly–a line extending perpendicularly between two parallel lines. The plural marker −*s* in *poles* represents the multiple instantiation of a 'pole'–understood as located at different points of space (not superimposed). By principles that govern the accommodation of different schemas occurring through a discourse to each other, the resulting conception includes the understanding that the poles are located at points on the transverse line and that these points have a representative distribution over this line (and are not, for example, all adjacent to each other in one spot).

While the first schematic system, configuration, establishes the basic delineations by which a scene or event being referred to is structured, the second schematic system, perspective, directs one as to where to place one's "mental eyes" to look out at the structured scene or event. This perspective system includes at least these conceptual categories:

A perspective point's spatial or temporal positioning within a larger frame, its distance away from the referent entity, its change or lack of change of location in the course of time as well as the path it follows in the case of change, and the viewing direction from the perspective point to the regarded entity.

And the third schematic system, attention, establishes how one is to distribute one's attention over the structured scene or event from the selected perspective point. Different strengths of attention in this distribution can form a pattern. And patterns of different types underlie various conceptual categories within this schematic system, such as scope of attention, focus of attention (in a center-surround pattern), level of attention, and the windowing of attention.

An example that involves both these second and third schematic systems, as with the previous example, rests on the distinct schemas of more than one closed-class form appearing throughout a sentence and on the interaction and integration of these schemas. Sentences (1) and (2) can both refer to the same scene. But in sentence (1), the marker for plurality (multiple instantiation) on *house* along with its plural verb agreement, the collectivity of the determiner *some*, and the stationariness represented by the spatial preposition *in* together call for a conceptual structuring in which one in effect regards the referent scene from a stationary distal perspective point with a global scope of attention. But in sentence (2), the singularity (unitary instantiation) of *house* along with its singular verb agreement, the distributedness of the temporal phrase, and the motion represented by the spatial preposition *through* together call for a moving proximal perspective point with local scope of attention–as if one were in succession regarding a series of houses from up close.

1. There are some houses in the valley.
2. There is a house every now and then through the valley.

These first three schematic systems might together be thought to comprise a group of architectonic systems because they can all operate together designating static or changing geometric-like patterns in a single spatiotemporal matrix (as just seen in the last example). If so, then a fourth schematic system, force dynamics, might be thought to complement the architectonic systems. While the first three systems deal with geometric-type delineations, the fourth system deals with the forces exerted by and the causal interactions among the entities marked out by the delineations. The schematic system of force dynamics includes an organized set of basic patterns–both steady-state and changing–that involve the exertion of force by one entity on another. It covers concepts like an entity's natural tendency toward motion or rest, an outside entity's opposition to such a tendency, resistance to this opposition, and overcoming of such resistance, as well as of helping and hindering, causing and letting. To illustrate, a sentence like *John doesn't leave the house* is force dynamically neutral and simply reports on a state of affairs. If a camera were set up outside the house, it would not record John's presence. Now consider the sentence *John can't leave the house*. The same camera would still show John's absence. But here this absence is conceptualized as the resultant of two opposing forces, John's tendency (here, desire) to leave and some obstacle that opposes that tendency, where the latter is stronger and so prevails.

A fifth schematic system of "cognitive state" could also be readily posited. Although I have written much about different aspects of such a system, I have not yet tried to work out how it might as a whole gather together and organize the extensive array of relevant closed-class representations. Actually, the schematic systems of perspective and attention are properly divisions within the system of cognitive state, but they are themselves so extensive that I have spun them off as separate schematic systems in their own right. Another extensive division within cognitive state, one that also might easily be spun off as a separate schematic system, comprises volition and intention, the criterial attributes of a sentient agent. Let me call this the "agency" division. Much as perspective and attention interact closely with configurational structure to comprise the architectonic systems, so agency interacts closely with force dynamics in what might together be dubbed the "ergal" systems. My analysis of agency appears mainly in Talmy (2000, Vol. 1, ch. 4 and 8 and Vol. 3, ch. 3), and it distinguishes between volition and intention. Volition is a cognitive event in a sentient agent that causes some motion of the agent's body or body parts, where this in turn can initiate a causal chain of events in the physical realm that culminates in a certain so-conceived final event. As a separate cognitive state, the agent's scope of intention is the amount of such a causal chain that the Agent intends to happen, necessarily starting with the volitional act, but able to terminate at various events before the final event, or to extent so as to include it, or even to extend beyond the final event. The three sentences in (3) illustrate these relationships. In the throwing situation of (3a), the length of the reported causal chain, involving a path of motion for a branch, is coextensive with the scope of John's intention for that chain. In the hunting situation of (3b) the actual actions carried out, such as moving about to inspect tracks, fall short of John's full scope of intention, which extends beyond those with the intent that they lead to finding and capturing the rat. And in the misplacing situation of (3c), whether or not it accords with a causal-chain account, at least it can be said that the length of the reported succession of events exceeds John's scope of intention. The latter only extends through John's placing the trowel down at some spot, not to his subsequent inability to remember that spot and find the trowel again (I term the subject of such a sentence the "Author" rather than the "Agent" of the final event). While such agency relationships can be lexicalized in open-class verbs (as they are for example, in *hide / hunt / spill*, respectively), they can also be represented by closed-class forms, as they are in (3a) by *down behind*, in (3b) by *for*, and in (3c) by *mis-*.

3. a. John threw the dead branch down behind the bush in his back yard.

3. b. John hunted for the rat that had been bothering him in his back yard.

3. c. John misplaced his trowel in his back yard.

Another major division within the schematic system of cognitive state can be termed "epistemics", which covers characterizations of a sentient entity's states of knowledge. This division certainly includes the evidential systems found in many languages, but it also includes many indicative-subjunctive type distinctions, factivity, forms for probability and possibility, and the like. Perhaps the most general characterization of this division is that it addresses the gradient from certainty to uncertainty. The forms within an evidential system in a language might well fall into two main classes with respect to this gradient, one class located at the certainty end and the other near it at the 'considered probable' location–in particular, where the speaker either knows or infers the stated proposition. More specifically, for one class of forms, the speaker considers the proposition to be a fact, while for the other class of forms, the speaker infers that the proposition is likely to have occurred, to be occurring, or to be going to occur. Within these classes, the forms differ as to the basis for concluding this factuality or likelihood. Thus, some languages distinguish three factual forms, one for where the speaker has witnessed the reported event ("John was chopping wood–I saw him"), another for where the speaker performed the action herself ("The beads are on the string"), and the third for situations considered common knowledge ("Horses eat grass"). And distinctions among the types of inference that some languages make include one for where the speaker has non-visually perceived the reported event ("John must have been chopping wood–I heard the whacks"), one for where the speaker observes telltale evidence (John must be chopping wood–the ax is gone from the house"), one based on observed periodicity ("John must be chopping wood–it's 3 PM and he usually chops wood now"), and one based on hearsay ("John is out chopping wood I hear").

Cognitive state includes still further divisions, such as "expectation" which covers both the expected and the surprising, as represented by the closed-class mirative systems found in some languages, as well as in such 'surprise' forms as the *how / so* forms in English as in *How big your eyes are! / Your eyes are so big!*. And there is certainly the affective division, which includes hypochoristic (diminutive) and pejorative closed-class forms although, as discussed in Talmy (2000, Vol. 1, ch. 1), affect never seems to become organized in a language as a replete closed-class system. But an overall analysis of the schematic system of cognitive state is still pending. Beyond the five schematic systems just proposed, others no doubt await positing. One candidate is a schematic system of "quantity". But more research is needed.

5. What are the most important open problems in this field and what are the prospects for progress?

What I outlined earlier–the overlapping systems model of cognitive organization–I see as a roadmap for directions in which the field of cognitive linguistics can and should expand. The procedure involves identifying cognitive systems sufficiently distinct from each other, determining the particular structure and dynamic processing that each such system has, and comparing these particular forms of structure and processing for their commonalities and differences. The promise of this procedure is to map out the overall structure and dynamics of human cognition.

This program has guided my previous work and is guiding my current research. I am working on a book on the attention system of language. Language has over 100 factors that raise or lower attention on one or another aspect of language and its use. These factors combine and interact in larger attentional patterns. There seem to be some dozen fundamental parameters whose combinations yield the numerous factors and which, accordingly, constitute the underlying attentional system. Trying to work this out is currently what is occupying my, uh, attention.

The above text is based on an interview by Iraide Ibarretxe-Antuñano (Ibarretxe-Antuñano 2005, 2006). We are grateful that she allowed us to remix her admirable and extensive interview with Len Talmy.

26

Eero Tarasti

Professor of Musicology
University of Helsinki

---

1. Why were you initially drawn to the theory of signs and meaning?

Certainly I have to thank for Claude Lévi-Strauss, who became the great idol of my young years after having read his brief booklet Myth of Asdiwal, as a Swedish translation. But of course much had happened before in my life, before this 'revelation'. As early as in my last classes at Helsinki Normal Lyceum, I got interested in German philosophy, which for me meant names like Hegel, Schiller, Goethe, and even Heidegger. When I then entered University of Helsinki with theoretical philosophy as my major I was upset by noticing that philosophy was not all like that but instead strongly dominated by the so-called Anglo-analytic school, formal logic, calculus of truth values etc. I got training in that - which later was useful in my Greimassian period - but was missing something. Simultaneously I wanted to become a musician, pianist, and studied at Sibelius Acadmy, the local conservatory.

Then in my year in the Finnish army I got interested in social affairs and after change my major into sociology, and started also ethnology. And then, in the summer of 1970 I read the aforementioned book and noticed that the two major themes of my life hitherto could be united: namely the abstract - philosophy - and the concrete - music, or as Lévi-Strauss put it: *l'intelligible et le sensible*. Then I established among my fellow students from many disciplines a study group or club which started to call itself 'Helsinki Structuralist Group'. We wanted to get familiar with continental thinkers but because no one of us mastered French or Italian well, we read them as Swedish translations - like Umberto Eco's *La struttura assente*. However, the first academic course in which I heard about semiotics was given by prof Vilmos Voigt from Budapest at Helsinki University Department of folkloristics in 1972.

Soon, after music and German language studies in Vienna, I wanted to leave for Paris, where I studied both music and structuralism. I played piano at Prof Jules Gentil at Ecole Normale de Musique, an institute established once by Alfred Cortot, and went to seminars and lectures which Parisian academic life could offer to me as an *auditeur libre*. I had become Master of Arts at Helsinki University in 1972 with a thesis "On the possibiltiy of a structuralist musicology" which I wanted to show to Lévi-Strauss himself. To my great surprise it was relatively easy to make an appointment at College de France, the plase of the 'immortals' which I visited, to interview him.

In fact the contact was helped by the friendship between Lévi-Strauss and a Finnish anthropologist Elli-Kaija Kîngos-Maranda, who was then professor at Laval uniersity in Quebec, so that I could bring greetings from the latter. I remember this moment very well and particularly how it ended: to conclude I said that certainly structuralism of such a small country like Finland could not be but a reflection of such big center like Paris. He interrupted: no, you are wrong, the center is always where you are yourself! That was of course very encouraging.

A little later I entered Ecoles des Hautes Etudes en Sciences Sociales with my PhD plan as an awardee of the French government. There the supervisor of my thesis became A.J.Greimas who immediately sympathized with me since I was from Finland and he from Lithuania. He introduced me to his great seminar which could easily gather two hundred students from all over the world, as 'the compatriot of George Henrik v. Wright'. But at that time there was also in Paris at Bld. St. Germain a *bureau d'acceuil* for foreign scholars whose services I could use. So I also got in touch with Roland Barthes whom I interviewed twice, and many others.

In my music studies I changed my teacher to Jacques Février, legendary pianist, and friend of Francis Poulenc. I felt that I could truly realize myself in the Parisian ambiance with a lot of various stimuli. But I also noticed how scholars rather spoke about of "sémiologie" or "sémiotique" than of sructuralism. I could see how Barthes, Foucault and Kristeva started their 'second periods' as poststructuralists, and how Lévi-Strauss's lectures gathered only some thirty listeners whereas in Foucault's lectures one had to be present almost one hour before in order to get a seat. So I became a semiotician.

2. What do you consider your contribution to the field?

I have undergone three periods in my scholarly career so far. The first period was strongly dominated by Lévi-Strauss, as said, and its main work was Myth and Music (Berlin: Mouton 1979) in which I scrutinized the mythical works in the Western erudite music and compared three major composers and their analogous mythical compositions, namely Wagner (*Siegfried*), Sibelius (*Kullervo*) and Stravinsky (*Oedipus Rex*). This orientation towards myths and what I called 'primal mythical communcation' brought me even to Brazil where I lived for one year in 1976 in order to study the Indians and myth and music in their aboriginal life. I was supposed to examine the flute orchestras by Suya Indians at river Xingu, guided by the American anthropologist Anthony Seeger who had been there for years and whom I then met in the anthropological section of Universidade Federal in Rio de Janeiro.

Yet, except a few transcriptions which I made for Anthony of the akias, melodies sung by the suyas, this plan was never realized - but instead I wrote an extensive study on Heitor Villa-Lobos, the greatest composer of Brazil, which had nothing to do with semiotics, a work which appeared in 1995 at Mcfarland, North Carolina. There we see how unexpeted and capricious the paths of a scholar can be!.

Anyway, my second 'life' in semiotics was dominated by the Paris school and Greimas. That culminated in the treatise *A Theory of Musical Semiotics* at Indiana University Press. My theory with its modal grammars etc. was—semiotically speaking—mostly based on a free interpretation of Greimas's generative course whereupon I built my 'system' and which I applied to musical works of various style periods - to show that the 'method' was universal and not bound with a certain stylistic framework.

But at the same time I became active in organisational issues thanks to my friendship with Thomas A Sebeok, a relationship which lasted unmitigated until his passing away in 2002. Sebeok invited me to the United States to visit annual meetings of the American semiotic society, which I did in Bloomington, Buffalo, Lubbock (Texas) and San Francisco. Yet Bloomington became my fortress in the US and its famous Research Center for Language and Semiotic studies. This may sound strange, thinking of my Greimassian background, but Sebeok never paid attention to school differences on this level. Yet the American meetings gave me a model how to organize similar conventions in my own country where I got the chair of musicology at the Helsinki University in 1984. The Semiotic Society of Finland had been founded as early as in 1979 but only now started its more active functioning which then led in the establishing of the International Semiotics Institute at Imatra in 1988, again thanks to Sebeok and a 'collegium' of 40 international semioticians. The ISI became then one of the most important centers of semiotics whose annual summer congresses gathered every June 200-300 participants. They culminated in the world congress of the IASS/AIS in Helsinki and Imatra in the summer of 2007. However, all this has been also very time and energy consuming, but has had a certain rewarding impact on our science even in global sense. Locally the ISI enabled foundation of our own series of monographs *Acta semiotica fennica* which we for some volumes published together with the Indiana University Press. Well, maybe such administrational activities can also be considered a 'contribution' to the field, at least it has meant a prepared platform for many semioticians, young and old, to present their ideas to others.

Simultaneously with these functions in general semiotics, I have been running my own specialty in musical semiotics, in which as early as in 1986 a research group entitled *Laboratoire européen de la recherche en Signification Musicale* was established at a direct emission in the French Broadcasting company in Paris. The title itself 'musical signification' was invented by Marcello Castellana, and present in the meeting were at least Gino Stefani, Costin Miereanu Francis Delalande and Luis Heitor Correa de Azevedo. The title was a clever choice since talk about 'signification' instead of 'semiotics' made the project more acceptable to broader circles. Later I asked from Greimas how to continue and he advised: take the project to Finland, we here in Paris are little bit like 'artists' in the management. So it happened, and the project has grown into the largest community of music semioticians in the world with its 550 members from all over the world. It has organized already ten major congresses, two in Finland, two in Paris, and one in Edinburgh, Roma, Bologna, and Aix en Provence. Next one will be in Vilnius in October 2008. The proceedings have been published as anthologies in major academic publishing houses from Mouton to Sorbonne series, CLUEB in Bologna and *Acta semiotica fennica*. As a side product of all this, 13 international doctoral and postdoctoral seminars in musical semiotics have been organized at Helsinki University, providing young scholars with a forum to enter the field. The proceedings of these have likewise appeared as anthologies like *Musical semiotics in growth* (1996) and *Musical semiotics revisited* (2003).

Yet my third period is perhaps 'the' original one, I call it 'existential semiotics'. It meant for me a return to the German speculative philosophy - which also in the meantime had become fashionalbe thanks to movements like deconstruction by Derrida . However, it did not mean any return to historically earlier period but rather finding a source of inspiration for semiotic epistemological reflections in the light of certain classics from Hegel to Kierkegaard, Heidegger to Jaspers, Sartre to Marcel, Soloviev to Royce. My first own book in this field was *Existential Semiotics* which appeared at Indiana University press in 2000. I remember, when choosing the title, the director John Gallman asked from me: what is existential semiotics? Is it the same as existential life? There is half a truth in that, namely in the sense that the role of a subject is reconsidered and on the other hand entirely new concepts are brought to semiotics like transcendence, metamodalities, *Moi/Soi*, being-in-and-for-itself/myself, new categories of signs from pre-act- and post-signs to geno-and phenosigns, endo- and exo-signs to quasi-signs and trans-signs.

Signs are considered in a constant movement between *Dasein* and transcendence via the 'journeys' of our existential subject, negation and affirmation. After all the existentiality of signs emerges in such encounters between transcendence and *Dasein*. Now 'transcendence' should be understood in a philosophical Kantian sense (evoking both his *transzendent* and *transzendental*). To put it simply: transcendent is anything which is absent but present in our minds. Every act of communication is a transcendental act since it means a leap into the unknown, to the 'alien psychic' of the Other.

Yet by no means the classical semiotics has lost its value, I am still faithful to Greimas, Lévi-Strauss and others, but they are now put in the framework of a new broader theory, which surrounds them (which is *englobant* to use the term by Greimas). This new theory is not at all yet ready and completed system, but is now under development and next treatise is appearing soon in Italian, French, Spanish, Russian and Bulgarian versions. It is also evoking anthologies dealing with reactions from the field. So the theory itself - as it says about signs in general - is in a state of 'becoming'.

3. What is the proper role of a theory of signs and meaning in relation to other academic disciplines?

There has been heavy debates on the essence of semiotics, whether it is an independent discipline or only an approach among many others. These discussions have then had their echoes in the practical academic life i.e. in the form of questions whether semiotics can be taught at all. Some classics were not very hopeful in this sense like Lotman or even Sebeok who taught a lot in other parts of the world except in Bloomington, where he never established semiotics as a discipline albeit had all the support from leaders from his university like from the legendary dean Herman B Wells. But others have been of school creating nature like Greimas and the fact is that semiotics nowadays strongly exists as an academic discipline all over the world.

But although semiotics certainly is a discipline with its own concepts, methods and epistemologies, it is very interdisciplinary by its nature. It is still probable that the utility of semiotics is only revealed when a scholar already has relatively much acquaintance with various empirical fields. Semiotics in most cases still grows from some concrete empirical or theoretical field, say linguistics, anthropology, arts, philosophy - which orients its exercise as the intuitive 'ground' or 'isotopy' for further reflections and methods.

On the other hand, the success of semiotics has lied in its adaptability to various local academic traditions in various countries, and also in its ability to change and be transformed all the time. Sebeok for instance had several phases: linguistics, anthropology, zoosemiotics, biosemiotics, Greimas shifted from lexicography and philology to a general theory of signs, Kristeva has been faithful to her psychoanalytic orientation, Lotman et alii are strongly linked to Slavic texts and Russian culture etc. In Finland, semiotics has been supported by folkloristics (Krohn Aarne, the' Finnish ' school of folklore with its impact on the Russians like Vladimir Propp or Hungarians from Bartok to Kodaly).

Moreover, semiotics has mirrored certain general intellectual trends - but fortunately not too much by losing its identity. So it has become one element in postmodern approaches from gender studies to postcolonial analyses and to British 'cultural theories', to deconstruction, media studies and 'mediologies', cognitive studies etc. It has often been combined with these as if it were not able to stand on its own i.e. communication and semiotics, cognitive studies and semiotics, media and semiotics. There are empirically oriented scholars in the field who see semiotics as a study of empirically observable and measurable signs and behaviours. But there are also philosophers and theoreticians who live in their discourses, getting inspiration from rather esoteric thinkers, even from Kant and Hegel, who for the first mentioned are only' conceptual poetry'. It is amazing how a peaceful cohabitation could be possible with such diverse standpoints. But perhaps we should believe in semiotics in the motto of the New Bulgarian University in Sofia, which runs manifold semiotic activities, namely in: *Ne varietatem timeamus*.

It is true that in the glorious days of structuralism semiotics was considered an 'efficient' discourse and metalanguage compared to traditional approaches. Semiotics was something of an avant-garde of thought - and in a certain sense it still is! I consider semiotics still an intellectual adventure which has a tremendous theoretical power when applied to many concrete problems of mankind - as biosemiotics, ecosemiotics and semioethics show.

Also existential semiotics takes the challenge of contemporary world seriously and ponders the role of values in our existential lives - as I have tried to show with my theories on resistance and postcolonial semiosis.

4. What do you consider the most important topics and/or contributions in the theory of meanng and signs?

This is very difficult to answer, let us say 'objectively' since the answer depends very much from your own scholarly history, temperament and taste, but let it then be subjective! I would divide this question into two aspects; one is theoretical and the other is practical.

Theoretically speaking there are many simultaneous theoretical options in the field of semiotics. Reflecting the fact we live more and more in a synchronic and not in a diachronic world characterized by historical succession, but rather in the field of 'omnitemporality' (a term by the Russian cultural philosopher Lev Karsavin, once a great idol of Greimas in his youth in Lithuania) or like music history in Latin America in which old styles do not vanish but continue their lives as superimposed levels of the whole culture (an idea by the Argentinian Carlos Vega) - in the same manner in semiotics which have inherited many theories from the classics which still maintain their full validity. Thus for instance Peirce was a genius - who has his position in philosophy - not highly recognized as a part of the so-called Anglo-analytic philosophical style to use the term by Nathan Houser - but rather as an independent figure, personalized greatness in philosophy, who will always stand on its own even without the semiotic movement. Then there is Greimas who has his believers in countries, scholars to whom his words are like engraved epigrams in an antique statue, the truth discovered once - which we only have read and interpret. Like Goethe said: *Das Wahre war schon längst gefunden, hat edle Geisterschaft erfunden, das alte Wahre fass es an!* Lotman created his cultural semotics school which still distinguishes itself as one theoretical alternative- but now applied to all possible cultures not only to the Slavic ones. But if we look after really new theoretical challenges in semiotics there are not many indeed, Biosemiotics stemming from the Estonian biologist Jakob von Uexkull, certainly is one among them. In philosophy and epistemology there is also a need for continuous redefinition of the foundations of the science of semiotics. Personally my modest effort has been to launch a theory of existential semiotics. but it is of course beyond my position to say how important it is or will be.

5. What are the most important open problems in this field and what are the prospects for progress?

First, the fact is that the history of semiotics in the twentieth century and now in the twenty-first has been an amazing intellectual adventure and success story. The basic ideas and concepts of our discipline, which were discovered and defined over centuries ago, since our classics in the Antiquity and Middle Ages, were grouped into various schools in the nineteenth and twentieth centuries...and now they appear in almost any congress organized in the humanities, social sciences and biosciences.

Semiotics has been victorious even to such an extent that those who have not followed its paths since its origin, are often even not aware of speaking the international scholarly language called 'semiotics'. Some may say that semiotics has blended together with other trends and schools, such as media and communication studies, cognitive approaches, biosemiotics, cultural studies, philosophy and so on. If you go to congresses of these fields and many other, the mere titles are pure semiotics stemming from our tradition. Others may see that semiotics has undergone an 'explosion' into different galaxies, into detailed special fields.

If we shortly try to define who we are and what are the prospects for progress, we could say: semiotics is a science which is always two steps in advance to others, it has served as the field of innovation in a true sense, not as a *pensée domestiquée* to produce immediate economic profits, but as a *pensée sauvage*, to quote Claude Lévi-Strauss whose centenary we celebrate in 2008.

In one word: semiotics has kept itself as the avant-garde of sciences. It has always been looking forwards, aspiring for the new, discovering new territories, asking new questions, making new explorations.

Let us look at the history. What made semiotics something new in the 1960, in the time of structuralism when it became institutionalized? On the one hand, regarding traditional high-culture topics in the arts, history, mythology, cultural heritage, the new, modern thing was to apply radically new viewpoints of information theory, linguistics, cybernetics, computer studies. This new viewpoint and aspect provided these topics with an estrangement effect, they were suddenly seen in a totally new light, fulfilling the epistemic ideals of efficiency, formalization, structural analysis. Yet on the other hand, as radical the idea to study popular, lower culture phenomena, lesser arts, like cinema, advertising, fashion, food, media with a rigorous and formal discourse sounded; they were so to speak elevated to a status of sublime and noble objects worth of serious academic studies. That was also a novelty.

But what could be the 'news' semiotics is bringing to us in 2007? Structuralism gave place for poststructuralism, and postmodernism, yet I have the feeling we are no longer living in any 'post- world', but rather facing new challenges. My conviction is also that science, even in its most abstact and theoretical branches, is ultimately done and written at its own time reflecting in a filtered version also the personal experiences of the world by the scholars exercising it. This new science I have taken the liberty to call *neosemiotics*. What it is and will be remains to all semioticians of the world, from many countries and traditions, to decide.

In some countries it is thougt that semiotic is kept alive and avant-garde by studying fresh phenomena of our new cultural environment. Thus one focuses on media, new forms of communication, internet, mobile phones, cyberthings, consumption, urban and posturban places, futurology etc. This is one possible avenue - but we have to remember that we are not only scholars studying such issues. They are dealt with by others whose discourses may have more direct appeal to larger audiences; we semioticians tend to be intellectuals who with our abstract concepts rather disturb the cheerful life in the globalized world.

Science is also an ideological activity. Is there then anything like 'semiotic' ideology or worldview which would guarantee its interest as a progressive science? Here we step into the area of values, which by no means can be excluded from any semiotics. It has been too much criticized for clarifying merely how things function instead of pondering vital questions like what we should do? Semioethics is a new subdiscipline trying to take this challenge seriously.

The theme of last world congress of the IASS/AIS reflected this situation with its emphasis on understanding of signs. Ultimately the idea came from a speech by prof Walbura von Raffler-Engel long time ago, in 1983 at a symposium of the Finnish semiotic society in Jyväskylä (also attended by Greimas), where she dealt with cross-cultural misunderstandings.

If such issues could be analyzed in a semiotical metalanguage and if there were enough educated people to understand and use such a discourse, semiotics could become, in the future, a living intellectual force, a theory of the global world of the 21st century. But not in the sense I would believe in any kind of rebirth of 'unified science' claiming that all problems are only results of wrong language use; if we get rid of badly defined concepts, the problems will disappear. Such naive beliefs do not sound very semiotical. Yet undeniable is it that semiotics could serve in a kind of 'emancipatory' function. Signs interact in the field tensions of freedom and necessity.

What we believe first to be 'necessary' or 'given by nature' appear in fact to be social constructions which might also be otherwise. The subject has the freedom to pursue semiotic acts in the world, i.e. 'actualize' virtual values and ideas, but when doing so he is totally responsible of his choices. He cannot say any longer *ca parle* or only observe how system thinks in him - he is an active agent in his world. Semiotics is there to help him to become conscious of it in order to fulfil his 'semiotic self'.

27

Mark Turner

Institute Professor
Professor and Chair of Cognitive Science
Case Western Reserve University
http://markturner.org

Signs of Intelligent Life

1. Why were you initially drawn to the theory of signs and meaning?

My interest in the singular cognitive abilities of human beings dates from my years growing up on the beach in California. Life was sweet. I had no directed intellectual purpose and paid no attention to anything intellectual at all, mostly because I was never exposed to anything intellectual at all. I had a tan, I ate Mexican food for breakfast, lunch, and dinner, and snack, and I swam all the time in the ocean. Mostly, I just watched the waves and the people. During a full day of doing nothing, after some long spell of just watching, or maybe very late that night, some riddle would spring fully formed into my head, I never knew why. The riddles always concerned some particle of everyday behavior I had witnessed, sometimes that day, sometimes in a more distant memory that had surfaced inadvertently to mind. I seemed to myself to have no control over the process, no warning, no choice, no insight into how it happened, and this posed a particularly hard riddle, but I liked it. Willy-nilly, my head became full of riddles, forming a list like Hilbert's problems in mathematics. I had no concept of research aside from my own thinking about these riddles. My school textbooks were unsatisfying. I did not know of any alternative within the world of education to the boredom these books offered. I found the riddles that popped into my mind much more interesting than anything I studied in school, and so I pretty much lived inside my own thoughts. I went to the library at times and read around randomly, but in those teenage years, I did not even know that academic fields like cultural anthropology and philology existed, much less what their names might be. I thought about beauty, desire, order, symmetry, art, music, chess, beef tacos, swimming, and surfing. Often I thought about mathematics, but my thoughts on any particular point of mathematics usually ended not with the mathematics itself but rather with the riddle that human brains could do mathematics. It seemed like magic to me that one could recognize a mathematical relationship for the first time, and understand it, and even extend it. But I knew it wasn't magic. Somehow, it was being done by brains, and I wanted to know how.

When I went to college, I took a B.A. and an M.A. in mathematics, but I also studied languages and took a B.A., M.A., and a Ph.D. in the English language. This sounds as if I was organized, but I was not. Most of my courses were not in any of my degree programs, and most of my degrees were taken only because I discovered that I had met most of the requirements. I took whatever courses I could find that treated aspects of the human mind. I tried psychology courses but found them dull. Those were still the days of rats and mazes. Various professors introduced me to rhetoric, philology, evolutionary biology, organic chemistry, neurobiology, artificial intelligence, computer simulation, languages, and linguistics. I also took two years off after college and went right back to the same beach to walk around and think and read while I sorted my ideas out. That was a wonderful two years, and I would not be in this field today if I had not spent those two years pondering riddles and hanging out on the beach. During that break in my education, I became interested in computing, especially artificial intelligence and natural language processing. When I went back to graduate school, in simultaneous but separate graduate degree programs, I had no mentors. Even my dissertation was self-directed. The problems I found interesting were almost universally judged by my professors to be intractable, maybe unanswerable. It was routinely conveyed to me that my interest in them was weird. I never understood these reactions and was frustrated with my professors.

I was exceptionally fortunate to encounter Hans Bremermann during my first year in graduate school. Bremermann was a professor in the department of mathematics who focused on biological systems, and particularly brains, but he also had a rich cultural education and was interested in everything. He was the first person I met on earth who was equipped to talk about brains and meaning and language in the same evening. His wife was smart, cultured, and warm. She carried the fabulous name "Maria Isabel Lopez Perez de Ojeda," which I loved saying. She was a professor of Romance languages. Their conversations fascinated me. They obviously loved each other very much, and their love was woven throughout their talk. Bremermann included me in his graduate research groups, where I was able to hear not only his own dissertation students (he had twenty-six of them in his lifetime) but also other dissertation students and postdocs from around the world talk about projects in the study of human cognition.

The phrase "cognitive science" had not yet been invented, but soon an informal group arose in "cognitive studies," where I met many psychologists, anthropologists, computer scientists, and linguists, but not as many biologists as I expected. Bremermann directed me to the nascent work in what we would now call cognitive neuroscience. The neurobiologists I was able to meet had much to say that was quite interesting about the nuts and bolts of the brain, and anatomy, which I dutifully studied, but it seemed as if they on principle declined to think about meaning, sign systems, or creativity. This was long ago—the mid-1970s. Passive brain imaging on normal subjects did not even arise on the scientific scene until much later, the late 1980s.

During that first year of graduate school, I arrived at the overarching view that still guides my research more than thirty years later, a view that is essentially an organized and better-grounded version of my beach reveries of the 1960s. It goes like this: Human beings are in their behavior, and especially in their ubiquitous creativity, dramatically unlike members of other species, despite the genetic and anatomical similarities. We rapidly develop new ideas, construct new meaning, and create symbolic systems. No other species has such abilities. Border collies, tursiops truncatus, bower birds, pan troglodytes, and mice are truly impressive, but, puzzlingly, human beings are so thoroughly different from members of other species as to be in a different galaxy of creative cognitive performance. This manifest grand difference in our behavior does not necessarily mean that we are qualitatively so different in our mental operations from other species. We are on a gradient with them, and in principle, it could be that we are simply farther up the gradient of ability. Nonetheless, the *effect* of our mental differences from other species is astounding. How can our distinctive cognitive abilities be explained? How did they originate in our species? How do they develop in individuals? How do they operate? What neurobiology subtends them?

Within science, it seemed to me then and it seems to me now that there is pretty much only silence in response to these questions. One long-standing shot at an answer—which has recently been revived under the name *evolutionary psychology*—consists of the claim that we evolved brains that give us this power. That answer, certainly true, is not per se very helpful. Except for dualists (if there are any left, who imagine that mind comes from non-physical stuff, such as muses or mythical ravens whispering in our ear, or souls spectrally instructed by unknown spirits), virtually everyone in the current scientific community has always been an evolutionary psychologist in just that sense: human beings evolved brains that enable us to perform these wonders. The easy embrace of this obvious principle brings no knowledge of the nature and details of the mental operations that constitute these abilities, or how the abilities evolved in the descent of our species, or how such abilities develop in individuals over the lifecourse, or the neurobiology that subtends them, and this is just the knowledge we want.

There is a more profound reason that the otherwise true and beautiful answer, "evolution did it," is inadequate. Evolutionary capacities like vision, pain, and hunger are nearly uniform across our species, not only in the *mechanisms* of their basic operation but also in the *products* of their operation. But the opposite is true for the basic mental operations that give us the ability for nuanced meaning and sign systems: although their *mechanisms* appear to be virtually universal across our species, their *products* are in important ways stupendously non-uniform across human cultures and human beings. The ideas, manners, rituals, and language used in one village can be quite different from those used in the village on the other side of the bay. The ideas, manners, rituals, and language used in one generation can be quite different from those used just a few generations ago. Human beings show staggering creativity, innovation, and variation in their meaning and sign systems. Vision, hunger, and pain show nothing like this creativity, innovation, or variation.

On one level, meaning and sign systems are indeed like vision, hunger, and pain: evolution produced vision, hunger, and pain, and evolution produced the mental operations we use in meaning and sign systems. The mechanisms of all these capacities are largely shared across the members of our species. But on another level, meaning and sign systems are quite unlike vision, hunger, and pain. Since they show great divergence in their products, we must discover not only the universal *mechanisms* that make meaning and signs possible and that result in regularities, but also how these mechanisms should make us so creative.

If three human beings all look at the same fruit tree when they are all very hungry, and then one of the fruits falls on each of their heads, they are going to see pretty much the same thing, experience pretty much the same interest in eating, and feel pretty much the same pain. But there can be extraordinary differences in what they think about it, what they say about it, the stories they tell later about it, the inquiries that result from it. The first might merely grumble, the second conclude that there is a spirit in the tree trying to communicate by sending down fruit on our heads, and the third invent a theory of gravity.

Evolutionary capacities like vision, hunger, and pain are extremely old in our evolutionary descent, but again, the opposite is true for nuanced meaning and sign systems, which are, in evolutionary terms, new. Writing systems, for example, are at most only a few thousand years old. Morse code and the English language were unknown only some hundreds of years ago. Digital systems and communication, including digital sign systems, which have swept the world, have developed for the most part only in my lifetime.

It would be a major scientific advance to know the details of how evolution produced the basic mental operations that make it possible for us to have meaning and sign systems. Yet it is obvious that those mental operations, which produce new meaning and sign systems very rapidly, are not themselves the evolutionary mechanisms of genetic variation, inheritance, and selection: those mechanisms require evolutionary time scales running across many generations, while meaning and signs, by contrast, can change within seconds. Meaning and sign systems develop in cultural time (that is, mere thousands of years or less) rather than evolutionary time. Meaning and sign systems can evolve so quickly that cultures often invent procedures, such as institutions, to govern the pace of invention, so as to enforce a useful level of stability, regularity, and expectation (Engel 2005).

Knowing that human beings are governed by systems of physics (gravity), chemistry (the chemical bond), or evolution (natural selection) gives us some insight: we fall to earth, our bodies can be damaged by free radicals, our differential genetic representation depends upon reproduction patterns. But these basic constraints do not tell us how language or art or scientific discovery or mathematical thinking work, or how they originated, or how they develop in individuals, or how human meaning and signs can change so quickly.

Did evolution "give" us meaning and signs? Perhaps a number of them. That is to say, it is conceivable and plausible that some highly-important frames of meaning and some meaningful signs could be carried by a genotype, in the complicated and limited sense that the structure of the genotype combines with reliable ontogenetic experience to produce during development those privileged frames and signs. No doubt evolution does this not only for us but also for dogs, dolphins, chimpanzees. For example, so goes the logic, human beings have a genetically-instructed capacity for recognizing certain kinds of predators and taking appropriate evasive action, and perhaps laughter is a species-wide sign. The hypothesis that such frames of meaning and such signs must arise for any human being with the requisite biology and the requisite experience is acceptable and interesting. But, first, this hypothesis of *genetic carriage* tells us nothing about the nature or principles of the underlying capacities. Second, it can apply to only a relatively small number of widespread frames of meaning and signs. Third, it offers no explanation for the meanings that vary dramatically from culture to culture or person to person. Indeed, it offers no explanation for the meanings that have developed during only the last five thousand years.

Granted that human beings, like lizards, are built to distinguish predators from potential mates, what we want to know is how the vast world of diverse human meaning could arise, and there is relatively little answer to be found in the hypothesis that natural selection has built human beings to develop a relatively few widespread frames and signs. What we need to know is how evolution built species-wide basic mental operations that make it possible for us to develop new conceptual meaning and sign systems, and quickly, too, without the need of further genetic evolution. We also need to know how those basic mental operations work. It is yet another project to show how those operations did in fact work in a particular cultural context to create particular ranges of local meaning.

Another promising approach in the explanation of human abilities is the field of *statistical extraction*. The field of statistical extraction is actually a sub-branch of the field of evolutionary psychology, not a rival, despite the adversarial positioning of the two fields, since the theory that human beings have capacities for statistical extraction relies on the assumption that phylogenetic descent evolved just those capacities (Poggio et al. 2004, Boucheron et al. 2004). Theorists of statistical extraction are to this extent evolutionary psychologists to the core. Theories of statistical extraction range from the notion that we develop conceptual frames and schemas by abstracting inductively from experience to, e.g., contemporary models of the formation of lexical categories and grammatical constructions by statistical extraction from the data we hear.

Again, it would be exceptionally valuable to know how our evident abilities for statistical extraction evolved, what operations in fact take place mentally during on-line statistical extraction, and what neurobiological processes subtend those operations, but even in the fantasy scenario in which we knew all those answers, we still would not know what we want to know: knowing that statistical extraction works on what already exists does not explain how it is that what already exists came into existence.

How do new meanings and new signs arise in our experience, so that we can recognize their regularities? To say that the individual knows meaning and sign systems by statistical extraction from experience is to assume the existence of the very systems whose origin we want to explain. Theories of statistical extraction propose that when the world changes, we detect new regularities and then represent those regularities in compressed templates. But most change in the world arises because people—individuals and groups—engage in mental invention of new meaning and signs, and this new meaning *results* in new regularities in the world. The new meaning is often available before it has produced new regularities in the world. Clearly, an account of the invention of meaning cannot assume as its beginning point that the world has already changed, for the invention of meaning is, in good measure, prior to those changes in the world. We need a theory of signs and meaning that accounts for the kind of invention that precedes the changes it induces in the world. To say, "there are meaning systems and sign systems, and we use statistical extraction to detect and model their regularities" does not explain how those meaning and sign systems can arise or change. For that, we need an account of the origin and development of meaning and signs that does not consist exclusively of extraction of regularities already evident in environments.

The riddle of meaning and signs seemed to me back when I was a beachcomber to be the most interesting, challenging, and important scientific problem we face, as well as perhaps the hardest, given that our minds are not ideal instruments for understanding how our minds work. The riddle only grows more attractive with time.

2. What do you consider your contribution to the field?

I once titled an article, "A Mechanism of Creativity." I did not ponder the title. I thought it was inevitable, unexceptionable, even pedestrian. Reviewers and readers since its publication have responded with the opposite attitude, asking, in various words, "Is that not an oxymoron?" The collation of "mechanism" and "creativity" has been regarded as aggressive, violent, reductive, insulting. I did not anticipate that reaction, and I have reflected on it since. Historically, it turns out, there has been great resistance to a science of imagination, creativity, and signs. It is almost as if there is a widespread view that the fundamental distinction of human beings lies by rights within the realm of the mysterious. This resistance has been based on a set of related erroneous views, which we should transcend:

- The erroneous view that creativity is a special, rare, psychologically costly event. On the contrary, creativity and innovation are the hallmark of our species. Our everyday, moment-to-moment activity, from infancy, shows an extraordinary creativity across all the behaviors that distinguish human beings. Every normal child is born a creative genius. Our brains run these creative processes constantly. Creativity is not unusual or psychologically costly. Given the brains we have, it comes for free.

- The erroneous view that there are special creative processes in the mind that are distinct from those we use for the rest of our activities.

- The erroneous view that only a fraction of human beings— Shakespeare, Mozart, Leonardo da Vinci—are creative.

- The—by my lights—unlikely view that our capacities for meaning are fundamentally different from our capacities for symbolic systems.

27. Mark Turner

I have worked on the science of what makes human beings human: a science of imagination, creativity, and symbolic systems. Human beings are biologically very close to other species. We have the common mammalian brain and the common primate brain, with their many detailed pathways. The human genome is much closer to the genomes of other species than was imagined even a decade ago. Anatomically, we look like a great ape. But fifty thousand years ago, more or less, during the Upper Paleolithic, unmistakable archeological evidence began to accumulate of a remarkable set of human singularities: art, science, religion, refined tool use, advanced music and dance, fashions of dress, language, mathematics, sign systems. Human beings began to demonstrate an unprecedented ability to be imaginative in whatever they encountered. Cognitively modern human beings throughout the world since that time have demonstrated this remarkable ability, as a routine part of what it means to be human.

What mental operations made these human abilities possible? How do those operations develop? Evolutionarily, what happened?

My work has centered on the principles of cognitive mapping. The overarching theory that combines the various aspects of my work and the work of others on cognitive mapping is known as the theory of "conceptual integration networks," which originated in a collaboration between me and Gilles Fauconnier. The principal presentation of this work to date is our 2002 book, *The Way We Think*. Perhaps hundreds of researchers from many different fields of formation have moved the work forward in many interesting directions. I try to list important new work at http://blending.stanford.edu, but the field is by now too large for me to monitor thoroughly.

The theory of conceptual integration analyzes the way in which conceptual projection occurs between different conceptual elements. The mental operation of conceptual integration has a set of constitutive principles and a set of governing, competing, optimality principles. Conceptual integration produces conceptual integration networks that include *blended spaces*, that is, mental arrays which receive selective projection from other conceptual arrays and develop emergent meaning of their own. Although rudimentary forms of conceptual integration seem to lie within the ken of many species, the most advanced form of conceptual integration is unique to human beings. It is called "double-scope conceptual integration" or "double-scope blending." Double-scope blending is the operation that makes it possible for us to invent and deploy new meaning rapidly, and equally the operation that makes it possible for us to have language and other sign systems. The capacity for new meaning and the capacity for sign systems are subspecies, I propose, of the same capacity.

A double-scope integration network—the most advanced form of conceptual integration network—has input conceptual arrays with different, often clashing, organizing frames and an organizing frame for the blend that includes parts of each of those organizing frames and emergent structure of its own. In such networks, both input organizing frames make central contributions to the blend, and their sharp differences offer the possibility of rich clashes. Far from blocking the construction of the conceptual integration network, such clashes offer conceptual challenges that lead to creative solutions. The resulting blends can turn out to be highly imaginative. Fauconnier & Turner 2002 offer analyses of the way in which grammar, speech, and writing systems derive from double-scope integration networks. Scott Liddell (Liddell 1998, Liddell 2000, Liddell 2003) and others (Parrill & Sweetser 2004, Wulf & Dudis 2005) have analyzed the derivation of sign and gesture from conceptual integration networks. Turner (2007) analyzes some of the ways in which signs compress conceptual arrays connected by *representation* links or *analogy* links, or both, into signs that are double-scope blends.

3. What is the proper role of a theory of signs and meaning in relation to other academic disciplines?

The supple forms of meaning construction and sign construction unique to human beings derive from our ability for double-scope blending. The study of meaning and signs is accordingly a part of cognitive science. Because higher-order human cognition derives from our abilities for blending, a discovery made about any one form of higher-order human cognition can tell us something about blending in general and accordingly something about other forms of higher-order human cognition. Via blending theory, the study of signs and meaning has evident connections to cognitive social neuroscience, developmental psychology, distributed cognition, rhetoric and poetics, and medical fields such as the study of cognitive disorders. It has equally evident connections to all the other fields that investigate human thought and action, as well as to art, language, literature, dance, theater, politics, economics, law, and society.

It is perhaps worth emphasizing the connection to history. Scholars of meaning and sign systems in the humanities have for the most part focused on cultural and sociological history as they operate over relatively brief temporal spans of a few decades or centuries. Cognitive science shares that interest in brief cultural and social history, but equally considers two other crucial aspects of human history. The first is phylogenetic history, as it runs over thousands and millions of years. The second is ontogenetic history—the development of the individual mind and brain, from conception to advanced age. Cultural, phylogenetic, and ontogenetic history are typically viewed in cognitive science as aspects of human history that do not operate independently. That is the view of history we should take in the study of meaning and signs. The meaning and sign systems we have are made possible by our evolution and the basic mental operations of cognitively modern minds, which is to say, minds of the sort that human beings have had for at least fifty thousand years. The products of those operations arise in ways that are path-dependent, non-foundational, contingent, non-teleological, and non-necessary. Historical systems develop emergent structure, and they rely on accidents. For example, our being alive at all probably depends upon an accident 65 million years ago in which a meteor hit the sea off the coast of Yucatán, giving mammals a leg up in the competition with dinosaurs.

There are many systems that develop through time that are path-dependent, non-foundational, contingent, non-teleological, and non-necessary. They include all living terrestrial things over all time; a given gene pool; all conceptual systems in all individuals over all time; a conceptual system shared by a community and all the conceptual systems that are ancestors of that conceptual system; a conceptual system within a single individual and all the conceptual systems that were, in the individual, ancestors of the current conceptual system; human language, all of it, over all historical time; a human language shared by a linguistic community and all the diachronic linguistic structures that are ancestors of that language; a human language, in an individual, and all the linguistic systems that were, in the individual, ancestors of that current linguistic system; and an individual central nervous system during its ontogenetic development. Systems of this sort also include communities and cultures. One of the things cognitive science is most interested in studying is how various human historical systems interact. The three aspects of human history I have listed—the phylogenetic, the ontogenetic, and the cultural—are, it seems, only some of the inseparably interacting historical systems that go into constituting meaning and sign systems.

4. What do you consider the most important topics and contributions in the theory of meaning and signs?

I provide a partial survey of these topics and contributions in (Turner 1998). The work that I find most useful consists of the studies of conceptual mapping and integration, but this work draws on traditions as varied as classic rhetoric, frame theory, cognitive linguistics, and cognitive scientific fields dedicated to representation, art, and semiosis. There is considerable hope that computational, developmental, neuro-medical, genetic, and brain imaging approaches might contribute to the study of meaning and signs. We should dedicate ourselves to bringing these fields together with the investigation of the nature, mechanisms, and principles of meaning and signs.

5. What are the most important open problems in this field and what are the prospects for progress?

V. S. Ramachandran has encouraged us to ask three particular questions when we discuss mental operations: What?, How?, and Why?

The What? question is the one on which I have chiefly worked: what are the principles of the mental operations that make higher-order human cognition possible? Double-scope blending, in particular, makes the origin, development, and deployment of meaning and sign systems possible, but how exactly does it work? Initial work on the subject is in place but there are many open problems to be solved.

The How? question is daunting, since our ignorance about the cognitive social neuroscience of higher-order thought is profound. Brain mapping is very intriguing, but mapping gives us indication only about location, and even then, only through subtractive and averaging means, and quite indirectly, such as through Blood Oxygen Level Dependent (BOLD) effects arising from the paramagnetic properties of differing proportions of deoxyhemoglobin in the blood over time in microvascular capillaries and venules in the brain. This is extremely far from knowing how the neurobiology is actually effecting the mental operations. It is a little bit like having a little data on where current is flowing in a computer without understanding what operations the computer is running. Moreover, the varieties of brain mapping that have been available to date are not suited to the investigation of the complexities of meaning and sign systems. Yet I am full of hope. Not only are fMRI and PET investigations unearthing interesting data, even if that data is somewhat remote from questions of cognition, but also work like Seana Coulson's (2000) Event-Related Potential (ERP) experiments on reaction to language, gesture, music, and so on—such as the role of the P300 component in incongruity, the N400 component in processing meaning, and the P600 component in processing grammaticality—are very interesting.

The Why? question—the question of phylogenetic descent—is presumably much harder to answer because we do not have a time machine to take us back fifty or one hundred thousand years or more to obtain the evidence. The answers to the Why? question are entirely speculative under present methods, and the obvious evidence related to the Why? question has vanished from the earth. The proposal that Gilles Fauconnier and I have made is that evolution produced an advance in conceptual integration properties, carrying us up the cline to the level of double-scope integration, at which point higher-order human cognition and culture become possible. At that point, human beings used the double-scope capacities they had to produce ranges of cultural products, meaning and sign systems. Double-scope integration need not have been a huge stride for it to have had enormous effects. Even small increments in the mental ability for blending would have conferred advantage, and so the natural selection just-so story taking us from more rudimentary forms of conceptual integration to full double-scope blending integration is plausible, if perhaps like all the other just-so stories impossible to prove at the moment.

I see a few hypothetical sources for answers to the How? question. The first is obvious. We do neural binding in everyday perception, time-place collocation, and other mammalian integrations. The neural computation involved in these operations could have evolved into a hypertrophy capable of advanced forms of integration. The second is also obvious: synaesthesia is a kind of neural binding in restricted domains. Perhaps it could have evolved into an ability that is not restricted to one or another conceptual domain. There are other restricted-domain abilities that look as if they involve integration, such as chase play, a kind of simulation of aggression, which evidently is quite common throughout the mammalian world. During chase play, parent and offspring simultaneously activate motor patterns, attention patterns, and motivational structures that belong to two very disparate domains, such as parent-offspring and predator-prey. It seems not an unreasonable hypothesis that the neural circuitry subtending binding, synaesthesia, or special-purpose blending of the sort we find in chase play might have gotten the ball rolling in the run-up to full cognitive modernity.

One major open problem in blending theory is the determination of the conditions under which blending occurs. Very occasionally, we can see the results of blending. Mostly it operates below the horizon of consciousness. How frequent in the brain are unsuccessful attempts at blending, of the sort that never penetrate to thought or behavior? Is the human brain a kind of vast bubble chamber, constantly trying to blend different things? Perhaps very many of these attempts are being conducted in our brains all the time. Perhaps almost any two things that are activated simultaneously become candidates for an attempt at blending. Perhaps a motor pattern shared by many different activities can initiate an attempt to blend those activities. Indeed, perhaps our ability to perform routine motor actions in different surroundings comes from our ability to blend our knowledge of our current surroundings with our knowledge of the motor ability. I imagine that most of these attempts fail almost immediately because the constitutive principles of blending are not fulfilled or the governing principles of blending are contravened or the integration networks do not attach themselves to any purpose we have. Of the relatively very few conceptual integration networks that are successful, only fewer still ever percolate into consciousness. But this constant attempt at blending provides a robust way of introducing a strong engine of variation into our conceptual systems. Almost all of those products of variation are selected against by governing principles or by pressures and affordances of our environments or by the absence of utility of any kind. But some of them, although they begin by blending different structures that one might think have no business being blended, nonetheless provide quite powerful new conceptions, new meanings, new signs.

The role of distributed cognition is also crucial for the study of sign systems. The great virtue of any one human being's coming up with any double-scope integration is that all the other human beings stand ready to understand it, incorporate it, and propagate it. In this way, culture is an incomparably larger bubble chamber than is an individual brain. With the entire species running double-scope experiments in this vast bubble chamber, there are wonderful possibilities for sustained, effective, and accretive creativity in meaning and sign systems.

These final open questions are at the outer limit of what cognitive social neuroscience, evolutionary biology, cognitive science, and semiotics can at present investigate. An aggressive and sustained program of research is needed to explain how the brain is capable of double-scope integration for meaning and sign systems. This program of research will require intensive and sustained collaboration across researchers in many different disciplines.

28
Wolfgang Wildgen

Professor of Linguistics
University of Bremen

1. Why were you initially drawn to the theory of signs and meaning?

Before I finished high school, i.e., before 1964, I was attracted by the work of Norbert Wiener and the cooperation in interdisciplinary groups which brought together mathematicians, anthropologists, psychologists, neuroscientists, philosophers, and linguists. My intention was to combine the solid methods of mathematically based sciences with insights into language and literature. In my first years as a student in Munich (1966 to 1968) I added to the normal courses in the department of Germanic and Romanic philology, lectures and seminars in cybernetics (in physics), of mathematical logics (philosophy and logics) and philosophy of language (Plato). At this stage, semiotics was rather implicit to such an interdisciplinary enterprise focusing on language and mathematics; it became more explicit when I went to Cologne (Hansjakob Seiler) and Bonn (Gerold Ungeheuer), where I added General Linguistics and Science of Communication to my curriculum. I very soon joined the German Association of Semiotics (DGS) founded in the 70s and gave my first semiotic talk at the International Conference of Semiotics in Vienna (1979). At this period I was already working on my Habilitation-thesis: "Verständigungsdynamik" (Dynamics of Communication), based on the work of René Thom in linguistics and semiotics. By joining a European group of semioticians (the *groupe Sigma* with Jean Petitot, Per Aage Brandt, Herman Parret, Jean-Pierre Desclés, Paolo Fabbri, Jean-François Bordron, a.o.) I definitely became a semiotician.

2. What do you consider your contribution to the field?

My work in sociolinguistics and discourse analysis in the 70s (cf. my doctoral dissertation on semantic-pragmatic variation and communicative styles in different social classes) was only semiotic insofar different media: spoken and written discourse and the influence of social characteristics were considered. One could call it "socio-semiotics".

In the new line of a topological semantics suggested by Thom, spatial structures and dynamics came into the center of my interests and I began to develop topological and dynamic models of different aspects of communication. First, in the analysis of the grammar of verbs and verbal valences (cf. my book: *Catastrophe Theoretic Semantics*, 1982), later in narrative analysis (cf. Part II of my book: *Process, Image, and Meaning*, 1994) spatially and dynamically motivated semiotic schemata were applied to language and discourse.

In a parallel endeavor the history of spatial and cosmological models applied to language was treated in a book (1985; in German) and a special link to antique and Renaissance artificial memory was established. The Copernican type of art of memory by Giordano Bruno (1548-1600) was a historical turning point in this development (cf. my book on the semiotics of Giordano Bruno in his art of memory, 1998). Leibniz and Peirce are seen as followers of this trend.

Beyond a semiotic theory based on differential topology (catastrophe theory) other kinds of mathematical models were considered: chaos theory, synergetics and cellular automata (cf. Wildgen, 1994). In general a theory of self-organization was considered, which could unite these fields and explain the emergence of semiotic capacities in man. My latest book: *The Evolution of Human Language* (2004) brought the lines of this research together.

Other fields, which allow for fruitful applications of the geometrically founded tools of dynamic semiotics are: visual semiotics, semiotics of town (morphogenesis of towns) and semiotics of architecture. Currently several areas of this field have been treated in conference papers and a book on visual and urban semiotics is in preparation. In a course book published by de Gruyter in February 2008 (in German) I summarized the research on "Cognitive grammars"(Lakoff, Langacker, Talmy, Fillmore, Fauconnier) since the 80s and its contribution to a cognitively oriented theory of linguistic meaning.

3. What is the proper role of a theory of signs and meaning in relation to other academic disciplines?

In general, the treatment of signs beyond linguistic signs (i.e., of visual, musical among other signs) asks for a semiotic framework. In the philosophy of language there are similar frontier lines to a philosophy of mind, neuro-philosophy and philosophy of art (sciences of the image), which ask for a proper integration. As the history of modern sciences teaches us, such integration cannot be achieved simply by the introduction of new terminologies; instead a more general conceptual framework must be conceived from which the specific disciplinary aspects can be derived. As a consequence of different empirical strategies and standards in the disciplines involved (hermeneutic, observational, experimental) the integration must also change the methodological standards (mostly in the direction of more objective methods) and solve the problem of mixed strategies which use different types of empirical impact in order to "triangulate" the problem. Semiotic thinking along the lines of Peirce, Jakobson, Cassirer and Thom may provide a new type of philosophy of the symbolic beyond traditional structuralism (Saussure, Hjelmslev). At the same time the simplistic semiotics implied by Chomskian paradigms, which reduce the sign more or less to the "signifiant" interpreted by some readymade logic must be overcome, while scientific rigor, including ways of mathematical assessment (for which the generative tradition stood), must be guaranteed. The kind of folk-linguistic theory building advanced by cognitive linguists like Lakoff and Langacker can only be considered for a discovery procedure in the domain of cognitive semantics (cf. Wildgen, forthcoming 2008 as a critical summary).

In the case of Eco's proposal that cultures are systems of signs and semiotics is a science of human cultures, one should not forget the Peircean program which included large parts of the natural sciences into the field of semiotics (physics, chemistry, evolutionary biology). The growing field of biosemiotics shows how relevant semiotics can be in the field of natural sciences, mainly in the zone where the sciences of life interact with research in the organization of nonliving matter (in chemistry and physics). René Thom in his theory of *"prégnance"* and *"saillance"* has shown how questions of natural sciences and human sciences may be integrated. Cf. the forthcoming issue of "Zeitschrift für Semiotik" on: Prägnanter Inhalt - Prägnante Form (edited together with Martina Plümacher).

4. What do you consider the most important topics and/or contributions in the theory of meaning and signs?

The theoretical and classificatory work of Peirce is basic, although relevant semiotic theorizing had already been achieved since antiquity (e.g., by Augustine), in medieval philosophy (Lullus, the Modists and Ockham) and in the period when the new sciences emerged (cf. the major innovators: Copernicus, Kepler, Galilei, and Descartes). The contemporaries of Kepler and Descartes can also be considered as the founders of modern semiotics. Thus Giordano Bruno (1648-1600) took up proposals for a model of human memory in the tradition of antique mnemonics, combined it with the Lullean tradition of conceptual combinatorics (in his *Ars Magna*) and tried to apply the geometry of Copernican universes to it (cf. Wildgen, 1998). In the seventeenth century Port Royal grammars and logics applied the epistemological innovation of Descartes to linguistics and logics, and Leibniz (in his *Allgemeine Charakteristik/Characteristica Universalis*) developed a research program, which was taken up by Peirce's systems of logics. Since Peirce considered his generalized systems of logics as semiotics, this line leads immediately to the foundation of modern semiotics. In the tradition of structuralism, Jakobson's (and the Prague school's) and Greimas' works had lasting effects on semiotic thinking. The latter mainly developed applications to literature; whereas Barthes opened the way for a semiotic description of advertisement and public culture (in his *Mythologies* of everyday culture). As film and television became more and more dominant in the 20th century, film semiotics (cf. the work of Lotman and Christian Metz) became an important field of semiotics. Together all these developments which furthered our knowledge about how systems of signs and their meanings are organized, led to a divergence or even a diffraction of the field of semiotics which endangered its unity. Critics argue that semiotics tries to give an explanation for every thing and therefore doesn't explain anything. It is therefore important to develop strict standards for empirical validity and theoretical coherence in the field of semiotics. After Peirce the contributions by the French mathematician René Thom (Fields medal 1958) had the largest scope combined with intellectual (and mathematical) rigor. His hypotheses call however for empirical substantiation (e.g. in the field of neurocognition) and as catastrophe theory has further evolved giving rise to such different systems like those proposed by Prigogine, Haken and Kelso, mathematical semiotics must integrate these proposals and take the field of self-organizing systems as a general background (cf. Wildgen, 1987/2005). If discrete dynamics are considered (e.g. cellular automata and generative systems), even the advances in the Chomskian paradigms may become an integrated part of mathematical semiotics in the spirit of René Thom. As it stands this field is, however, still dormant given that the majority of researchers in the field of semiotics work in the humanities (literature, art, media, social sciences) and are rather reluctant to use mathematical tools in their search for generalization.

As to Jakobson's program of a literary semiotics (and Greimas' and Barthes's contributions to it), one has to wait until the literary sciences abandon their purely hermeneutic methodology and accept the standards of empirical objectivity and consistent model-building which have been accepted by all the other sciences. Current attempts to develop a neurobiology of music and art (cf. the field of *cognitive semiotics* initiated by Brandt) show that the barriers against scientific standards in the domain of literary criticism are moving, therefore I believe that sooner or later a rich field of semiotics using the path breaking proposals by Jakobson and others will become a central concern in the humanities.

5. What are the most important open problems in this field and what are the prospects for progress?

I shall enumerate some open problems, for which I already can see advances in current research:

The morphogenesis (emergence) of sign systems. Contrary to Saussure's rejection of questions about the origin or the historical becoming of linguistic (or sign) systems, I think that we cannot understand the architecture of these systems without plausible hypotheses about their becoming. The simplest laws inherent in semiotic systems stem from basic (local) restrictions on their genesis. These must be separated from the myriad of adaptations and mixtures, which have constituted the major steps in the emergence of semiotic systems.

The already mentioned juxtaposition of symbolic forms proposed by Cassirer in his *Philosophy of Symbolic Forms*, i.e., language, myth (religion), science, art, technology, law (ethics), etc., has consequences for semiotics, because we must find the common basis of all these cultural phenomena and possibly their biological roots (the conditions of their evolutionary genesis). What is the basic faculty for symbolic behavior and how is it distributed over the specific cultural forms? What are the criteria of distinction between the different symbolic forms and how are these linked to each other in human behavior and thinking?

The concept of sign which Saussure defined in the linguistic domain cannot be directly applied to visual or musical signs. Therefore new definitions or differentiations must be found. The same is true if, beyond images, also sculpture and architecture are considered. The dimensionality of the "signifiant" makes a dramatic difference because new structural choices and lines of reading of the sign are opened. In the case of architecture and urban semiotics the *substance* of meaning (technical, geographical) and the social use of signs, such as codified paths and ritual behaviors become prominent and ask for a new concept of meaning. Although the very general notions introduced by Peirce, mainly his triad: *icon, index, and symbol*, can be applied in these fields they must be further differentiated. Probably the implicit hierarchy: icon > index > symbol must be questioned. In general the terminological apparatus provided by general (Peircian) semiotics seems to be insufficient, if semioticians have to cope with the complexities of visual and musical semiotics. In the case of architecture and music, high level theories have been developed ever since antiquity, and architectural and musical semiotics must be able to integrate this corpus of knowledge. As the widely spread "Peirce-philology" is rather reluctant to innovations in the field of general semiotics, their thinking by authorities, which is typical for pre-modern scientific discourse (it characterizes the way Bellarmin argued in his process against Galiliei), must be abandoned.

Are there mathematical techniques, which can help to specify a unified model of the symbolic in humans (the "symbolic species", *"animal symbolicum"*)? What is the relation between logical-mathematical models (the type used in logical and generative grammars), topological-dynamic models (used in models of self-organization and emergence) and possibly statistical (stochastic) models? How can the relation between continua (in perception, cognition and language) and discrete structures like those of written languages, computer programs, etc. be conceived (by derivation or by parallel specification)?

29
References

Anachreon, see *Lyra Graeca*

Anderson, Myrdene, John Deely, Martin Krampen, Joseph Ransdell, Thomas A. Sebeok,

Aristotle, *The Categories, On Interpretation, Prior Analytics*, Harvard University Press, Cambridge, MA. (Quotation translated by J. F. Sowa).

Arnheim, Rudolf. 1969. *Visual Thinking.* Berkeley: University of California Press.

Augustine (397-426/1952 *On Christian Doctrine* (trans. J.F. Shaw). In *Augustine. Great Books of the WesternWorld*, (Robert Maynard, ed.) vol.18. Chicago/ London/ Toronto: William Benton, Encyclopædia Brittannica Inc.

Baer, Karl Ernst von 1864. *Reden gehalten in wissenschaftlichen Versammlungen und kleinere Aufsätze vermischten Inhalts.* Erster Theil. St. Petersburg: H.Schmitzdorff.

Barron, D. S. 2005. *There's No Such Thing as a Negative Emotion.* Denver: Outskirts Press.

Barthes, Roland. 1957 *Mythologies*, Paris: Seuil. English version, *The Eiffel Tower and Other Mythologies.* New York: Hill and Wang, 1979.

Barthes, Roland. 1967. *Système de la mode.* Paris: Seuil. English version, *The Fashion System.* Berkeley: University of California Press.

Bierman, Arthur K. 1963. That there are no iconic signs, *Philosophy and phenomenological research*, XXIII/2: 243-249.

Blake, William 1971. *The Complete Poems* (W.H. Stevenson, ed.). London: Longman.

Boucheron, S., O. Bousquet, and G. Lugosi. 2004. Introduction to Statistical Learning Theory. In O. Bousquet, U. Von Luxburg, and G. Ratsch (eds), *Advanced Lectures on Machine Learning.* Lecture Notes in Artificial Intelligence 3176, Heidelberg: Springer, 169-207

Brandt, Per Aage 1973. *L'analyse phrastique. Introduction a la grammatique*, Bruxelles, Paris: AIMAV.

Brandt, Per Aage 1983. *Sandheden, sætningen og døden. Semiotiske aspekter af kulturanalysen*. København: Basilisk

Brandt, Per Aage 1985. *Recherches semiotiques* (1971-1984), Aarhus: Romansk Institut

Brandt, Per Aage 1989. *Linguistique et semiotique: Actualité de Viggo Brøndal*, Conf. Proceedings (ed. Brandt), Travaux du Cercle Linguistique de Copenhague XXII

Brandt, Per Aage 1990. Semiosis No. 25, special issue dedicated to PAaB, ed. By A. Bundgaard, Jalapa, Veracruz, Mexico

Brandt, Per Aage 1991. *Qu'est-ce qu'une promesse?*, Paris VII Conference Proceedings, red. P. Aa. Brandt & A. Prassoloff, Aarhus Universitetsforlag

Brandt, Per Aage 1992. *La Charpente modale du sens. Pour une sémio-linguistique morphogénétique et dynamique*, Amsterdam, New York: John Benjamins

Brandt, Per Aage 1994. *Dynamiques du sens*, Aarhus: Aarhus Universitetsforlag

Brandt, Per Aage 1995. *Morphologies of Meaning*, Aarhus: Aarhus Universitetsforlag

Brandt, Per Aage (ed.) 1998a. *The Roman Jakobson Centennial Symposium*, Acta Linguistica Hafniensia, No. 29, København

Brandt, Per Aage 1998b. *Tegn, ting og tanker. Semiotiske essays*, København: Basilisk Sigma

Brandt, Per Aage 2005a. *Spaces, Domains, and Meaning. Essays in Cognitive Semiotics*, Bern: Peter Lang

Brandt, Per Aage 2005b. Form and Meaning in Art. In Mark Turner (ed.), *The Artful Mind. Cognitive Science and the Riddle of Human Creativity*. New York: Oxford University Press.

Brandt, Per Aage (with Line Brandt). 2005c. Making sense of a blend. A cognitive semiotics approach to metaphor. *Annual Review of Cognitive Linguistics*, vol. 3. Amsterdam: John Benjamins

Brandt, Per Aage.2007. On Consciousness and Semiosis. *Cognitive Semiotics* 1.

Bruner, J., Goodnow, J. & Austin, G. 1956. *A Study of Thinking.* New York: Wiley.

Bühler, Karl. 1934/1990. *Sprachtheorie.* Jena: Fischer. English Translation by Donald A. Goodwin, *Theory of Language*, Amsterdam: John Benjamins.

Butler, Judith. 1990. *Gender Trouble: Feminism and the Subversion of Identity.* New York: Routledge.

Canclini, Néstor Garcia. 1989. *Hybrid Cultures: Strategies for Entering and Leaving Modernity.* Minneapolis: University of Minnesota Press

Cassirer, Ernst. 1923-29/1953-57. *The Philosophy of Symbolic Forms.* Volume 1: Language; Volume 2: Mythical Thought; Volume 3: The Phenomenology of Knowledge, Yale UP, New Haven & London.New Haven: Yale University Press.

Cassirer, Ernst. 1930/1985. 'Form und Technik,' in *Kunst und Technik*, edited by Leo Kestenberg. Berlin: Wegweiser Verlag: pp. 15-61. Reprinted in Ernst Cassirer, *Symbol, Technik, Sprache.* Edited by Ernst Wolfgang Orth, John Michael Krois, and Joseph Werle. Hamburg: Felix Meiner Verlag.

Cassirer, Ernst. 1942. *Zur Logik der Kulturwissenschaften.* Göteborg: Elanders.

Cassirer, Ernst. 1944. The Concept of Group and the Theory of Perception, *Philosophy and Phenomenological Research* 5, 1-35 (original French version 1938).

Cassirer, Ernst. 1945. Structuralism in Modern Linguistics, *Word* 1.

Cassirer, Ernst. 1957. *Das Erkenntnisproblem in der Philosophie und Wissenschaft der neueren Zeit. Von Hegels Tod bis zur Gegenwart (1832-1932)*, vol. IV Hildesheim: Georg Olms (1991)

Colapietro, Vincent. 1989. *Peirce's Approach to the Self: A Semiotic Perspective on Human Subjectivity*, SUNY Press.

Comrie, Bernard. 1989. *Language Universals and Linguistic Typology: Syntax and Morphology.* 2nd ed. Chicago: U of Chicago P.

Coulson, Seana.. 2000. *Semantic Leaps: Frame-shifting and Conceptual Blending in Meaning Construction.* New York and Cambridge: Cambridge University Press.

Crystal, David. 2006. *Language and the Internet*, Cambridge: Cambridge University Press

Cummings, Naomi. 2000. *The Sonic Self: Musical Subjectivity and Signification*, Bloomington: Indianapolis University Press.

Damasio, Antonio. 1999. *The Feeling of What Happens: Body and Emotion in the Making of Consciousness*. New York: Harcourt Brace & Company.

Danesi, Marcel. 1993. *Vico. Metphor and the Origin of Language*. Bloomington. Indiana University Press.

Danesi, Marcel. 2002. *The Puzzle Instinct*. Bloomington: Indiana University Press

Danesi, Marcel. 2004. *Poetic Logic: The Role of Metaphor in Thought, Language, and Culture*. Madison WI: Atwood Publishing.

Danesi, Marcel. 2006. Alphabets and The Principle of Least Effort, *Studies in Communication Sciences* 6, 2006, 47-62.

Danesi, Marcel and Thomas A. Sebeok 2000 *The Forms of Meaning: Modeling Systems Theory and Semiotic Analysis*. Berlin: Mouton de Gruyter.

Deacon, Terrence. 1997. *The Symbolic Species: The Co-Evolution of Language and the Brain*. New York: Norton.

Deely, John. 1990. *Basics of Semiotics*. Bloomington: Indiana University Press.

Deely, John. 2001. *Four Ages of Understanding*. Toronto: University of Toronto Press.

Deledalle, Gérard. 2000. *Charles S. Peirce's Philosophy of Signs: Essays in Comparative Linguistics*, Indianapolis University Press.

Dewey, John. 1896/1998. The Reflex Arc Concept in Psychology. In Larry Hickman and Thomas Alexander (eds.), *The Essential Dewey*. 2 vols. Bloomington: Indiana University Press: 2:3-10 (originally published 1896).

Dewey, John. 1925/1988. *Experience and Nature*. Later Works, vol. 1. Carbondale: Southern Illinois University Press (originally published 1925).

Dewey, John. 1934/1987. *Art as Experience*. Later Works, vol. 10. Carbondale: Southern Ilinois University Press (originally published 1934).

Dines-Johansen, Jørgen 1993. *Dialogic Semiosis*. Indiana University Press.

Dines-Johansen, Jørgen 1993. Let sleeping signs lie: On signs, objects, and communication, *Semiotica* 97/3-4, 271-295.

Dines-Johansen, Jørgen. 1996. Iconicity in literature, *Semiotica* 110/1-2, 37-55.

Dines-Johansen, Jørgen. 1998a. Analogy and Fable in Poetry and Fiction, *RS/SI* (*Recherches sémiotique/Semiotic inquiries*).17/1-2-3, 255-69.

Dines-Johansen, Jørgen. 1998b. Hjelmslev and Glossematics. In Posner, Robering, Sebeok (eds.), *Semiotik/Semiotics. A Handbook on the Sign-Theoretic Foundations of Nature and Culture*. Berlin: Walter de Gruyter, 2272-89.

Dines-Johansen, Jørgen. 2000. Hypothese, Rekonstruktion und existentielle Analogie. Hermeneutik und semiotische Literaturinterpretation. In U. Wirth (ed.), *Die Welt als Zeichen und Hypothese. Perspektiven des semiotischen Pragmatismus von Charles S. Peirce*, Frankfurt/M: Suhrkamp Taschenbuch Wissenschaft: 181-210.

Dines-Johansen, Jørgen. 2002a. *Literary Discourse. A Semiotic-Pragmatic Approach to Literature*. Toronto: University of Toronto Press.

Dines-Johansen, Jørgen. 2002b. *Signs in Use* (with Svend Erik Larsen, English trans. of Danish edition 1994). London: Routledge.

Dines-Johansen, Jørgen. 2007. *Litteratur og intersubjektivitet. Tegn, bevidsthed og litteratur* (Literature and Subjectivity. Sign, Mind, Literature). Odense: Syddansk Universitetsforlag.

Dines-Johansen, Jørgen. 2007. *Semiotics of Literature* (Guest Editor: Jørgen Dines Johansen), *Semiotica*, 165/1-4, Special issue.

Dines-Johansen, Jørgen. 2008. Semiotisk-pragmatisk litteraturteori (Semiotic-Pragmatic theory of literature). In J. Fibiger, G. von Buchwald Lütken and N. Mølgaard (eds.), Academica: 175-208.

Dodge, Ellen and Lakoff, George. 2005. Image Schemas: From Linguistics Analysis to Neural Grounding. In B. Hampe (ed.). *From Perception to Meaning: Image Schemas in Cognitive Linguistics*. Berlin: Mouton de Gruyter, 57-92.

29. References

Donald, Merlin. 1991. *Origins of the Modern Mind. Three Stages in the Evolution of Culture and Cognition.* Cambridge, Mass.: Harvard University Press.

Duckitt, John H. 1992. *The Social Psychology of Prejudice.* New York: Praeger.

Dummett, Michael 1981. *The Interpretation of Frege's Philosophy,* London: Duckworth.

Dummett, Michael 1993. *Origins of Analytical Philosophy,* Cambridge, MA.: Harvard University Press.

Eco, Umberto. 1968: *La struttura assente.* Milano: Bompiani.

Eco, Umberto. 1976: *A theory of Semiotics.* Bloomington: Indiana University Press.

Eco, Umberto. 1997 *Kant and the Platypus.* New York: Harcourt Brace

Edelman, Gerald. and Tononi, G. 2000. *A Universe of Consciousness: How Matter Becomes Imagination.* New York: Basic Books.

Emmeche, Claus 2001. The emergence of signs of living feelings: Reverberations from the first Gatherings in Biosemiotics. *Sign Systems Studies* 29/1, 369-376.

Emmeche, Claus; Hoffmeyer, Jesper; Kull, Kalevi. 2002a. Editors' comment. *Sign Systems Studies* 30/1, 11-13.

Emmeche, Claus; Kull, Kalevi; Stjernfelt, Frederik. 2002b. *Reading Hoffmeyer, Rethinking Biology.* [*Tartu Semiotics Library* 3.] Tartu: Tartu University Press.

Emmeche, Claus., Simo Køppe, and Frederik Stjernfelt. 1997. Explaining emergence: Towards an ontology of levels, *Journal for General Philosophy of Science* 28/1, 83-119.

Emmeche, Claus., Simo Køppe, and Frederik Stjernfelt. 2000. Levels, emergence, and three versions of downward causation. In P. Bøgh Andersen et al. (eds.), *Downward Causation,* Copenhagen: Aarhus University Press, 13-34

Engel, Christoph. 2005. *Generating Predictability: Institutional Analysis and Design.* Cambridge University Press.

Fauconnier, Gilles. 1984. *Espaces mentaux: Aspects de la construction du sens dans les langues naturelles,* Paris: Les Éditions de Minuit. (Eng. version 1994.)

Fauconnier, Gilles. 1994. *Mental Spaces: Aspects of meaning construction in natural language.* Cambridge: MIT Press.

Fauconnier, Gilles. 1997. *Mappings in Thought and Language.* New York: Cambridge University Press.

Fauconnier, Gilles and Eve Sweetser (eds.). 1996. *Spaces, Worlds, and Grammar.* Chicago: Chicago University Press.

Fauconnier, Gilles & Mark Turner. 2002. *The Way We Think: Conceptual Blending and the Mind's Hidden Complexity.* New York: Basic Books.

Favareau, Don. 2005. Founding a world biosemiotics institution: The International Society for Biosemiotic Studies. *Sign Systems Studies* 33/1, 481-485.

Favareau, Don. 2007. The evolutionary history of biosemiotics. In Barbieri, M. (ed.), *Introduction to Biosemiotics.* Berlin: Springer, 1-67.

Feldman, J. 2006. *From Molecule to Metaphor: A Neural Theory of Language.* Cambridge, Mass.: MIT Press.

Fisch, Max H. 1986. *Peirce, Semeiotic, and Pragmatism* (Ketner and Kloesel, eds.), Indiana University Press.

Floch, Jean-Marie. 1984: *Petites mythologies de l'œil et l'esprit.* Paris: Hadès

Forceville, C. 1996. *Pictorial Metaphor in Advertising.* London: Routledge.

Frege, Gottlob. 1879. *Begriffsschrift.* English translation in J. van Heijenoort (ed), *From Frege to Gödel.* Cambridge, MA: Harvard University Press, 1-82 (1967).

Frege, Gottlob. 1884. *Die Grundlagen der Arithmetik: eine logisch-mathematische Untersuchung über den Begriff der Zahl.* Breslau: W. Koebner. Enlgish translation, *The Foundations of Arithmetic: A logico-mathematical enquiry into the concept of number.* Oxford: Blackwell, second revised edition 1974.

Frege, Gottlob. 1980. *Translations from the Philosophical Writings of Gottlob Frege.* Oxford: Blackwell, third edition.

Frost, Robert. 1963. *A Lover's Quarrel with the World,* film, WGBH Educational Foundation, Boston.

Gabora, L., Rosch, E. & Aerts, D. 2008. Toward an ecological theory of concepts. *Ecological Psychology* 20: 84-116.

Gallese, Vittorio and Lakoff, George. 2005. The Brain's Concepts: The Role of the Sensory-motor System in Conceptual Knowledge. *Cognitive Neuropsychology* 22, 455-79.

Gardiner, Alan. 1951. *The Theory of Speech and Language.* 2nd. ed. Oxford: Oxford University Press (originally published 1932).

Gibbs, Raymond. 1994. *The Poetics of Mind: Figurative Thought, Language, and Understanding.* Cambridge: Cambridge University Press.

Gibson, James. 1982. *Reasons for Realism. Selected Essays of James J. Gibson.* Edward Reed and Rebecca Jones (eds.). Hillsdale, New Jersey: Lawrence Erlbaum.

Goodman, Nelson. 1968. *Languages of Art.* London: Oxford University Press.

Gopnik, A. & Meltzoff, A. 1997. *Words, Thoughts, and Theories.* Cambridge, MA: MIT Press.

Gould, Steven J. and Richard C. Lewontin. 1979. The Spandrels of San Marco and the Panglossian Paradigm: a Critique of the Adaptationist Programme. *Proc. B. Soc. London* B 205, 581-598.

Grady, Joseph. 1997. *Foundations of Meaning: Primary Metaphors and Primary Scenes.* Ph.D. diss., University of California, Berkeley.

Greimas, Algirdas Julien. 1966. *Sémantique structurale.* Paris: Larousse. English version, *Structural Semantics.* University of Nebraska Press.

Greimas, Algirdas Julien. 1970. *Du sens.* Paris: Seuil.

Greimas, Algirdas Julien. 1976. *Maupassant* : La sémiotique du texte. Paris: Seuil.

Greimas, Algirdas Julien. 1983. *Du sens* II. Paris: Seuil. English version, *On Meaning: Selected Writings in Semiotic Theory.* University of Minnesota Press.

Greimas, Algirdas Julien and Joseph Courtés. 1979. *Dictionnaire raisonné de la théorie du langage.* Paris: Hachette.

Greimas, Algirdas Julien and François Rastier. 1968. The interaction of semiotic constraints, *Yale French Studies*, 41, 86-105. In Greimas 1970.

Grice, Paul. 1957. Meaning, *The Philosophical Review* 66, 377-388.

Grice, Paul. 1975. *Logic and Conversation.* In P. Cole and J. Morgan (eds.), *Syntax and Semantics*, Vol. 3, New York: Academic Press.

Grice, Paul. 1989. *Studies in the Way of Words.* Harvard Unviersity Press.

Groupe µ. 1970 *Rhétorique générale*, Paris: Seuil

Groupe µ. 1977 *Rhétorique de la poésie.* Bruxelles: Editions Complexe.

Groupe µ. 1992 *Traité du signe visuel.* Paris: Seuil.

Gurwitsch, Aron 1957 *Théorie du champ de la conscience.* Bruges: Desclée de Brouver.

Hampe, Beate. (ed.). 2005. *From Perception to Meaning: Image Schemas in Cognitive Linguistics.* Berlin: Mouton de Gruyter.

Hintikka, Jaakko. 1983. C.S. Peirce's "First Real Discovery" and its contemporary relevance. In E. Freeman (ed.), *The Relevance of Charles Peirce.* La Salle, Ill.: The Hegeler Institute, 107-118.

Hintikka, Jaakko. 1997a. The place of C.S. Peirce in the history of logical theory. In J. Brunning and P. Forster (eds.), *The Rule of Reason*, Toronto: University of Toronto Press 1997, 13-33.

Hintikka, Jaakko. 1997b. *Lingua Universalis vs. Calculus Ratiocinator. An Ultimate Presupposition of Twentieth-Century Philosophy*, Dordrecht: Kluwer.

Hjelmslev, Louis. 1928. *Principes de grammaire générale.* Copenhagen: Høst og Søn.

Hjelmslev, Louis 1943 *Omkring sprogteoriens grundlæggelse.* Copenhagen: Akademisk forlag. English version: *Prolegomena to a Theory of Language.* Baltimore: Inidiana University Publications in Anthropology and Linguistics, 1953 and Madison: University of Wisconsin Press, 1961.

Hoffmeyer, Jesper. 1995. The Swarming Cyberspace of the Body. *Cybernetics & Human Knowing* 3, 16-25.

Hoffmeyer, Jesper. 1996. *Signs of Meaning in the Universe.* Bloomington: Indiana University Press.

Hoffmeyer, Jesper. 2008. *Biosemiotics. An Examination into the Signs of Life and the Life of Signs.* Scranton: Scranton University Press.

Hoffmeyer, Jesper. (in preparation). *Biosemiotics: A New Approach to the Question of Meaning.* Gordon, B. (eds): *Wistar Retrospective Sympoisum.*

Hoffmeyer, Jesper and Claus Emmeche. 1991. Code-Duality and the Semiotics of Nature. Anderson, M. and F. Merrell (eds): *On Semiotic Modeling.* New York: Mouton de Gruyter. 117-166.

Hoffmeyer, Jesper and Kalevi Kull. 2003. Baldwin and biosemiotics: What intelligence is for. In Weber, B. and Depew, D. (eds.), *Evolution and Learning: The Baldwin Effect Reconsidered.* Cambridge: MIT Press, 253-272.

Hogan, Patrick Colm. 1996/2008. *On Interpretation: Meaning and Inference in Law, Psychoanalysis, and Literature.* Athens, GA: University of Georgia Press.

Hogan, Patrick Colm. 2000a. *Colonialism and Cultural Identity: Crises of Tradition in the Anglophone Literatures of India, Africa, and the Caribbean.* Albany, NY: State University of New York Press.

Hogan, Patrick Colm. 2000b. *Philosophical Approaches to the Study of Literature.* Gainesville, FL: University Press of Florida.

Hogan, Patrick Colm. 2001. *The Culture of Conformism.* Durham, N.C.: Duke University Press.

Hogan, Patrick Colm. 2002. A Minimal, Lexicalist/Constituent Transfer Account of Metaphor. *Style* 36/3, 484-502.

Hogan, Patrick Colm. 2003a. *Cognitive Science, Literature, and the Arts: A Guide for Humanists.* New York: Routledge.

Hogan, Patrick Colm. 2003b. *The Mind and Its Stories: Narrative Universals and Human Emotion.* Cambridge: Cambridge University Press and Paris: Editions de la Maison des Sciences de L'Homme.

Hogan, Patrick Colm. 2004. *Empire and Poetic Voice: Cognitive and Cultural Studies of Literary Tradition and Colonialism.* Albany, NY: State University of New York Press.

Hogan, Patrick Colm. 2007. Intent in Norms. In *Encyclopedia of Law and Society: American and Global Perspectives.* Ed. David Clark. Thousand Oaks, CA: Sage, 802-803.

Hogan, Patrick Colm. (Forthcoming). On the Very Idea of the Language Sciences. In *The Cambridge Encyclopedia of the Lan-*

guage Sciences. Ed. Patrick Colm Hogan. Cambridge: Cambridge University Press.

Houser, Nathan, Don D. Roberts and James van Evra (eds.). 1997. *Studies in the Logic of Charles Sanders Peirce*, Bloomington: Indiana University Press.

Husserl, Edmund. 1892. *Philosophie der Aritmetik*, Hua XII, Den Haag: Martinus Nijhoff (1970).

Husserl, Edmund. 1907. *Ding und Raum*, Hua XVI, Den Haag: Martinus Nijhoff (1973).

Husserl, Edmund. 1913/1968. *Logische Untersuchungen*. Tübingen: Niemeyer. Engl. translation, *Logical Investigations* (transl. J.N.Findlay), London and Henley: Routledge and Kegan Paul.

Husserl, Edmund. 1939 *Erfahrung und Urteil*. Prag: Academia Verlagsbuchhandlung. English translation, *Experience and Judgment*, London: Routledge and Kegan Paul (1975).

Husserl, Edmund. 1980 *Phantasie, Bildbewusstsein, Erinnerung*, Hua XXIII, Dordrecht: Martinus Nijhoff.

Ibarretxe-Antuñano, Iraide. 2005. Interview: Leonard Talmy. A windowing to conceptual structure and language. Part 1: Lexicalisation and typology. *Annual Review of Cognitive Linguistics*, 3, 325-347.

Ibarretxe-Antuñano, Iraide. 2006. Interview: Leonard Talmy. A windowing onto conceptual structure and language. Part 2: Language and cognition: Past and Future. Annual Review of Cognitive Linguistics, 4, 253-268.

Ingarden, Roman. 1931. *Das literarische Kunstwerk*.Tübingen 1965: Max Niemeyer (1965). Eng. translation, *The Literary Work of Art*. Evanston: Northwestern University Press.

Ingarden, Roman. 1965-74 *Der Streit um die Existenz der Welt* I-III, Tübingen: Max Niemeyer.

Ingarden, Roman. 1968. *Vom Erkennen des literarischen Kunstwerk*. Tübingen: Max Niemeyer. Eng. translation, *The Cognition of the Literary Work of Art*, Evanston 1973: Northwestern University Press.

Ingarden, Roman. 1969 *Erlebnis, Kunstwerk and Wert*, Darmstadt: Wissenschaftliche Buchgesellschaft.

Innis, Robert. 1977. Art, Symbol, and Consciousness. *International Philosophical Quarterly* 17/4: 455-476, 1977. Polish translation: Sztuka, Symbol, Swiadomosc. In *Semiotyka Dzis I Wczoraj. Wybór Tekstów*. Edited by Jerzy Pelc and Leona Koja. Wroclaw: Ossolineum, 1991: pp. 98-108

Innis, Robert. 1979. Translation, with introduction, of *The Central Texts of Ludwig Wittgenstein* by Gerd Brand. Oxford: Basil Blackwell, 1979. Published in the United States by Basic Books (1979) as *The Essential Wittgenstein*.

Innis, Robert. 1980. Review article on *A Theory of Semiotics* by Umberto Eco. *International Philosophical Quarterly* 20/2, 221-232.

Innis, Robert. 1982. *Karl Bühler: Semiotic Foundations of Language Theory*. New York: Plenum.

Innis, Robert. 1984. Perception, Abstraction and Subjectivity in Bühler's Language Theory. *Rassegna italiana di linguistica applicata* January/April, 2-23.

Innis, Robert. 1985. *Semiotics: An Introductory Anthology*. Bloomington: Indiana University Press. British edition: *Semiotics: An Introductory Reader*. London: Hutchinson, 1986.

Innis, Robert 1986. *Meaning and Context: An Introduction to the Psychology of Language*. New York: Plenum . A revised and supplemented edition of Hans Hörmann's *Einführung in die Psycholinguistik..*

Innis, Robert 1991. Critical bilingual edition, translated with introduction and notes, of Johann Christoph Hoffbauer, *Tentamina Semiologica* (1789), under the title *Semiological Investigations*. Amsterdam and Philadelphia: John Benjamins.

Innis, Robert 1994. *Consciousness and the Play of Signs*. Bloomington: Indiana University Press.

Innis, Robert 1999. John Dewey et sa glose approfondie de la théorie peircienne de la qualité. *Protée* (Winter 1998/1999), 89-98.

Innis, Robert 2002. *Pragmatism and the Forms of Sense: Language, Perception, Technics*. University Park: The Pennsylvania State University Press.

Innis, Robert 2004. The Tacit Logic of Ritual Embodiments. *Social Analysis* 48/2, 197-212. This issue published as a book, *Ritual in Its Own Right*, edited by Don Handelman and Galina Lindquist. New York: Berghahn Books, 2005.

Innis, Robert 2007. The Making of the Literary Symbol: Taking Note of Langer. *Semiotica* 165-1/4, 91-106.

Innis, Robert . 2009. *Susanne Langer in Focus: The Symbolic Mind.* Bloomington: Indiana University Press.

Jakobson, Roman. 1981. *Poetry of Grammar and Grammar of Poetry*, Selected writings, vol. 3. The Hague: Mouton de Gruyter.

Jakobson, Roman. 1990. *On Language* (Waugh and Monville- Burston, eds.), Harvard University Press.

James, William. 1902. *The Varieties of Religious Experience.* New York: Longmans, Green & Co. (Reprinted by Penguin Books 1985).

Johnson, Mark. 1987. *The Body in the Mind: The Bodily Basis of Meaning, Imagination, and Reason.* Chicago: University of Chicago Press.

Johnson, Mark. 1993. *Moral Imagination: Implications of Cognitive Science for Ethics.* Chicago: University of Chicago Press.

Johnson, Mark. 2007. *The Meaning of the Body: Aesthetics of Human Understanding.* Chicago: University of Chicago Press.

Johnson, Mark and Larson, S. 2003. Something in the Way She Moves: Metaphors of Musical Motion. *Metaphor and Symbol* 18, no. 2, 63-84.

Kamp, Hans. 2001. Levels of linguistic meaning and the logic of natural language, http://www.illc.uva.nl/lia/farewell_kamp.html

Krampen, Martin. 1981. Phytosemiotics. *Semiotica* 36, 187-209.

Krois, John Michael 1987 *Cassirer, Symbolic Forms and History*, New Haven and London: Yale University Press

Krois, John Michael 2004 More than a Linguistic Turn in Philosophy: the Semiotic Programs of Peirce and Cassirer, *Sats – Nordic Journal of Philosophy*, vol. 5, no. 2, 14–33

Krois, John Michael (ed.) 2007 *Embodiment in Cognition and Culture*, Amsterdam: John Benjamins

Kull, Kalevi. 1988. The origin of species: A new view. In Kull, Kalevi; Tiivel, Toomas (eds.), *Lectures in Theoretical Biology.* Tallinn: Valgus, 73-77.

Kull, Kalevi. 1992. Evolution and semiotics. In Sebeok, Thomas A.; Umiker-Sebeok, Jean (eds.), *Biosemiotics: Semiotic Web 1991*. Berlin: Mouton de Gruyter, 221-233.

Kull, Kalevi. 1999. Biosemiotics in the twentieth century: a view from biology. *Semiotica* 127/1-4, 385-414.

Kull, Kalevi. 2000a. Organisms can be proud to have been their own designers. *Cybernetics and Human Knowing* 7/1, 45–55.

Kull, Kalevi. 2000b. An introduction to phytosemiotics: Semiotic botany and vegetative sign systems. *Sign Systems Studies* 28: 326-350.

Kull, Kalevi. 2001. Jakob von Uexküll: An introduction. *Semiotica* 134/1-4, 1–59.

Kull, Kalevi. 2003. Ladder, tree, web: The ages of biological understanding. *Sign Systems Studies* 31/2, 589–603.

Kull, Kalevi. 2007. Biosemiotics and biophysics — the fundamental approaches to the study of life. In Barbieri, Marcello (ed.), *Introduction to Biosemiotics: The New Biological Synthesis*. Berlin: Springer, 167–177.

Lakoff, George. 1987 *Women, Fire, and Dangerous Things*. Chicago: University of Chicago Press.

Lakoff, George. 1996. *Moral Politics: What Conservatives Know that Liberals Don't*. Chicago: University of Chicago Press.

Lakoff, George. 2008. *The Political Mind: Why You Can't Understand 21st Century American Politics with an 18th Century Brain*. New York: Penguin/Viking.

Lakoff, George and Mark Johnson. 1980. *Metaphors We Live By*. Chicago: University of Chicago Press.

Lakoff, George and Mark Johnson. 1999. *Philosophy in the Flesh: The Embodied Mind and Its Challenge to Western Thought*. New York: Basic Books.

Lakoff, George and Rafael Nuñez. 2001. *Where Mathematics Comes From. How the Embodied Mind Brings Mathematics into Being* New York: Basic Books.

Lakoff, George and Mark Turner. 1989. *More than Cool Reason: A Field Guide to Poetic Metaphor*. Chicago: University of Chicago Press.

Langacker, Ronald. 1987-1991. *Foundations of Cognitive Grammar*, Vols. 1-2, Stanford, California: Stanford University Press.

Langacker, Ronald. 1991. *Concept, Image, and Symbol: The Cognitive Basis of Grammar*. Berlin & New York: Mouton de Gruyter.

Langacker, Ronald. 1999. *Grammar and Conceptualization*. Berlin and New York: Mouton de Gruyter

Langer, Susanne K. 1942. *Philosophy in a New Key*. Cambridge, Mass: Harvard University Press.

Langer, Susanne K.. 1988. *Mind: An Essay on Human Feeling*, abridged edition, by Gary Van Den Heuvel. Baltimore: The Johns Hopkins University Press.

Laurence, S. & Margolis, E. (eds.). 1999. *Concepts: Core Readings*, Cambridge, MA: MIT Press.

Lévi-Strauss, Claude. 1958. *Anthropologie structurale*, Paris: Plon.

Lévi-Strauss, Claude. 1964-1971. *Mythologiques* I-IV. Paris: Plon.

Lévi-Strauss, Claude. 1971 *L'homme nu. Mythologiques* IV, Paris: Plon.

Lévi-Strauss, Claude. 1973 *Anthropologie structurale*, II, Paris: Plon.

Lévi-Strauss, Claude. 1988 *De près et de loin*, Paris: Plon.

Leyton, Michael. 2001. *A Generative Theory of Shape*, Heidelberg: Springer.

Liddell, Scott K. 1998. Grounded Blends, Gestures, and Conceptual Shifts. *Cognitive Linguistics*, 9, 283-314.

Liddell, Scott K. 2000. Blended Spaces and Deixis in Sign Language Discourse. In David McNeill, editor. *Language and gesture*. Cambridge, MA: Cambridge University Press, 331-357.

Liddell, Scott K. 2003. *Grammar, Gesture and Meaning in American Sign Language*. Cambridge: Cambridge University Press.

Liszka, James Jakób.1990. *A General Introduction to the Semeiotic of Charles Sanders Peirce*, Indiana University Press.

Lorenz, Konrad. 1974. *On Agression*. New York: Harcourt Brace Jovanovich.

Lotman, Jurij M. 1977. *Probleme der Kinoästhetik* (Semiotika kino i problemi kinoestetiki, dt.). Frankfurt am Main: Syndicat

Lotman, Yuri M. 1990. *Universe of the Mind: A Semiotic Theory of Culture*. London: I.B.Tauris.

Lotman, Yuri M. 2005 [1984]. On the semiosphere. *Sign Systems Studies* 33/1, 215–239.

Lotman, Yuri M. 2008. *Culture and Explosion*. Berlin: Mouton de Gruyter (in press).

Lotman, Yuri M., Boris A. Uspenskij, Vjaceslav. V. Ivanov, V. N. Toporov and A. M. Pjatigorski. 1975. *Thesis on the Semiotic Study of Culture*. Lisse: The Peter de Ridder Press

Lyra Graeca I-III. 1922-27. (J.M. Edmons trans. & ed.). Cambridge MASS/London: HarvardUniversity Press/Heinemann: Loeb.

Maranda, Pierre and Ellis-Konga Maranda. 1971. *Structural Models in Folklore*, The Hague: Mouton de Gruyter

Malrieu, D. and François Rastier. 2001. Genres et variations morphosyntaxiques. *Traitements automatiques du langage*, 42, 2: 547-577.

Maritain, Jacques 1939 *Quatre essais sur l'esprit dans sa condition carnelle*, Paris: De Brouwer

Martinet, André 1955 *Économie des changements phonétiques*, Bern : Francke

McNeill, D. 1992. *Hand and Mind: What Gestures Reveal about Thought*. Chicago: University of Chicago Press.

Medin, D. 1989. Concepts and conceptual structure, *American Psychologist* 44, 1469-1481.

Merleau-Ponty, Maurice. 1945. *Phénoménologie de la perception*, Paris : Gallimard (1983).

Merleau-Ponty, Maurice. 1964. *Le visible et l'invisible*, Paris: Gallimard

Merleau-Ponty, Maurice. 1995. *La nature. Notes. Cours de Collège de France*. Paris : Seuil.

Metz, Christian, 1971. *Langage et cinéma*, Paris: Larousse.

Morris, Charles W. 1938. *Foundations of the Theory of Signs*, Chicago University Press, Chicago.

Morris, Desmond 1967. *The Naked Ape*. London: Jonathan Cape.

Mukarovsky, Jan. 1974. *Studien zur strukturalistischen Ästhetik und Poetik.* München: Hanser Verlag.

Mukarovsky, Jan. 1978. *Structure, sign, and function, Selected essays.* New Haven & London: Yale University Press.

Nicolis, Grégoire and Ilya Prigogine. 1989. *Exploring Complexity. An Introduction,* New York: Freeman.

Nöth, Winfried. 2000. *Handbuch der Semiotik.* Stuttgart: J.B.Metzler.

Ockham, William of 1323. *Summa Logicae,* Johannes Higman, Paris, 1488. (The edition owned by C. S. Peirce)

Ogden, C. K., & I. A. Richards 1923. *The Meaning of Meaning,* , New York: Harcourt, Brace, and World, 8th edition 1946.

Osherson, D. & Smith, E. 1981. On the adequacy of prototype theory as a theory of concepts. *Cognition* 9, 35-58.

Pape, Helmut 1989. *Erfahrung und Wirklichkeit als Zeichenprozess: Charles S. Peirces Entwurf einer Spekulativen Grammatik des Seins,* Frankfurt am Main: Suhrkamp Verlag.

Parmentier, Richard 1994. *Signs in Society: Studies in Semiotic Anthropology,* Indiana University Press.

Parrill, Fey & Eve Sweetser. 2004. What We Mean By Meaning. *Gesture* 4:2, 197-219.

Partee, Barbara H. 2005. Formal semantics, Lectures at a workshop in Moscow. http://people.umass.edu/partee/RGGU_2005/RGGU05_formal_semantics.htm

Paterson, Hugh E.H. 1993. *Evolution and the Recognition Concept of Species.* Baltimore: The J. Hopkins Univ. Press.

Piaget, Jean. 1945. *La formation du symbole chez l'enfant.* Neuchatel: Delachaux & Niestlé, (1967).

Piaget, Jean. 1970 *Epistémologie des sciences de l'homme.* Paris: Gallimard.

Peirce, Charles Sanders. 1931-1958. (CP) *Collected Papers of C. S. Peirce,* ed. by C. Hartshorne, P. Weiss, & A. Burks, 8 vols., Cambridge, MA: Harvard University Press.

Peirce, Charles Sanders. 1976. *New Elements of Mathematics)* I-IV. The Hague: Mouton.

Peirce, Charles Sanders. 1998. *The Essential Peirce, Volume I-II.* Ed. by the Peirce Edition Project. Bloomington and Indianapolis: Indiana University Press.

Peirce, Charles Sanders. *Unpublished manuscripts,* numbered and paginated by the Institute for Studies in Pragmatism, Texas Tech University, Lubbock, TX.

Petitot, Jean. 1985. *Morphogenèse du sens.* Paris: PUF.

Petitot, Jean. 1992. *Physique du sens.* Paris: Editions du CNRS.

Petitot, Jean. 1995. Morphodynamics and Attractor Syntax. Dynamical and morphological models for constituency in visual perception and cognitive grammar. In T. van Gelder and R. Port (eds.), *Mind as Motion.* Cambridge/ The MIT Press, 227-281.

Petitot, Jean. 1999. Morphological Eidetics for Phenomenology of Perception. In Jean Petitot *et al.* 5eds.), *Naturalizing Phenomenology.* Stanford: Stanford University Press, 330-371.

Petitot, Jean. 2003. *Morpogenesis of Meaning.* Bern: Peter Lang.

Petitot, Jean. 2004. *Morphologie et esthétique.* Paris: Maisonneuve et Larose.

Poggio, T., R. Rifkin, S. Mukherjee, and P. Niyogi. 2004. General Conditions for Predictivity in Learning Theory. *Nature* 428: 419-422.

Poinsot, John (John of St. Thomas) 1955 *Outlines of Formal Logic,* transl. F.C.Wade, Milwaukee: Marquette University Press

Poinsot, John 1985 *Tractatus de Signis/ Treatise on Signs,* bilingual edition, Berkeley: University of California Press

Polanyi, Michael. 1958. *Personal Knowledge: Towards a Postcritical Philosophy.* Chicago: University of Chicago Press.

Posner, Roland. 2004. Basic Tasks of Cultural Semiotics. In Gloria Withalm and Josef Wallmannsberger (eds.). *Macht der Zichen/ Zeichen der Macht.* Wien: INST., 56-89.

Posner, Roland, R.J. Jorna and B. van Heusden (eds.). 1993. *Signs, Search, and Communication: Semiotic Aspects of Artificial Intelligence* Berlin and New York: Walter de Gruyter.

Posner, Roland, Klaus Robering and Thomas A. Sebeok (eds.) 1997ff. *Semiotics–A Handbook on the Sign-theoretic Foundations of Nature and Culture,* vols. I-III, Berlin and New York: Walter de Gruyter.

Price, H.H. 1953. *Thinking and Experience,* N.Y..: Hutchinson's University Library.

Prieto, Luis J. 1975 *Pertinence et pratique.* Paris: Minuit.

Prodi, Giorgio 1988. Signs and Codes in Immunology. In E.E. Sercarz, et al. (eds.): *The Semiotics of Cellular Communication and the Immune System.* Berlin: Springer. 53-64.

Pulvermüller, Friedemann 2002. *The Neuroscience of Language: On Brain Circuits of Words and Serial Order.* Cambridge: Cambridge UP.

Ransdell, Joseph. 1977. Some Leading Ideas of Peirce's Semiotic, *Semiotica.*

Ransdell, Joseph. 1981. Semiotic Causation. In Ketner et al., *Proceedings of the C.S. Peirce*

Bicentennial International Congress, Texas Tech Press.

Rastier, François. 1974. *Essais de sémiotique discursive,* Paris, Mame. Reedited pdf.: http: //www.revue-texto.net

Rastier, François. 1997. *Meaning and Textuality,* Toronto, Toronto University Press.

Rastier, François. 1999. Cognitive Semantics and Diachrony. In Andreas Blank / Peter Koch (eds), *Historical Semantics and Cognition,* Mouton de Gruyter, Berlin (Cognitive Linguistics Research), 109-144.

Rastier, François. 2001a. L'action et le sens. — Pour une sémiotique des cultures, *Journal des Anthropologues* (85-86), 183-219.

Rastier, François. 2001b. *Arts et sciences du texte,* Paris, PUF.

Rastier, François. 2002. *Semantics for Descriptions,* Chicago University Press, 2002].

Rastier, François. 2005. *Ulysse à Auschwitz. Primo Levi, le survivant.* Paris, Éditions du Cerf.

Rastier, François 1991. *Sémantique et recherches cognitives,* Paris, PUF, 262 p. [second edition 2001].

Rastier, François. 2002. *Semantics for Descriptions,* Chicago: Chicago University Press, 2002.

Rastier, François. (ed.) 1995. *L'analyse thématique des données textuelles*, Paris: Didier.

Ricoeur, Paul. 1975. *La Métaphore vive*. Paris: Seuil. English version: *The Rule of Metaphor: Multi-Disciplinary Studies in the Creation of Meaning in Language*. London: Routledge and Kegan Paul 1978

Rogers, T. & McClelland, J. 2004. *Semantic Cognition: A Parallel Distributed Processing Approach*. Cambridge MA: MIT Press.

Rohrer, Tim. 2005. Image Schemata in the Brain. In Beate Hampe (ed.). From Perception to Meaning: Image Schemas in Cognitive Linguistics. Berlin: Mouton de Gruyter, 165-196.

Rosch, E. 1973. Natural categories. *Cognitive Psychology* 4, 328-350.

Rosch, E. 1978. Principles of categorization. In E. Rosch and B.B. Lloyd (eds.), *Cognition and Categorization*. Hillsdale, N.J.: Lawrence Erlbaum. [Reprinted in Laurence, S. & Margolis, E. (eds.) 1999, *Concepts: Core Readings*. Cambridge, MA: MIT Press.]

Rosch, E. 1999. Reclaiming concepts. *Journal of Consciousness Studies* 6/11-12, 61-77.

Rosch, E. 2002. How to catch James's mystic germ: Religious experience, Buddhist meditation, and psychology. *Journal of Consciousness Studies* 9/9-10, 37-56.

Rosch, E. 2004. "If you depict a bird, give it space to fly:" On mind, meditation and art. In J. Baas & M. J. Jacobs (eds.*), Buddha Mind in Contemporary Art*. Berkeley, CA: University of California Press. [Reprinted in M. McLeod (ed.*), The Best Buddhist Writing 2005*, Boston: Shambhala, 2005.]

Rosch, E. 2007a. More that mindfulness: When you have a tiger by the tail, let it eat you. *Psychological Inquiry* 18/4, 258-264.

Rosch, E. 2007b. What Buddhist meditation has to tell psychology about the mind. *Anti-Matters*1, 11-21. (http://anti-matters.org)

Rosch, E. In press a. Beginner's mind: Paths to the wisdom that is not taught. In Ferrari, M. & Potworowski, G. (eds.), *Teaching for Wisdom*, Hillsdale NJ: Erlbaum.

Rosch, E. In press b. Concepts. Prototypes. *The Cambridge Encyclopedia of the Language Sciences*.

Rosch, E. & Fallah, E. 2007, May 16. Science and religion, Dalai Lama style [A review of A. Harrington & A. Zajonc (eds.), *The Dalai Lama at MIT*]. *PsycCRITIQUES–Contemporary Psychology: APA Review of Books*, 52/ 20, Article 4.

Rosch, E. and Mervis. C.B. 1975. Family resemblances: Studies in the internal structure of categories. *Cognitive Psychology* 7, 573-605.

Rosch, E., Mervis, C.B., Gray, W.D., Johnson, D.M., and Boyes-Braem, P. 1976. Basic objects in natural categories. *Cognitive Psychology* 8, 382-439. [Reprinted in M. R. DePaul & W. Ramsey (eds.),1988, *Rethinking intuition: The Psychology of Intuition and its Role in Philosophical Inquiry*. Lanham, MD: Rowman & Littlefield.]

Rosen, Robert 1991. *Life Itself: A Comprehensive Inquiry Into the Nature, Origin, and Fabrication of Life*. New York: Columbia University Press.

Rotschild, Friedrich Solomon 1962. Laws of Symbolic Mediation in the Dynamics of Self and Personality. *Annals of New York Academy of Sciences* 96, 774-784.

Russell, Bertrand. 1905. On Denoting. *Mind*, New Series, 14/56. (Oct., 1905), 479-493.

Salthe, Stanley 1999. A Semiotic Attempt to Corral Creativity via Generativity. *Semiotica* 127, 481-495.

Santaella, Lucia (1983). *What is semiotics*. São Paulo: Brasiliense.

Santaella, Lucia (1992). *The signature of things*. Rio de Janeiro: Imago.

Santaella, Lucia (1993) *Perception*. A semiotic theory. São Paulo: Experimento.

Santaella, Lucia (1994). *General theory of signs*. São Paulo: Ática.

Santaella, Lucia (1994). *Aesthetics*. From Plato to Peirce. São Paulo: Experimento.

Santaella, Lucia (2001). *Matrices of language and thought*. Sound, vision and verbal. São Paulo: Iluminuras/Fapesp.

Santaella, Lucia (2004). *The anti-cartesian method of C. S. Peirce*. São Paulo: Unesp.

Santaella, Lucia (2004). *Applied semiotics*. São Paulo: Thomson.

29. References

Santaella, Lucia and Nöth Winfried (1998). *Image. Communication, semiotics, media.* São Paulo: Iluminuras.

Savan, David 1987. *An Introduction to C.S. Peirce's Full System of Semeiotic,* Victoria College in the University of Toronto.

Saussure, Ferdinand de. 2006. *Writings in General Linguistics,* Oxford, Oxford University Press.

Searle, John 1964 "How to Derive 'Ought' from 'Is'", *Philosophical Review* vol. 73, January 1964

Searle, John 1969 *Speech Acts: An Essay in the Philosophy of Language,* Cambridge: Cambridge University Press

Searle, John. 1975. A Taxonomy of Illocutionary Acts. In, Keith Gunderson (ed.), *Language, Mind and Knowledge,* Minnesota Studies in the Philosophy of Science, Vol. VII Minneapolis: University of Minnesota Press (reprinted in Searle 1979).

Searle, John. 1979. *Expression and Meaning,* Cambridge: Cambridge University Press, 1979.

Searle, John. 1983. *Intentionality: An Essay in the Philosophy of Mind,* Cambridge: Cambridge University Press.

Searle, John. 1995. *The Construction of Social Reality.* New York: The Free Press

Searle, John (in preparation) "What is Language? Some Preliminary Remarks", http://ist-socrates.berkeley.edu/~jsearle/articles.html

Sebeok, Thomas A. 1963. Communication in Animals and Men. *Language* 39, 448-466.

Sebeok, Thomas A. 1991. *A Sign is just a Sign.* Bloomington: Indiana University Press.

Sebeok, Thomas A. 2001a. Biosemiotics: Its roots, proliferation, and prospects. *Semiotica* 134/1-4, 61-78.

Sebeok, Thomas A. 2001b. *Global Semiotics.* Bloomington: Indiana University Press.

Sebeok, Thomas (ed.).1986. *Encyclopedic Dictionary of Semiotics* I-III. Berlin: Mouton de Gruyter

Sebeok, Thomas A. and Jean Umiker-Sebeok (eds.). 1992. *Biosemiotics: The Semiotic Web 1991.* Berlin: Mouton de Gruyter.

Sercarz, Eli E., Franco Celada, N. Avrion Mitchison and Tomio Tada (eds.). 1988. *The Semiotics of Cellular Communication in the Immune System*. Berlin and Heidelberg: Springer.

Shapiro, Michael. 1983. *The Sense of Grammar*. Bloomington: Indiana University Press, 1983.

Shapiro, Michael. 1991. *The Sense of Change: Language as History*. Bloomington: Indiana University Press 1991.

Short, T.L. 1997. Hypostatic abstraction in self-consciousness. In Brunning and Forster (eds.), *The Rule of Reason*. Toronto: University of Toronto Press.

Short, Thomas. L. 2007. *Peirce's Theory of Signs*. Cambridge, US: Cambridge University Press.

Smith, Barry 1988. Gestalt Theory—an essay in philosophy. In Barry Smith (ed.), *Foundations of Gestalt Theory*. Munich-Vienna: Philosophia, 11-81.

Smith, Barry 1994 *Austrian Philosophy*, LaSalle and Chicago: Open Court.

Smith, Barry. 1979. Roman Ingarden: Ontological foundations for literary theory. In J. Odmark (ed.), *Language, Literature & Meaning* I. Amsterdam: Johns Benjamins, 373-90

Smith, Barry. 1980. Ingarden vs. Meinong on the logic of fiction, *Philosophy and Phenomenological Research* 16, 93-105

Smith, Barry. 1992. An essay on material necessity. In P.Hanson and B. Hunter (eds.), *Return of the A Priori (Canadian Journal of Philosophy*, Supplementary Vol. 18).

Smith, Barry. 1996. In defense of extreme (fallibilistic) apriorism, *Journal of Libertarian Studies,* 12, 179-192.

Smith, Barry. 1998 (with Achille Varzi). The Niche, *Nous,* 33/2, 198-222

Smith, Barry. 2000. Logic and formal ontology, *Manuscrito* 23, 275-323

Smith, Barry. 2003. Ontology. In Luciano Floridi (ed.), *Blackwell Guide to the Philosophy of Computing and Information*. Oxford: Blackwell, 155-66.

Smith, Barry. 2004. Beyond Concepts, or: Ontology as Reality Representation, Achille Varzi and Laure Vieu (eds.), *Formal On-*

tology and Information Systems. Proceedings of the Third International Conference (FOIS 2004), Amsterdam: IOS Press, 2004, 73–84.

Smith, Barry, Werner Ceusters and Rita Temmerman. 2005a. Wüsteria, *Medical Informatics Europe* (MIE 2005), Geneva, *Stud Health Technol Inform.* 2005;116:647–652.

Smith, Barry. 2005b. Against Fantology, in M. Reicher and J. Marek (eds.), *Experience and Analysis*, Vienna: ÖBV & HPT.

Smith, Barry and Werner Ceusters. 2006. HL7 RIM: An Incoherent Standard (MIE 2006), *Studies in Health Technology and Informatics*, vol. 124, 133–138.

Smith, Barry 2006 Against Idiosyncrasy in Ontology Development, in B. Bennett and C. Fellbaum (eds.), *Formal Ontology in Information Systems* (FOIS 2006), Amsterdam: IOS Press, 2006, 15-26.

Smith, Barry 2008 "Searle and De Soto: The New Ontology of the Social World", Barry Smith, David Mark and Isaac Ehrlich, *The Mystery of Capital and the Construction of Social Reality*, Chicago: Open Court, 2008, 35-51.

Solomon, Jack. 1988. *The Signs of Our Time*

Sommer, Doris 1990. Irresistible Romance: The Foundational Fictions of Latin America. In *Nation and Narration*, ed. Homi Bhabha. New York: Routledge, 71-98.

Sonesson, Göran. 1988 *Methods and models in pictorial semiotics.* Semiotics Project: Lund University.

Sonesson, Göran. 1989 *Pictorial Concepts. Inquiries into the Semiotic Heritage and its Relevance for the Analysis of the Visual World.* Lund: Aris/Lund University Press.

Sonesson, Göran. 1992 The semiotic function and the genesis of pictorial meaning. In Eero Tarasti (ed.), *Center/Periphery in representations and institutions. Proceedings from the Conference of The International Semiotics Institute, Imatra, Finland, July 16–21, 1990*, 211–156. Imatra: Acta Semiotica Fennica.

Sonesson, Göran. 1993 Pictorial semiotics, Gestalt psychology, and the ecology of perception. *Semiotica* 99/3–4, 319–399.

Sonesson, Göran. 1995 On pictorality. The impact of the perceptual model in the development of visual semiotics. In Thomas Sebeok and Jean Umiker–Sebeok (eds), *The Semiotic Web 1992/93:*

Advances in Visual Semiotics, 67–108. Berlin & New York: Mouton de Gruyter.

Sonesson, Göran. 1996 An essay concerning images. From rhetoric to semiotics by way of ecological physics. *Semiotica* 109/1-2: 41–140.

Sonesson, Göran. 1998 /entries/. In Paul Bouissac (ed.) *Encyclopaedia of Semiotics*. New York & London: Oxford University Press.

Sonesson, Göran. 2001 From Semiosis to Ecology. On the theory of iconicity and its consequences for the ontology of the Lifeworld. In Andrew W. Quinn (ed.), Cultural Cognition and Space Cognition/Cognition culturelle et cognition spatiale. *VISIO*, 6/2–3: 85–110.

Sonesson, Göran. 2003 Why the mirror is a sign–and why the television picture is no mirror. Two episodes in the critique of the iconicity critique. *S. European Journal for Semiotic Studies* 15/2-4, 217–232.

Sonesson, Göran. 2000a. Ego meets Alter: The meaning of otherness in cultural semiotics. *Semiotica* 128/3-4, 537-559.

Sonesson, Göran. 2000b. Action becoming art: "Performance" in the context of theatre, play, ritual–and life. *VISIO* 5, 3, 105-122.

Sonesson, Göran. 2003. Spaces of urbanity. From the village square to the boulevard. In Sarapik, Virve, & Tüür, Kadri (eds.), *Place and location III: The city — topias and reflection*. Talinn: Estonian Academy of Arts, 25-54.

Sonesson, Göran. 2004. The globalization of Ego and Alter. An essay in cultural semiotics. *Semiotica*, 148- 1/4, 153-174.

Sonesson, Göran. 2004b. Rhétorique du monde de la vie. In Anne Hénault, & Anne Beyaert (eds.), *Ateliers de sémiotique visuelle*, Paris: PUF, 83-100.

Sonesson, Göran. 2006a. *Current issues in pictorial semiotics. Lecture one: The Quadrature of the Hermeneutic Circle*. First conference of a series published online at the Semiotics Institute Online. Revised version in August 2006: http://www.chass.utoronto.ca/epc/srb/cyber/Sonesson1.pdf

Sonesson, Göran. 2006b. The meaning of meaning in biology and cognitive science. A semiotic reconstruction. *Sign Systems Studies*, 34:1, 155-214.

Sonesson, Göran. 2007 Den allra nyaste Laokoon. Lessing i ljuset av modern semiotik. In Göran Rossholm, & Göran Sonesson (eds), *Konstverk och konstverkan*, Stehag & Stockholm: Symposion, 96-128..

Sowa, John F. 1976. Conceptual graphs for a data base interface. *IBM Journal of Research and Development* 20/4, 336-357.

Sowa, John F. 1984. *Conceptual Structures: Information Processing in Mind and Machine*, Reading, MA: Addison- Wesley.

Sowa, John F. 1997. Matching logical structure to linguistic structure. In Robert Houser et al. (eds.) 1997.

Sowa, John F. 2000. *Knowledge Representation: Logical, Philosophical, and Computational Foundations*, Pacific Grove, CA: Brooks/Cole Publishing Co.

Sowa, John F. 2005. The Challenge of Knowledge Soup. In J. Ramadas & S. Chunawala, *Research Trends in Science, Technology, and Mathematics Education*, Homi Bhabha Centre, Mumbai, 55-90.

Sowa, John F., & Arun K. Majumdar 2003. Analogical reasoning. In A. de Moor, W. Lex, & B. Ganter (eds), *Conceptual Structures for Knowledge Creation and Communication*, LNAI 2746, Berlin: Springer, 16-36.

Stjernfelt, Frederik. 1992a. *Formens betydning. Katastrofeteori og semiotik*, ['The Meaning of Form. Catastrophe Theory and Semiotics'], Copenhagen: Akademisk Forlag

Stjernfelt, Frederik. 1992b. Categorical perception as a basic prerequisite to the formation of signs. In Sebeok and Umiker-Sebeok 1992, 427-454

Stjernfelt, Frederik. 1995. Récits de l'âgon: leur description linguistique. In Michèle Porte (ed.), *La Passion des formes* , vol. II. Paris: C.N.R.S.

Stjernfelt, Frederik. 2000. Die Vermittlung zwischen Anschuung und Denken bei Kant, Cassirer und Peirce, *Zeitschrift für Semiotik* 22/ 3-4, 341-68

Stjernfelt, Frederik. 2001. The vulgar metaphysics of transgression, *Text und Kontext* 23/1, 144-55

Stjernfelt, Frederik. 2002. A Biosemiotic Building: 13 Theses. Emmeche, C., K. Kull and F. Stjernfelt (eds.): *Reading Hoffmeyer, Rethinking Biology*. Tartu: Tartu University Press.

Stjernfelt, Frederik. 2006. Two iconicity notions in Peirce's diagrammatology, *Proceedings from 6th International Conference on Conceptual Structures.* Vienna: Springer Verlag

Stjernfelt, Frederik. 2007a. *Diagrammatology. An Investigation on the Borderlines of Phenomenology, Ontology, and Semiotics*

Stjernfelt, Frederik. 2007b (with Nikolaj Zeuthen). The representation of consciousness in language and fiction. A cognitive theory of enunciation, *Semiotica* 165/1-4.

Stjernfelt, Frederik (in press). Simple animals and complex biology. The double von Uexküll inspiration in Cassirer's philosophy, *Synthese*

Stumpf, Carl. 1873. *Über den psychologischen Ursprung der Raumvorstellung.* Leipzig: Hirzel.

Talmy, Leonard. 2000. *Toward a Cognitive Semantics.* Vol. 1-2. Massachusetts: The MIT Press.

Tarasti, Eero 1979. *Myth and Music. A Semiotic Approach to the Aesthetics of Myth in Music, especially that of Wagner, Sibelius and Stravinsky.* 1979 Berlin: Mouton de Gruyter (in Finnish by Helsinki: Gaudeamus 1994, and French Paris: Michel de Maule).

Tarasti, Eero 1987. *Heitor Villa-Lobos* (in Finnish Helsinki: Gaudeamus 1987; in English North Carolina: McFarland 1996)

Tarasti, Eero. 1994. *A Theory of Musical Semiotics.* Bloomington, Indianapolis: Indiana University Press

Tarasti, Eero. 1996. *Sémiotique musicale.* Limoges: Presses Universitaires de Limoges. Trad. par B. Dublanche.

Tarasti, Eero 1998. *Snow, Forest, Silence. The Finnish Tradition of Semiotics.* ed. publ. by Indiana University Press (Bloomington) and *Acta Semiotica Fennica* ASF (Imatra).

Tarasti, Eero 2000. *Existential Semiotics.* Bloomington, Indianapolis: Indiana University Press,

Tarasti, Eero 2002. *Signs of Music, A Guide to Musical Semiotics.* Berlin, New York: Mouton de Gruyter 2002

Tarasti, Eero 2003. *Musical Semiotics Revisited.* Ed. *Acta Semiotica Fennica* XV, Imatra: ISI 2003

Tarasti, Eero 2004. *From Nature to Psyche. Proccedings from the ISI Congresses 2001-2001.* ed. Acta Semiotica Fennica XX. Imatra: ISI, 2004

Tarasti, Eero 2006a. *La musique et les signes*. Paris: L'Harmattan.

Tarasti, Eero 2006b *Music and the Arts I-II*, ed. Acta Semiotica Fennica XXIII.

Talmy, Leonard 2000 *Towards a Cognitive Semantics*, 2 vols. Cambridge MA: MIT Press.

Taub, S. 2001. *Language from the Body: Iconicity and Metaphor in American Sign Language*. Cambridge: Cambridge University Press.

Taylor, J. 2003. *Linguistic Categorization*. Oxford: Oxford University Press.

Thom, René. 1972. *Stabilité Structurale et Morphogénèse*. Paris: Ediscience. English translation,
Structural Stability and Morphogenesis, Reading MA: Benjamin.

Thom, René. 1983. *Mathematical Models of Morphogenesis*, New York: Horwood (Wiley).

Thom, René. 1988 *Ésquisse d'une sémiophysique*, Paris.

Thom, René. 1992. *Apologie du logos*. Paris: Hachette.

Thomsen, Søren Ulrik and Frederik Stjernfelt. 2005. *Kritik af den negative opbyggelighed* ["A Critique of Negativism"]. Copenhagen: Vindrose.

Thürlemann, Felix, 1990: *Vom Bild zum Raum. Beiträge zu einer semiotischen Kunstwissenschaft*. Köln: DuMont.

Tomasello, Michael. 1999. *The Cultural Origins of Human Cognition*, Camb. Mass.: Harvard University Press.

Torop, Peeter 2000. New Tartu semiotics. *European Journal for Semiotic Studies* 12/1, 5-22.

Tucker, D. 2007. *Mind From Body: Experience From Neural Structure*. Oxford: Oxford University Press.

Turner, Mark. 1996. *The Literary Mind: The Origins of Thought and Language*. New York: Oxford University Press.

Turner, Mark. 1998. Figure. In Cristina Cacciari, Ray Gibbs, Jr., Albert Katz, and Mark Turner (eds.), *Figurative Language and Thought*. New York: Oxford University Press.

Turner, Mark. 2007. The Way We Imagine. In Ilona Roth (ed.), *The Imaginative Mind*. London: Oxford University Press & The British Academy.

Turner, Marker and Gilles Fauconnier. 1998. Conceptual Integration Networks. *Cognitive Science* 22/2, 133-187.

Uexküll, Jakob von. 1928 [1920]. *Theoretische Biologie.* 2te Aufl. Berlin: J.Springer.

Uexküll, Jakob von. 1940. *Bedeutungslehre.* Leipzig: J.A.Barth.

Uexküll, Jakob von. 1982. [1940]. The theory of meaning. *Semiotica* 42/1, 25–82.

Uexküll, Thure von 1984. A semiotic perspective on the sciences: Steps toward a new paradigm. *Semiotica* 52/1-2, 7–47.

Vailati, Giovanni. 1980. *Scritti filosofici.* Edited by Giorgio Lanaro. Florence: La nuova Italia editrice (selected texts from *Scritti di G. Vailati.* Edited by Mario Calderoni, Umberto Ricci, and Giovanni Vacca. Leipzig: Barth; Florence: Successori B. Seeber, 1911).

Varela, Francisco., Evan Thompson. & Eleanor Rosch. 1991. *The Embodied Mind: Cognitive Science and Human Experience.* Cambridge, MA: MIT Press.

Vygotskij, Lev. 1962. *Thought and language.* Edited and translated by Eugenia Hanfmann and Gertrude Vakar. Cambridge, Mass.: M.I.T. Press.

Whitehead, Alfred North 1937. Analysis of Meaning, *Philosophical Review*, reprinted in A. N. Whitehead, *Essays in Science and Philosophy*, New York: Philosophical Library, 122-131.

Wierzbicka, Anna. 1996. *Semantics: Primes and Universals*, Oxford: Oxford University Press

Wildgen, Wolfgang. 1977a. *Differentielle Linguistik, Entwurf eines Modells zur Beschreibung und Messung semantischer und pragmatischer Variation*, Tübingen: Niemeyer.

Wildgen, Wolfgang. 1977b. *Kommunikativer Stil und Sozialisation. Eine empirische Untersuchung*, Tübingen: Niemeyer.

Wildgen, Wolfgang. 1982. *Catastrophe Theoretic Semantics: An Elaboration and Application of René Thom's Theory*, Amsterdam: John Benjamins Publishing Co.

Wildgen, Wolfgang, 1985a). *Archetypensemantik. Grundlagen für eine dynamische Semantik auf der Basis der Katastrophentheorie*, Tübingen: Narr.

Wildgen, Wolfgang. 1985b/2005. *Dynamische Sprach- und Weltauffassungen (in ihrer Entwicklung von der Antike bis zur Gegenwart)*. Publications of the Center: Philosophical Foundations of Science, vol. 3, Bremen. Electronic version with augmented bibliography: http://elib.suub.uni-bremen.de/ip/docs/00010029.pdf

Wildgen, Wolfgang and Laurent Mottron. 1987. *Dynamische Sprachtheorie. Sprachbeschreibung und Spracherklärung nach den Prinzipien der Selbstorganisation und der Morphogenese*, Bochum: Brockmeyer.

Wildgen, Wolfgang. 1987/2005. *Das dynamische Paradigma in der Linguistik*, electronic version of part 1 In Wildgen and Mottron, 1987, with augmented bibliography: http://elib.suub.uni-bremen.de/ip/docs/00010028.pdf.

Wildgen, Wolfgang. 1994. *Process, Image, and Meaning. A Realistic Model of the Meanings of Sentences and Narrative Texts*, Amsterdam: Benjamins.

Wildgen, Wolfgang. 1998. *Das kosmische Gedächtnis. Kosmologie, Semiotik und Gedächtnistheorie im Werke von Giordano Bruno (1548-1600)*, Frankfurt: Lang.

Wildgen, Wolfgang. 2004. *The Evolution of Human Languages. Scenarios, Principles, and Cultural Dynamics*, Amsterdam: Benjamins.

Wildgen, Wolfgang. 2006. The Dimensionality of Text and Picture and the Organization of Content Based Complexes. In Reinhard Köhler and Alexander Mehler (eds.). *Aspects of Automatic Text Analysis*. Festschrift in Honor of Prof. Dr. B. Rieger, Berlin: Springer, 421-442.

Wildgen, Wolfgang. 2008. *Kognitive Grammatik. Klassische Paradigmen und neue Perspektiven*, Berlin: de Gruyter.

Wilson, Edward O. 1975. *Sociobiology. The New Synthesis*. Cambridge/London: Belknap Press.

Wittgenstein, Ludwig 1922. *Tractatus Logico-Philosophicus*, London: Routledge and Kegan Paul

Wittgenstein, Ludwig 1953. *Philosophical Investigations*, Basil Blackwell: Oxford.

Wulf, Alyssa & Paul Dudis. 2005. Body Partitioning in ASL Metaphorical Blends. *Sign Language Studies* 5/3, 317-332.

Zbikowski, L. 2002. *Conceptualizing Music: Cognitive Structure, Theory, and Analysis.* Oxford: Oxford University Press.

About the Editors

Peer Bundgaard

Peer F. Bundgaard (b. 1967) is an Associate Professor and PhD in General Semiotics at the University of Aarhus. His research interests include cognitive linguistics and phenomenology of language, as well as semiotics of visual and literary art. His recent publications include *Kunst — semiotiske beskrivelse af æstetisk betydning og oplevelse*; (2004) "The ideal scaffolding of language — E. Husserl's fourth logical investigation in the light of cognitive linguistics", "Principles of linguistic composition below and beyond the clause: Elements of a semantic combinatorial system", and "The cognitive import of the narrative schema".

Frederik Stjernfelt

Frederik Stjernfelt (b. 1957) is Ph.D., Dr.Phil. and Full Professor at the Center for Semiotics, Aarhus University. Member of the Danish Academy and the Danish Royal Society of the Sciences. Editor of the journal KRITIK, critic at the weekly Weekendavisen. Reserach interests: general semiotics, cognitive semiotics, theory of science, theory of literature, biosemiotics, political philosophy. Recent Danish publications include two volumes on the Balkan wars and a book on multiculturalism (with Jens-Martin Eriksen) as well as the 3-vol. history of ideas "Tankens magt" (The Power of Thought, edited with H.S.Jensen and O. Knudsen). English publications include the post.doc. dissertation Diagrammatology. An Investigation on the Borderlines of Phenomenology, Ontology, and Semiotics (2007) and numeruous papers in international journals.

Index

aesthetics, 4, 51, 88, 98, 105, 111, 171, 189, 291, 305
anthropology, 6, 19, 47, 55, 58, 80, 92, 98, 110, 133, 149, 222, 223, 230, 237, 252, 258, 287, 295
artificial intelligence (AI), 6, 130, 135, 173, 219, 220, 222, 258, 279, 296

biology, iv, 14, 19, 21, 22, 27, 42, 48, 61–64, 76, 82, 113, 114, 116, 117, 120, 127, 132, 133, 148, 172, 175, 190, 201, 217, 223, 231, 234, 235, 258, 262, 271, 275, 284, 291, 292, 303–305
biosemiotics, 13, 14, 28, 64, 65, 70, 111, 113–115, 117–119, 172, 198, 217, 218, 231, 234, 235, 252–254, 275, 284, 285, 287, 288, 292, 300
blending, 2, 8, 46, 235, 236, 265, 266, 268–270, 281, 285

catastrophe theory, 5, 230, 274, 276, 304
categorization, 71, 79, 81, 84, 120, 153–155, 158, 159, 161, 162, 298, 306
closed-class forms, 238, 239, 243, 244
cognition, 4, 7, 8, 11, 22, 46, 48, 49, 55, 102, 105–107, 109, 110, 112, 140, 141, 162, 208, 222, 226, 235–238, 245, 259, 266, 268–270, 276, 278, 289, 298, 303, 306
cognitive grammar, 46, 48, 293, 296
cognitive linguistics, iv, 2, 46, 48, 105, 107, 108, 141, 203, 231, 245, 268, 280, 283, 287, 289, 293, 297, 298
cognitive psychology, 140, 216, 217, 220, 298, 299
cognitive science, 1, 45, 46, 48, 58, 71, 106, 110, 112, 140, 153, 158, 208, 217, 219, 222, 232, 257, 259, 266, 267, 271, 280, 288, 291, 303, 307
cognitive semantics, iv, 48, 228, 236, 275, 297, 305, 306
cognitive semiotics, 3, 55, 129, 232, 277, 280
communication, 3, 6, 9, 15–17, 20, 22, 30, 31, 33–35, 52, 54, 58, 92,

108, 111, 114, 116, 128, 130, 132, 133, 139, 140, 144, 147, 149, 167, 168, 170, 172, 175, 181, 196, 208, 212, 251, 252, 254, 255, 261, 273, 274, 282, 283, 296, 297, 300, 301, 304
complex (systems), 19, 64
compression, 15–17, 46, 47
computational linguistics, 140, 219
conceptual integration, 2, 48, 49, 265, 266, 269, 270, 307
consciousness, 1, 2, 6, 66, 68, 70, 88, 93–98, 189, 194, 197, 210, 215, 218, 235, 238, 270, 280, 282, 284, 290, 298, 301, 305
creativity, 4, 49, 104, 115, 167, 213, 225, 259, 260, 264, 265, 271, 280, 299
culture (semiotics of culture, cultural semiotics), 3, 9–12, 14–16, 21, 26–28, 34, 36, 39, 49, 115, 116, 118, 119, 125, 127–129, 131, 132, 135, 137, 144, 148, 149, 157, 160–162, 165–167, 170, 173, 177, 208–210, 215, 228, 237, 252, 253, 255, 262, 269, 270, 276, 282–284, 288, 291, 294, 296, 297, 303
cybernetics, iv, 19, 255, 273, 287, 292

cybersemiotics, 14

diagram, 31, 40, 42, 56, 174, 234
double-scope blending, 265, 266, 268, 269
dynamical (object), 32–34

embodiment, 90, 93, 94, 96, 97, 103, 108, 110, 112, 191, 236, 291
emotion, 75, 76, 81, 105, 108, 162, 279, 282, 288
evolution, 7, 20, 21, 25, 28, 43, 63, 65, 66, 70, 117, 128, 145, 201, 211, 218, 234, 260–262, 267, 269, 274, 282, 284, 288, 292, 295, 308

fictive motion, 46, 48
firstness, 94, 95, 169, 171, 172, 224
force dynamics, 46, 48, 242
frame, 48, 166, 241, 266, 268, 281

grammar, 1, 8, 46, 48, 52, 148, 155, 190, 207, 227, 239, 240, 266, 274, 285, 291, 293, 296, 301

habit, 20, 65, 192

icon, 3, 57, 130, 168, 172, 278
iconicity, 2, 3, 37, 95, 110, 112, 169, 209, 213, 214, 231, 234, 283, 303, 305, 306
immediate (object), 32–34
index, 54, 130, 147, 168, 172, 193, 278

information, 14, 16, 19, 22, 23, 42, 62–64, 74, 80, 81, 130, 131, 133, 134, 136, 140, 168, 173, 175, 198–203, 205, 215, 235, 255, 301, 302, 304
intentionality, 70, 82, 83, 180, 181, 187, 194, 196, 300
interpretant, 32–34, 171, 190, 192–194
interpretation, iv, 3, 14, 20–22, 29, 31, 34, 37, 41–43, 56, 58, 64, 69, 74, 75, 79, 117, 120, 126, 131, 139, 142, 145, 149, 169, 190, 191, 193, 194, 196, 197, 223, 229–231, 249, 279, 284, 288
isotopy, 53, 57, 140, 252

language, iii, iv, 1, 6–9, 15, 16, 20, 21, 25, 26, 39, 46, 47, 49, 52, 63, 71–75, 79, 83, 88–93, 96, 101–103, 105, 107–109, 111, 112, 125, 140, 146, 148, 149, 151, 153, 155, 159–162, 171, 172, 179–184, 186, 187, 198, 207, 208, 210–214, 216–220, 222–228, 230, 232, 235–240, 244, 245, 248, 249, 254, 256, 258–262, 265–267, 269, 273–275, 277, 278, 281, 282, 285–291, 293, 297, 298, 300, 301, 305–308
linguistic turn, 25, 72, 96, 109, 232, 236, 291
linguistics, iv, 1, 2, 6, 7, 9, 19, 22, 26, 31, 37, 45–48, 51, 53, 54, 58, 72, 91, 92, 102, 105–108, 114, 122, 132, 140–142, 145, 147–151, 154, 155, 165, 179, 203, 207, 209, 217, 219, 220, 222, 223, 230–232, 235–237, 245, 252, 255, 258, 268, 273, 276, 280–283, 287, 289, 293, 297, 298, 300
literary semiotics, 277
literature, 25, 27, 29–31, 37–40, 42, 48, 66, 71, 73, 101, 122, 125, 126, 139, 145, 153, 167, 168, 171, 207, 229–231, 266, 273, 276, 277, 283, 288, 301
logic, 9, 19, 21, 53, 56, 88, 96, 102, 103, 118, 128, 130, 132, 135, 136, 173, 174, 177, 178, 184, 190, 191, 199, 201, 214, 219–221, 223–228, 230, 234, 247, 262, 275, 282, 287, 289–291, 296, 301

mapping, 6, 35, 84, 102–104, 106, 221, 265, 268, 269
mathematics, iv, 1, 11, 12, 45, 47, 49, 51, 56, 121, 122, 168, 219, 220, 226, 227, 229, 230, 234, 237, 257, 258, 265, 273, 292, 295, 304

316   Index

mental space, 46
metaphor, 4, 9–11, 37, 38, 41, 46, 48, 63, 74, 75, 90, 97, 101–106, 108, 136, 180, 183, 236, 280, 282, 285, 288, 291, 292, 298, 306
metaphor (conceptual), 48, 74, 75, 102, 103, 105, 106, 108
metaphysics, iv, 2, 178, 185, 189, 190, 195, 216, 222, 304
musical semiotics, 249, 250, 278, 305
musicology, 98, 132, 133, 247–249

neuroscience, 7, 47, 83, 84, 105, 107, 108, 150, 186, 222, 232, 259, 266, 268, 271, 297
neurosemiotics, 123

ontology, iii, 4, 64, 150, 174, 182, 187, 188, 199–202, 204, 226, 230–232, 284, 301–303, 305

phenomenology, 4, 25, 83, 90–92, 169, 170, 175, 177, 189, 208, 209, 214, 215, 231, 281, 296, 305
philosophy, iv, 1, 4–6, 11, 20, 25, 26, 29, 31, 47, 48, 51, 55, 56, 71–75, 79, 87–89, 92, 93, 96–98, 101, 102, 107, 109–112, 118, 125, 126, 132, 133, 135, 141, 145, 148, 150, 151, 154, 155, 168–170, 174–177, 179–187, 189, 191, 192, 194, 197–200, 205, 210, 214, 215, 217, 219, 220, 222, 223, 225, 228, 229, 231, 232, 234, 236, 247, 251–254, 273, 275–277, 279, 281, 282, 284, 287, 291–293, 296, 300, 301, 305, 307
phonetics, 1, 8, 90
phonology, 90, 155, 207, 238
physics, 1, 5, 19, 23, 27, 48, 56, 61, 82, 118, 125, 128, 133, 175, 192, 229, 261, 273, 275, 303
physiosemiosis, 26, 28, 70
poetics, 7, 29, 37, 48, 51, 266, 286
poststructuralism, 30, 165, 255
pragmaticism, 31, 173
pragmatics, 31, 105, 108, 112, 134, 136, 147, 187, 207, 227, 228
pragmatism, 20, 93, 96, 178, 227, 285, 290, 296
prototype, 76, 81, 156, 178, 295
psychologism, 20, 74, 224, 230
psychology, 1, 6, 14, 21, 22, 29, 47, 55, 58, 71–74, 79, 80, 84, 91, 97, 98, 107, 108, 132, 144, 153–155, 158, 208–210, 214–217, 220, 222, 223, 230, 232, 237, 258, 260, 263, 266, 282, 284, 285, 290, 298, 299, 302
puzzle, 11, 18, 282
pyramid (semiotic), 35, 36

rhetoric, iv, 31, 51, 52, 61,

190, 213, 227, 228, 258, 266, 268, 303

schema, 95, 103, 110, 239, 240
schematic systems, 239–242, 244
secondness, 66, 95, 171, 172, 224
semantics, iv, 5, 6, 30, 31, 48, 58, 77, 83, 101, 105, 108, 112, 136, 140, 142, 143, 145, 149, 151, 155, 187, 224, 226–228, 233, 236, 238, 239, 274, 275, 286, 287, 295, 297, 305–307
semeiotic, 67, 111, 189, 190, 192–197, 219, 285, 293, 300
semioethics, 28, 253, 256
semiology, 2, 45, 67, 190
semiosis, iv, 13, 18, 21, 23, 31, 33–35, 37, 58, 66, 69, 90, 93, 95, 116–120, 129, 172, 174, 177, 178, 210, 212, 215, 216, 218, 253, 268, 280, 283, 303
semiotics, iv, 2, 3, 6–13, 15, 17, 18, 20, 21, 23, 26–31, 43, 47–49, 52–59, 64, 65, 68, 69, 89–99, 106, 113–116, 118, 119, 122, 123, 125, 128–137, 140, 142, 144–151, 165–178, 189, 197, 207–211, 213–218, 229–236, 247, 249–256, 271, 273–278, 280, 282–284, 288, 290, 292, 296, 297, 300–306
sign, iv, 2, 5, 6, 10–13, 15, 17, 18, 21, 27, 30–39, 42, 43, 49, 54, 56, 65, 88, 90, 92–95, 98, 107, 112, 126–137, 144, 145, 147, 149, 150, 167, 170–173, 179, 190, 192–194, 196–198, 209–212, 214, 217, 223, 224, 234–236, 259–263, 265–271, 275, 277, 278, 283–285, 292–296, 300, 303, 306, 308
social ontology, 182, 187, 188
society, 7, 26, 36, 43, 84, 106, 115, 125, 127, 128, 147, 159, 177, 184, 187, 210, 212, 213, 215, 216, 249, 250, 256, 266, 285, 288, 295
sociology, iv, 47, 51, 55, 80, 98, 148, 210, 230, 232, 247
speech act, 5, 6, 130, 181
structuralism, 2, 7, 29–31, 46, 53, 56, 71, 72, 121, 122, 150, 165, 231, 248, 253, 255, 275, 276, 281
structuralist, 29–31, 45, 51, 114, 126, 207, 209, 247, 248
structure, iii, 2–4, 6, 11, 13, 16, 19, 38–40, 47, 51, 54, 62, 73–75, 82, 94, 96, 102–106, 116, 126, 132, 153, 156, 157, 167, 181, 193, 228, 229, 236–240, 242, 245, 262, 266, 267, 289,

294, 295, 299, 304, 306, 309
symbol, 3, 6, 21, 54, 68, 88, 93, 103, 130, 135, 147, 168, 172, 193, 223, 225, 235, 278, 281, 290, 291, 293
symbolic form, 110
symbolization, 7, 68, 91, 97
syntax, 2, 7, 31, 83, 105, 108, 112, 146, 155, 167, 227, 235, 236, 281, 287, 296

thirdness, 66, 67, 95, 172, 224
threshold (semiotic), 28, 69, 117, 119
topological semantics, 274
topology, 5, 274
triad, 91, 168, 224, 227, 228, 278
type, 14, 21, 33, 34, 40, 52, 91, 93, 97, 106, 107, 122, 126, 127, 136, 146, 181, 182, 185, 193–196, 240, 242, 243, 274, 275, 278

visual semiotics, 52–54, 58, 173, 208, 274, 302, 303

zoosemiotics, 64, 119, 172, 252

www.ingramcontent.com/pod-product-compliance
Lightning Source LLC
Chambersburg PA
CBHW021135230426
43667CB00005B/129